Thinking
Color
in Space

Kerstin Schultz
Hedwig Wiedemann-Tokarz
Eva Maria Herrmann

Thinking Color in Space

Positions
Projects
Potentials

Birkhäuser
Basel

Authors

Kerstin Schultz (*1967)
Prof. Dipl.-Ing. Architect
Darmstadt University of Applied Sciences
Studied architecture at Darmstadt Technical University,
since 1997 shared practice with Werner Schulz
in Reichelsheim, since 2008 Professor at the Faculty
of Architecture and Interior Design of Darmstadt
University of Applied Sciences

Hedwig Wiedemann-Tokarz (*1975)
Dipl.-Ing. Architect
Darmstadt University of Applied Sciences
Studied architecture at the Mackintosh School of
Architecture, Glasgow and Stuttgart University,
since 2010 Scientific Assistant at the Faculty of
Architecture and Interior Design of Darmstadt
University of Applied Sciences

Eva Maria Herrmann (*1975)
Dipl.-Ing. Architect
Studied architecture at Darmstadt University of
Applied Sciences, 2007-2009 Scientific Assistant at
the Endowed Chair for Housing Design and Housing
Management, Munich Technical University, since 2005
independent practice in Munich

h_da
HOCHSCHULE DARMSTADT
UNIVERSITY OF APPLIED SCIENCES

fb a
FACHBEREICH ARCHITEKTUR

**The book was prepared at the Faculty of Architecture
at Hochschule Darmstadt, University of Applied Sciences**
www.fba.h-da.de

Endowed Chair
Caparol Farben Lacke Bautenschutz GmbH and
Knauf Gips KG

Contents

Part 1

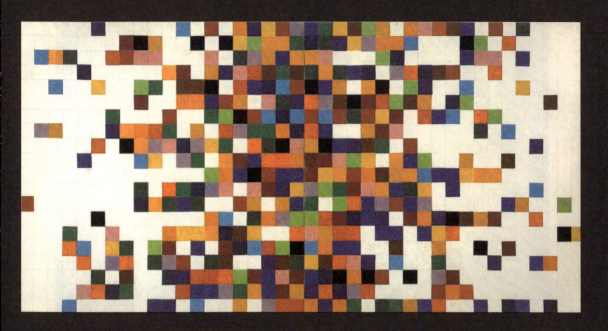

The autonomy
of color

Ellsworth Kelly,
"Spectrum Colors Arranged by Chance I", 1951,
graphite and collage on paper, 49.5 × 99.1 cm

Titian emphasized color as the real substance of the painting and made it the key design element.

Color as the real substance of painting

For centuries, artists and architects have been preoccupied by the fascinating potential of color's expressive ability, the way it creates depth in space, and its interactive mechanisms. Throughout art and architectural history, controversial views have been held, because there is a tendency to relate the perception of color to one's feelings and subjective view. Even Immanuel Kant felt that, beyond a shadow of a doubt, color was overshadowed by drawing, which was considered to be suitable for objective assessment and hence was the preferred medium.[1]

This ambivalent relationship with color can already be detected in ancient times—seeing that, on the one hand, it represented all that was illusory and incidental and, on the other hand, it also stood for life and truthfulness.[2] In spite of a sometimes exuberant use of color, the discussion was therefore based more on assumptions than on scientific findings, and the exact determination of color shades was not relevant. With his extensive theories on color, Aristotle is one of the pioneers who tried to explore a fundamental understanding of color, and presumably he was the first to focus on the subject of color combinations in an experimental and scientific way (see p. 77–95). He strongly criticized the use of color for purely decorative purposes and considered color rendering secondary to drawing.

The discussion of whether contour drawing should be considered superior to color was revived in the Italian Renaissance. The representatives of the two Italian centers of art, Venice and Rome, argued about the primacy of the line, *disegno*, versus color, *colore*. Drawing, which was associated with a reflective, rational, and analytical approach to images, was favored by Rome and Florence, whereas in Venice color was used highly expressively and with great passion. We must remember, however, that drawing was considered not only a manual skill but also an intellectual achievement.[3]

At that time, the range of colors used was still rather limited, because the selection of colors heavily depended on availability. Venice, however, owing to its strategic location, benefited from lively international trade, which meant that artists had access to the rarer pigments. One of the leading representatives of Venetian painting in the sixteenth century, Titian, whose real name was Tiziano Vecellio (1488–1576), used color with a versatility and nuance never seen before. Titian omitted contours, outlines, and lines.

The most beautiful colors, laid on confusedly, will not give as much pleasure as the chalk outline of a portrait.[4] Aristotele

In an almost abstract way, he determined the message of the image purely by the colored forms applied with the brush. These colored forms also bring the picture together. The range of colors is full of contrast and has many subtle nuances. With the detail-rich color composition, he generates

1 Kant 1970, in Weischedel 1996, 141ff.
2 Gage 1993, 15.
3 Brunner 2003, 17–35.
4 Aristotle, Poetry, in Gage 1993, 15.

his own radiant colorfulness in the sense of a "color signature." Given the limited availability of color pigments at the time, and compared with his later works, which are dominated by brown color shades, Titian's early work is particularly fascinating when viewed in the light of later developments in modern painting.

The path toward a new picture language—
Color and light as important conveyors of expression

From the end of the eighteenth century, artists increasingly worked more independently of patrons and turned toward new artistic themes and content. The Christian view of the world was undergoing change, and in an endeavor to liberate themselves from traditional ideas the thinkers of the time planted the seeds of the modern world. Society strived for more autonomy and self-determination. Structures that had existed since the Middle Ages were broken up, and different ideas took hold in art as well as in the fields of architecture, music, literature, and philosophy. The increasing independence from old thinking patterns and traditions found its resonance in a break with traditional painting and coloring techniques in art, as is particularly evident in the work of Eugène Delacroix (1798–1863). In his paintings, light, color, and contrast vibrate with one another, and the drawing is completely dissolved in favor of powerful and expressive strokes of the brush. Delacroix was not so much interested in perfecting the purely manual skill of painting; rather, his focus was on bringing luminosity, radiance, and light to the painting.

The predominant understanding of art in France in the middle of the nineteenth century was heavily influenced by the École des Beaux-Arts (the Salon) in Paris, which was presided over by the classicist painter Dominique Ingres (1780–1867). He worked on cool, clear compositions with sparse shading and reduced background, emulating the ideas of Antiquity and the Italian Renaissance. Ingres and his followers were considered the protagonists of the classical school, and criticized what, in their eyes, were chaotic picture compositions—the radiant, vibrant coloring, the exuberant passion, and the unencumbered drawing technique of the French Romantics. A dispute developed about the theory of art, between Ingres and Delacroix and his followers, rekindling the Renaissance discussion on the meaning of line and color in painting, and dominating the French art scene for almost half a century.

In the meantime, Delacroix continued to develop his pictorial language using the elements of color and light as important conveyors of expression. He was an outstanding draftsman, but it was not until he acquired his exact knowledge of the optical behavior of colors that he was able to achieve a pictorial effect, such as in the *Women of Algiers* painting of 1834. Color became the expression of the artist's subjective feeling; it went beyond the correct depiction of reality, achieving an autonomy that had never been seen before.

5   Signac 1908, 37.
6   Ibid., 40.
7   Bocola 2013, 128.
8   Ibid.

Delacroix had studied the color theories of Michel Eugène Chevreul (1786–1889) in some depth (see p. 77–95). He used complementary colors and color contrast in the form of defined color compositions, adopting a very focused and almost mathematical approach.[5] The picture composition was determined by the arranged distribution of lines and colors. Through the juxtaposition of related color shades with small strokes of the brush, and through hatching, the colors combine for the spectator in a typical fashion, creating nuanced, complex, mixed shades that in some areas result in increased lucidity (see p. 13).

"He knows that the effect of the complementary colors is heightened when they are placed next to each other, and that it is destroyed when they are mixed on the palette [...]"[6] Paul Signac on Delacroix

Subsequent generations of artists were much intrigued by the fact that colors can exist only through the viewer's perception and are experienced changeably, subjectively, and interactively. They espoused the principles of the complementary contrast and the subdivision of the picture surface into numerous pure color pigments that harmonize with each other, and developed them further. Decades later, in his Pointillist manifesto *D'Eugène Delacroix au néo-impressionnisme*, the painter Paul Signac thanked the artist for "having liberated" color and painting techniques "from all tradition." Signac was much inspired by the way Delacroix used color.

Representatives of Impressionism, Expressionism, and Fauvism, as well as the abstract artists working around the middle of the twentieth century, drew their inspiration from Delacroix's work. In addition, the means of artistic expression were being drastically reduced. The seeming contradiction between artistic intention and means of expression appeared to have been eradicated, and this led to a completely new artistic approach in which the painting process itself took on paramount importance.[7]

Breaking with the past—Color as a means of abstraction

In the case of the Impressionists in particular, colors were now made to resonate with one another and to generate a pulsating and vibrating ensemble of light, color, and atmosphere. Applying patches of color without contours releases the color from its bond with objects and allows it to vibrate freely. From a distance, these colors appear indeterminate; seen from close up, they consist of innumerable elements of pure color of a similar size. The color dialogue does not arise until seen from a distance, and makes the picture accessible. The interaction of uncountable molecules of color results in an impression of the picture that appears to be the most fitting in the light of nature—based on Delacroix's theory of complementary contrast.[8]

The artists of the nineteenth century broke radically with the past. Along with scientific and technical progress, a more rational way of thinking developed on the basis of measurable findings that stood in contrast to emotional, and at times irrational, attitudes. Furthermore, artists moved away from the strict rules of the academies. Traditional, sacred, or mythological picture subjects were forsaken, and the depiction of nature and its relationship with humankind became the determining motif of the Impressionist painters. Along with the Impressionists' idea that objects are only accessible to human perception in the form of their changeable appearance, color was rejected as a determined local color, as was taught in the Italian Renaissance. Shape and color were experienced as personal sensations depending on the conditions of light, air, and time; this was seen to correspond to the changeability of the world and how it is experienced at a given moment. As a result, the subjective process of perception became essential to experiencing the picture. The differentiation between color, shape, and content prepared the way for abstraction. The motif and drawing became less and less interesting. The act of seeing was the subject of the work, not the motif; the moment and the process were important rather than any notion of a persistent, durable nature of the image.

The subject is something secondary, what I want to reproduce, is what lies between the subject and myself. [9]
Claude Monet

At the same time, there was a change in the presentation of perspective, which up until then had been taught in the form of a classical foreground and background concept and had been considered an important structural principle. Atmospheric perspective, which contrasts the dark and full color shades of what is near with the light and blurred colors of the background, and color perspective, which places warm colors in the foreground and cool colors in the background, were now replaced by the situational appearance, rich in color. Light and dark points of color were used in the foreground and in the background with the same sharpness. Shadows appear in the colors as they are seen.

The interaction of the lucid, pure colors that resonate with one another helped the language of painting to acquire new expression and exerted a major influence on future generations of painters. From this point on, color acquired an autonomous and aesthetic quality and became the central means of design. The scientific approach underlying the "mood pictures" of the Impressionists was systematically developed in a color theory by Pointillists such as Georges Seurat (1859–1891). Physical processes of perception were systematically analyzed with a cool head; above all, it was the rational, clear, technical composition that determined the picture. Georges Seurat was concerned with the type of painting itself, which followed clearly defined rules in accordance with a formal structure of the painting and precluded

9 Monet 1880, in fondation-monet.com.

Eugène Delacroix,
"Landscape Near Champrosay",
1850s, oil on paper on board,
38.3 × 46.2 cm

In the years 1892 and 1893, Monet painted twenty-eight pictures of the west facade of the Cathedral of Rouen, thereby introducing the concept of the series in fine art. Monet captured the everyday nature and perception of the appearance of light in many series of pictures. This subjective experience of perception at a certain moment demanded sketch-like quick, small strokes of the brush.

Claude Monet,
"West Facade of the Cathedral of Rouen",
oil on canvas, 106 × 73 cm

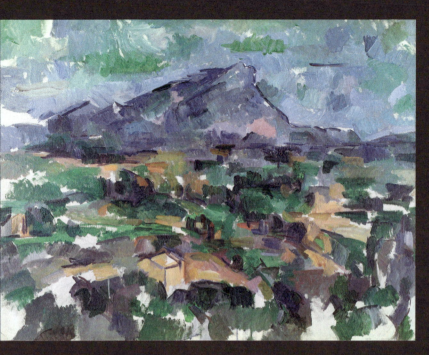

Paul Cézanne (1839–1906),
"Montagne
Sainte-Victoire",
ca. 1904–6,
oil on canvas, 63.5 × 83 cm

Cézanne develops the basic motif of the picture like
a colorful fabric using broad, flat patches of
color and combines the individual abstract elements
into a meaningful whole.

Manet's work, with its strong reliance on flat area, has
been abstracted to such a considerable extent in his
painting "Olympia" that Gustave Courbet compared it to a
playing card owing to its flatness.

Édouard Manet,
"Olympia", 1863,
oil on canvas,
130.5 × 190 cm

all spontaneity. Point grids and diamonds were placed methodically exact in the primary colors; the picture language was mechanical and impersonal. The search for an autonomous image with its own inherent laws determined everything. Even though the Pointillists' method of painting served many artists as an experimental example and the method of color segmentation provided important stimuli, the major criticism was that the technique of producing the image was replacing the image's message.

"As for stippling, making halos or other things, I find that a real discovery, but it can already be foreseen that this technique won't become a universal dogma any more than another."[10] Vincent van Gogh

Vincent van Gogh (1853–1890) responded to the cool and rational painting of Pointillism with individual expression. His own signature and pure color joined together to create larger forms returned to the image. The color areas of the painting became a dense matrix of excessively thick applied lines, points, and waves without any loss of creative control and order. The object of the observation, in its changeability, was no longer the motif; instead, the unbroken color took the lead.

Van Gogh was conscious of the liberal way he worked with color. He stated: "And I wouldn't be very surprised if the Impressionists were soon to find fault with my way of doing things, which was fertilized more by the ideas of Delacroix than by theirs. Because instead of trying to render exactly what I have before my eyes, I use color more arbitrarily in order to express myself forcefully."[11]

In addition to the desire for personal expression or an independent artistic reality, many artists were looking to reestablish a cohesive effect in the picture, which seemed to have been dissolved in the process of the strong color segregation. Paul Gauguin (1848–1903) generated the cohesion of his color areas using luminous fields of color set into strong contour lines.

Paul Cézanne (1839–1906), in whose pictures color and the colored/formal picture composition became the most important elements, replaced the small, pixel-like patterns of the Impressionists with broader brushstrokes, and introduced an interlaced way of painting that gathered all the elements, interweaving the individual forms into a dense matrix. Form, dimension, and proportion characterized his work. He developed a strong, relief-type spatial depth in the picture by layering different planes of color, and worked color into intense three-dimensionality and density. According to Gottfried Boehm, the colored "taches, tons, plans" are reminiscent of the "planimetry of a carpet."[12] Cézanne delineated the forms in the picture by creating contrast or clear contours. The strict separation of color and drawing was abandoned.

"The contrast and the relationship between the color shades: therein lies the secret of drawing and of modeling. When the color shades are in harmony next to each other and there are no gaps, the picture models itself. One should not say model, but modulate instead."[13] Paul Cézanne

10 Van Gogh 1888, letter 528 in vangoghletters.org.
11 Van Gogh 1888, letter 520 in vangoghletters.org.
12 Baumann 2000, 17.
13 Cézanne 1980, 76.

Cézanne worked with serial, staggered, and repeat arrangements and brought them into tension and balance. By placing compact blocks of color, he achieved a new type of spatial effect and the impression of three-dimensionality. Green color shades of the ground are repeated in the sky, color reflections are used in order to create a synthesis between object and space. Motifs are "to be born out of the color," and what color shades are linked with one another is not based on any rules or rigid system but is rediscovered in every picture. The shapes themselves were developing purely through the contrasting colors.

The freedom of color and shape

"Color must be thought, dreamt, imagined."[14] With these words, Gustave Moreau (1826–1898), painter and teacher at the École des Beaux-Arts in Paris, addressed his students, who were strongly influenced by his approach to color, which was to have a profound effect. It was important to Moreau that his students develop an idea of color in order to articulate this in a personal picture language, and follow less their visual perception than their feelings. One of his students was Henri Matisse, who, as a member of the group of Fauvists, used color to give new weight to painting.

The Fauvists formed themselves as a countermovement to the flightiness of Impressionism, and wanted to counteract the dogmatic and theoretical Pointillism. At the exhibition of the third Salon d'Automne in Paris that opened on October 18, 1905, color and shape exploded. Areas saturated by color and defined by contours were declared to be of the essence. Purple-colored rivers, red/blue forests, and landscapes steeped in saffron shades—the colors' own dynamism outshone any intention to imitate reality. Illustrations appear thus in the painter's view; the "wrong" colors of objects are free from being assigned to specific characters, contents, or realistic depictions. The shapes were simplified; light and shadow disappeared. The Fauvists also relied on the teachings of Signac and Seurat with great liberty, although completely unfettered by dogma. Even though the most important stimuli were adopted from Impressionism, the focus was on the search for the elementary connection between color and shape, rather than on a search for theoretical understanding. Lines and colors were always used subjectively. Van Gogh also influenced the work of the Fauvists. A way of painting with flat shapes, often lacking any depth or perspective, became the characteristic feature of the Fauves. Amongst the Fauvists, it was Henri Matisse (1869–1954) in particular who constructed his pictures in a unique way with color, sometimes filling the entire canvas. The flat shapes of subject and background were given equal value. Paul Gauguin (1848–1903) and Édouard Manet (1832–1883), whose painting with flat shapes led to a complete loss of depth and modeling, exerted a big influence over Matisse.

Matisse also heavily simplified his shapes; light and shadow were omitted. The flat colored areas were not supposed to suggest a pretend depth of space to the onlooker; the intention was that the picture be viewed superficially and to make the applied color visible. All depth of space and volume was translated into a decorative arrangement, with areas lacking all depth. In this way, the object and interior space are equally weighted.

Matisse, who continued to use contour lines that further enhanced the poster-like effect, was heavily criticized, above all by Paul Signac. However, Matisse defended the unity of his picture effect and considered the composition with colored areas as the key part of his work. "The breaking up of color lead to the breaking up of form, of contour. Result: a jumpy surface. There is only a retinal sensation, but it destroys the calm of the surface and of the contour."[15]

Whereas the Pointillists had isolated and freed up the color, Matisse brought it into equilibrium and constructed with color. Color abstraction and balance determined the composition; naturalistic depictions were modified by using different colors. All color planes were reduced to a flat form, which, independent of foreground and background, was superimposed throughout by large colored forms or ornamental patterns. The *L'Atelier rouge* painting (1911) clearly shows how three-dimensionality and the perception of perspective can be not only changed but even completely omitted by the use of color. In this way, monochrome color is given weight and density. Through it, all other parts appear scattered and, at the same time, fixed. In this picture, Matisse reduced everything to the color red.

Owing to its radical approach to shape and color, *L'Atelier rouge* heralded the advent of pure Color Field painting, in which the first priority was the interaction of the painter with the surface, the viewpoint of the viewer, and the monochrome color. Mark Rothko (1903–1970) once recounted that he had spent "hour upon hour" sitting in front of Matisse's painting and that it had significantly influenced his own work. The reduction of shape and content introduced by Matisse was further developed by Rothko as early as 1949–50. In 1954, the year Matisse died, Rothko painted *Homage to Matisse*.

In his later work, Matisse translated the merging of flat form and image carrier into space and, in this way, combined space, form, architecture, and painting. He produced a large mural, *La Danse II* (first version, 1931–33). Matisse pointed out the difficulty of scale that is involved when applying large colored forms to a surface in a room. The figures point beyond the limits of the picture and evoke the idea of infinity. The boundaries of the room are abolished: "Perhaps it would be important to indicate that the composition of the panel arose from a struggle between the artist and fifty-two square meters of surface of which his spirit had to take possession, and not the modern procedure of the compositions' projection on the surface, multiplied to the size required and traced. A man looking for an airplane with a searchlight does not explore the vastness of the sky in the same way as an aviator. If I have made myself clear, I think you will grasp the essential difference between the two conceptions."[16]

14 Hofstätter 1978, 162.
15 Matisse 1929
    in Matisse 1995, 84.
16 Matisse 1956
    in Matisse 1995, 160.

Henri Matisse,
"L'Atelier rouge", 1911,
oil on canvas,
181 × 219.1 cm

With "L'Atelier rouge" of 1911, Henri Matisse achieved
a maximum of flatness without depth using the all-
enveloping color red. In spite of the two-dimensionality
shown, the idea of the space of the studio is created.

Robert Delaunay,
"Les Fenêtres sur la ville
(1ère partie, 1ers
contrastes simultanées)",
The Windows on the City
[1st part, simultaneous
contrasts], 1912,
oil on canvas, 53.4 × 207 cm

The quest for objectivity and truth

"In painting, nothing is true other than the color," wrote Theo van Does-burg (1883–1931) in 1930 in his manifesto *Basis of Concrete Painting*. At the beginning of the twentieth century, artistic views and forms of expression existed that could not have been more different. The Cubist method of deconstructing shape clearly demonstrates the dismantling of a hitherto perceived reality, concomitant with strongly abstracted depictions and a maximum liberation from classically studied application techniques. As a form of art that corresponds to the artist's expression of the soul, it was Expressionism that dominated the art scene in Germany; this fact was directly related to the effects of World War I, the collapse of the political order, and growing anonymity and poverty in the large cities. The "new world" that the Impressionists had still depicted as a color event full of light appeared to the painters in the form of increasing loneliness and iso-lation. The feelings and sensations of the painters were expressed through unbroken color shades of deep intensity and strong contrast within large areas. Artists such as Franz Marc developed their own symbol language with color.

In Germany, the Expressionist painters mostly came together in two groupings: *Die Brücke* (The Bridge), founded in 1905 and based in Berlin, and *Der Blaue Reiter* (The Blue Rider), founded in 1911 in Munich. In 1910 the painter Wassily Kandinsky (1866–1944) published his treatise *On the Spiritual in Art* and painted his first abstract improvisations. From 1904 Kandinsky had occupied himself with the effect, definition, and quality of color, primarily in the written form.[17] Kandinsky was convinced that color "had to be liberated from the real shape" in order to be effective.

At nearly the same time, artists and scientists throughout Europe, and later also in America, abandoned nature as a subject and developed similar ideas. As one of the first, Robert Delaunay (1885–1941) constructed his *Windows* pictures of 1912 solely based on relationships between colors, using the simultaneous effect of the colors. His pictures seem to be in a state of movement and developed a transparent depth. "I have dared to create a simultaneous architecture using colors in the hope of fostering the stimuli, the state of dynamic poetry, and to still remain exclusively in the medium of the painter, devoid of any literature, of any descriptive anecdote."[18]

An increasing systemization of image components became more and more apparent in art, and artists such as Delaunay focused on the newly gained findings.

17 Kandinsky, in Friedel 2007, 237ff.
18 Delaunay 1957, 98.

I felt that color is a dynamic element, which has its own laws, with height and breadth...[19]
Robert Delaunay

Most artists aimed for a universal art—not only in order to create new image worlds but also to satisfy the idealistic desire for renewal of the world in a utopian sense. All principles of arranging, modeling, and structuring were reconsidered.

The radical way in which the respective image components were applied was unique to this period. Giving up central perspective, the flattening method of Fauvist and Expressionist painting, the radical limitation of the means of depiction, and finally visionary ideas of three-dimensionality led to the abstract art that dominated the twentieth century. František Kupka (1871–1957) had already written in a letter in 1905 that he did not believe "that it is necessary to paint trees, because on their way to the exhibition people could see better trees." With Kazimir Malevich's *Black Square*, dated 1915, Suprematism developed as the first totally abstract art direction, staking the claim for an art that is free from purpose and logic. The black color, tied to the shape of a square, did not seek to establish any relationship with other image elements, and freed itself of all ties. The supposed generated "emptiness" was the exemplification of nonrepresentational art per se. Malevich said "This was no 'empty square' which I had exhibited but rather the feeling of non-objectivity."[20] In this, Malevich saw a philosophical concept that should influence all spheres of life and from which a new realism of painting arose. "By contrast, I have found a new *Gestalt* in the zero of shapes, and beyond the zero have arrived at the creative, that is, at Suprematism, the new realism in painting—at creation without object. Suprematism is the beginning of a new culture."[21]

Floating, simple, or complex objects in space did away with the idea of top and bottom, finite and infinite. Reality was no longer described but constructed, and henceforth color forces filled the picture compositions. The interaction between the different ways of handling abstraction, which could be observed since Cézanne, had led to a constructive art. Between the two world wars, the Constructivists also continued to work on the principle of rigidly geometric compositions, which were often based on tectonic thinking. Firmly defined relationships and elements, the laws governing color, the theory of proportion, and new knowledge on the processes of seeing determined the images.

There was an affinity with the Bauhaus and De Stijl. Only primary colors were used in addition to black, white, and gray. Important representatives of international Constructivism, such as the Swiss artist Johannes

Itten, taught the Constructivist color theory at the Bauhaus and occupied themselves with color graduation and color distribution in space that had a spatial and perspective effect, one example being the work of German/American painter Lyonel Feininger (1871–1956), who was also at the Bauhaus. Artists such as Theo van Doesburg and Piet Mondrian (1872–1944) were, according to Theo van Doesburg in his 1930 manifesto *Foundations of Concrete Painting*, "in search of the ultimate purity." They even disavowed abstract painting: "That is to say, concrete painting rather than abstract, because nothing is more concrete, nothing more real than a line, a color, a flat surface."[22]

The Dutch painter Piet Mondrian, who initially turned to Cubism, later developed his way of painting without any formation of shape whatsoever. He called his own style Neoplasticism. He constructed painted forms without creating any three-dimensionality in the picture. "Both in their dimensions (line) and their tonality (color), the forms are capable of designing space without expressing space visually in a perspective."[23] Colors were reduced to the primary colors and organized in a web of relationships of vertical and horizontal lines. "It was the line that liberated the color,"[24] writes curator Hans Janssen of the Gemeentemuseum, The Hague, in 2015 in the catalogue for the *Piet Mondrian: The Line* exhibition in the Gropius building in Berlin. Under the influence of philosopher Jan Schoenmaeker, whose idea of the world was based on mathematical principles, Mondrian established his understanding of functionality, geometry, and logic, which, for the first time in the history of art, was developed on the basis of asymmetry. Like Kandinsky, Mondrian wanted to find theoretical answers to the questions raised by his work. The idea was to exclude all randomness and arbitrariness in favor of a precisely arranged equilibrium of all parts. The objective was to make universal harmony visible.

In order to draw a clear distinction between his work and abstract art, Max Bill (1908–1994) coined the term *concrete art* in the middle of the 1930s to refer to all those proponents in the modernist movement who developed supposedly objective and reproducible criteria on the basis of rational concepts and strictly mathematical approaches. In spite of these image components, their works express playful and free handling of color and shape. "The means of design are colors, light, movement, the volume, the space," said Bill.[25]

The representatives of concrete art set strict, self-created design rules for themselves. Design no longer started with the process of abstraction, but was based on the direct objective and autonomous interaction with concrete image components such as line, color, form, and space.

The group of artists known as De Stijl, which had been founded by Mondrian and Van Doesburg, pursued the mission of articulating completely new, generally applicable design principles for all spheres of life and genres. Similarly, they emphasized the transfer of this artistic aesthetic to sculpture, painting, architecture, and interior design. Van Doesburg even went so far as to stipulate that, in the common interest, the individual, personal viewpoint be subordinated to the universal new awareness of

19 Delaunay 1957, 229.
20 Malevich 1927,
    in Malevich 1959, 118.
21 Malevich 1916,
    in Baurmeister 1983.
22 Doesburg 1930,
    in Danzker 2000, 113.
23 Gassen 1994, 28.
24 Janssen 2015.
25 Bill 1936 in Du 872
    2016, 34.

beauty. The De Stijl artists felt that their aesthetic principles were linked with the development of a new culture of mankind. Like others of their generation, they not only drove forward their own artistic work with extreme seriousness but also worked on a theoretical justification of their creative oeuvre.

Richard Paul Lohse (1902–1988), Max Bill, and Camille Graeser (1892–1980) belonged to the Zurich-based Schule der Konkreten (Zurich School) that had formed during the 1930s and was also active after 1945. According to the idea of these artists, anything subconscious or spiritual could in no way be linked with concrete art. Lohse, for example, preferred to use terms such as *systematic, methodical, or rational* in relation to his art. Bill, who in 1950 founded the Ulm School of Design using the Bauhaus as example, pleaded for exact, repeatable, and controllable means of design. In his paintings, Camille Graeser explored themes such as rotation, rhythmical reduction and addition, and progression and degression, and formulated these by subdividing the area in relation to the ratios of color quantities. Furthermore, Graeser focused intensely on the visualization of rhythms, sounds, and musical structures (see p. 27).

There was, however, also skepticism regarding the through-composed and constructed images. Many artists refused to accept the logic of the rational and performed a radical U-turn to embrace the material presence of color as an image-forming component per se. In this way, another approach to the search for a new art led to monochrome painting, in which the color alone became the message. In retrospect, the artist Alexander Rodchenko, who was one of the driving forces of the Russian avant-garde and developed the manifestos of Constructivism, is seen as the precursor of monochrome painting. The triptych *Pure Color Red, Pure Color Yellow, and Pure Color Blue* of 1921 is completely without any structure or traces of its process; the pictures become the color matter. Looking back, Rodchenko said in 1939: "I reduced painting to its logical conclusion and exhibited three canvases: red, blue, yellow … it's all over. Basic colors. Every plane is a plane and there is to be no more representation."[26] For the development of monochrome painting, however, this was to be only the beginning; with his work, Rodchenko preceded the later developments of Abstract Expressionism and Color Field painting. On this subject, Benjamin Buchloh writes: "With Rodchenko's introduction of monochrome color we are becoming witnesses not only of the liberation of relational composition, but also—and more importantly—of the liberation from conventional instructions regarding the meaning of colors in favor of the pure materiality of color."[27]

The indeterminability of color

As a result of the outbreak of World War II and persecution at the hands of the National Socialists, many European artists, architects, scientists, and philosophers immigrated to the USA. With them they brought valuable stimuli to the local world of art, working as teachers or founding their own schools. Josef Albers (1888–1976), whose work occupies an outstanding position within concrete art, had taught at the Bauhaus for thirteen years and, after its closure in 1933, moved to Black Mountain College in North Carolina. In 1959 he became director of the Department of Design at Yale University. With his teaching activity, Albers laid the theoretical foundations for his later geometrical abstract painting. The profiling of its poetically prominent characteristics distinguishes him from most of his colleagues. Albers's statement "What I teach is not a system, is not a theory, but an inspiration to see, to become more discerning, to sharpen visual perception" explains his real objective: to train perception and seeing. Albers's preoccupation with the interactive effects and relationships of colors made him one of the most important color theorists and color artists of the twentieth century. "In order to use color effectively, it is necessary to recognize that color deceives continually,"[28] was his thesis. Instead of mechanically applying laws and rules of color harmony, he pleaded "distinct color effects are produced—through recognition of the interaction of color—by making for instance two very different colors look alike or nearly alike. The aim of such study is to develop through experience—by trial and error—an eye for color. This means, specifically, seeing color in action as well as feeling color relatedness."[29]

Albers's interest was in color per se, its autonomy and elevation, and less in the formal and structural subjects of most constructive painters. Albers extolled the discrepancy between perceptibility, plannability, and inexplainability, as well as the ambiguity of visual phenomena, using color as the medium, and he continued to produce different versions, series, and variations of his works. In view of the fact that our visual memory of color and understanding of color is relatively weak compared with our perception and hearing, color appears indeterminate and ungraspable, leading Albers to make its enigma in particular the subject. "Only appearances are not deceptive,"[30] was Albers's hypothesis, based on which he characterized the changing identities of colors.

Albers's series of pictures *Homage to the Square* developed from 1949 is based on an arrangement in which the squares, in spite of their flatness, appear with an imaginary depth and a three-dimensional perspective. The image is determined by the organization of the color alone. The effect of the image changes only through the change of color. Even though the colors can be distinguished in spite of their very fine gradation, not all the nuances of these colors can be recognized. The effects of the color on the spectator are unfathomable; the neutrality of the subdivision of areas is retained, and bold image structures are present.

"In the colors there are hidden harmonies or contrasts which contribute of their own accord, and which if left unused are of no benefit."[31]

26 Chilova 2013.
27 Buchloh 1986, 44.
28 Albers 1963
    in Albers 2006, 1.
29 Ibid.
30 Liesbrock 2010.
31 Van Gogh 1882,
    letter 226,
    in vangoghletters.org.

is what Vincent van Gogh had previously said. Albers, who was interested in the interaction of color nuances, including disharmonious and unconventional ones, in 1963 compiled his thoughts in the book *Interaction of Color*. He assigns a meditative, mystical character to the mutual interaction between colors, to the radiation of color beyond the edges, and to their mutual changeability. In this context, the statement by painter Philipp Otto Runge is interesting: "The strict regularity is most necessary in those works of art that originate from the imagination and the mysticism of our soul, without outer matter or history."[32]

In his work, Albers considers seeing to be highly relevant as a process of perception and an act of concentration. Albers emphasized that he did not want to establish dogmas with his work. It was intended to serve greater understanding amongst others, and demonstrated all the more clearly that color cannot be determined too rigidly and fixedly. For this reason, Albers's painter colleague Ad Reinhardt (1913–1967) radically rejected color. "There is something wrong, irresponsible and mindless about color, something impossible to control."[33]

From the 1950s, Reinhardt worked with monochrome paintings, mostly in red and blue, that had subtle color differences within slightly nuanced rectangles that were applied in several layers of scumble. This meant that they were only seemingly monochrome. From 1953, most of Reinhardt's paintings were black. At first glance it is not possible to detect a compositional principle or a discernible form of expression. On closer inspection, however, one can see extremely delicate, almost velvety color gradations and, after a prolonged period of time, similar to Albers, also a simple, anonymous scheme of forms beneath the black—in blue, red, or green. With his pictures that challenged the viewer to look closely and that reveal the subtlest of differentiations, Reinhardt penetrated to the core of color. (see p. 35)

Pushing the boundaries of perception with color

Even a decade after the end of World War II, abstract painting, which was devoid of any spontaneity and gesture by the artist, was not able to find much resonance in the USA. Abstract Expressionism, known under the name of the New York School, dominated the art world and hence the individual form of artistic expression. The term was an umbrella for a wide range of different approaches. The focus was on emotion and improvisation; strict rules and laws were rejected. Particularly impressive was the method of action painting that equated to an expression of liberation from the limitations of traditional art concomitant with the liberation from small formats, imposed strictures, rules, and repression. Its most famous representative, Jackson Pollock (1912–1956), wildly sprayed and flung the paint onto the canvas. This spontaneous and free painting turns the act of painting with full physical involvement into the picture itself.

At the end of the 1950s, artists turned away from the expressionism of gesture, and unique art directions sprang up, such as that of Mark Rothko or Barnett Newman (1905–1970), whose works are classified under Color

Field painting. The place of generally applicable rules or impulsive, expressive modes of expression was taken by an experience of color, which opened the space for personal experiences. Rothko's monochrome painting developed a type of floating state, in which the space between was just as important as the color fields themselves. The permeable character of the pictures, which were subdivided into two or three colored areas that flow into each other without contours, spread a special and mysterious mood. The terms *breathing* and *pulsating* were often used for the light-flooded and nebulous impression of his images.

At the same time, in order to create a state of intimacy, Rothko increased the format of his pictures until they reached such dimensions that the viewer's entire field of vision is filled when looking at the works close up. This produced a new relationship with three-dimensionality. Rothko wanted to make it possible to experience the sensation of color and to eliminate the distance between the viewer and the image. In a certain sense, his world of feelings was the subject of his expressive painting.

In their large monochrome pictures, the group of Color Field painters focused exclusively on color as image-forming component, its expressive inherent value, and different forms of appearance. The involvement with expanding behavior, with processes of limitation, with dynamizing force vectors, or with the development of three-dimensionality through color became just as relevant as the preoccupation with the processes of perception. Color Field painting deliberately withdrew from any social references. Canvases were created that contained nothing but color. Monochrome painting opened up the possibility of designing images without visible principles of composition, free from myth, memories, associations, or interpretation options. In this context, the engagement with experiences and transgressions that go beyond conventional boundaries played an important role. The idea was that the viewer should experience the effect of the color overwhelmingly and incomprehensibly, triggered by the painting itself. Color, surface, and space were perceived as a physical unit.

The painter and sculptor Barnett Newman also focused on the quality of color, particularly in terms of his practical work. He writes: "What bothers me is color as color, as material, as local."[34] Any kind of personal artistic expression was avoided, any trace of the application of paint disappeared. Even artists such as Piet Mondrian were not immune to Newman's criticism. He held that Mondrian's paintings were not pure abstraction and that he was purely representing the geometric image of nature.[35]

Newman saw the beginning of a new direction for art only in nongeometric art, and considered artistic self-determination to be more important than academic sets of rules. All references, either in reality or its presentation, however abstract, were to be avoided in order to create an experience based purely on visual perception. Newman was focused on pure painting in order to reestablish therein the aesthetics of the "sublime." With this picture from a series of four paintings, *Who's Afraid of Red, Yellow and Blue III* (see p. 28), Newman presents the three primary colors and imbues color with a semantic quality. Red stands for the exalted; it expands

32 Haftmann 1965, 292.
33 Rowell 1980, 23.
34 Newman 1992, 292.
35 Ibid., 163.

beyond the edges of the image and develops an overwhelming effect. The colors yellow and blue serve to emphasize even further the luminosity of the red color. Barnett Newman's interest was always in the encounter between the viewer and the picture, in a personal interaction. He was less concerned with the spatial effect of his painting than with "experiences of sensations in time."[36] Nevertheless, the overwhelming presence of color in Newman's pictures exerted a strong spatial fascination.

At this time, it was a logical development for painting to eventually extend into the room itself. In 1965 Ellsworth Kelly (1923–2015) installed monochrome color panels in the form of a spatial arrangement. Some of the color panels Kelly simply leaned against the wall, thus creating the impression of a floating state. Kelly's unconventionally shaped canvases were an example of the interaction between form, color, and space and included the architectural context through their three-dimensional presence. When working on his groups of color panels (1968), Kelly used trapezoid or rectangular shapes as picture supports in order to achieve the illusion of distorted space in perspective.

Kelly was considered a realist in the way he handled color, and he rejected any mystification or spiritualization of art. He was interested in the three-dimensionality of painting at the boundary with sculpture, between image and object. For Kelly, the relationship between form and the extent of color was essential; he often used wood or aluminum as a carrier material, which had a significant effect on the perception of the picture and its quality of light and shadow. During his lifetime, Ellsworth Kelly was associated with many different art movements, including concrete art, hard-edge painting, post-painterly abstraction, and Color Field painting. When minimal art became established in New York in the 1960s, Ellsworth Kelly was considered its precursor.

Donald Judd (1928–1994), one of the most important representatives of minimal art, developed his work in parallel to Color Field painting. In his 1993 essay "Some aspects of color in general, and red and black in particular," which was based on a lecture he had given, Judd declared: "Color to continue had to occur in space."[37]

Judd criticized painting because, at best, in contrast to sculpture, it would only create spatial illusionism. With his freestanding objects in space, he liberated the picture from the wall, and omitted any kind of association with pictures. For Judd, color and space only ever appeared together. He used bright cadmium red as a favorite color, since it most clearly defined the shape of his objects, created a three-dimensional presence in space, and emphasized edges.[38] In contrast to the Constructivists, who were aiming for proportion, balance, and charged relationships based on an individual approach to order and modeled arrangement, Judd rejected any expression that appeared to be based on composition. His involvement with color was closely related to the material. He used aluminum, transparent and colored acrylic glass, copper sheets, or plywood in equal weighting with the color, which he used vigorously and applied in a way that retained the characteristic properties and texture of the material. The different

36 Newman 1949,
    in Newman 1992, 175.
37 Elger 1999, 115.
38 Ibid., 17.

26

Camille Graeser,
"Sinfonie der Farbe" (Symphony of color),
1946–50, oil on canvas,
70 × 105 cm

Working from the square as basic element, Graeser's
"Sinfonie der Farbe" is based on a strict ordering
principle, which is interrupted by a single disruptive
element in the left half of the picture.

Mark Rothko,
"Orange, Red and Red", 1962,
oil on canvas, 237 × 235 cm

Barnett Newman,
"Who's Afraid of Red, Yellow and Blue III",
1967–68, acrylic on canvas, 224 × 544 cm

Color Field painting set out to question fundamental traditional approaches to the art of painting. The area colored in cadmium red dominates the image surface, with size, format, and color determining each other.
The dimensions that make it impossible to comprehend the whole picture in one glance lead to a modified perception and add to the overwhelming power of the color. The monumentality and degree of abstraction of the picture go beyond familiar ways of seeing. Viewers, who are completely surrounded by the red color space, are referred back to themselves.

Ellsworth Kelly,
"White Angle", 1966,
painted aluminum,
181 × 91.4 × 183.5 cm

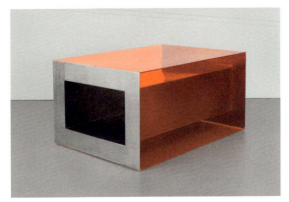

Donald Judd,
"Untitled", 1968,
stainless steel and orange
acrylic glass,
83.82 × 172.7 × 121.9 cm

Imi Knoebel,
"Genter Raum", 1979–80,
449 painted wood panels in
variable arrangement

Gerwald Rockenschaub,
"Embrace Romance Remodeled",
Exhibition Space Halle,
Salzburg, Austria, 2012

Gerwald Rockenschaub produces his work digitally
and uses industrial materials such as PVC.

John M. Armleder,
"Untitled (Furniture Sculpture)", 1986,
acrylic and enamel on canvas and chests of drawers,
250 × 400 × 50 cm max.

qualities of the materials created unpredicted effects due to the color's power of reflection and the different surface textures: radiant, reflective, glowing, filling the interior space. At times the surfaces dematerialized, and then physical presence interacted with emptiness. Additions, series, and variations were created while anonymizing principles of order to the greatest possible extent.

Departure from the picture—
Color in the context of material and space

An exhibition in Zurich entitled *Concrete Art*, presented by Max Bill in 1960, showed the first examples of American Color Field painting as well as work by the Zero group. All works of the artists involved with Zero were of a serial nature. In music too, serial structures were developed at this time. The dynamic of the picture surface was increasingly emphasized using light, movement, and material. Instead of composition, fields of energy, grids, and repetition in space became important. Zero promoted a "departure from the picture."

Color was further reduced toward monochromy, and plain color was used owing to its purity. The maxim of "rethinking everything" led to the artists' using new industrial products, and even everyday items such as nails or waste products of space travel were included. The American Robert Ryman (born 1930), one of the key figures of monochrome art, practiced his art during the time of Zero. For Ryman, the essential elements of art are light, the physical substance of the material, and space. Ryman experimented in particular with oil, enamel, and lacquer on a wide variety of substrates, such as canvas, fabric, metal, wood, wax paper, and plastic. The color white held particular fascination for Ryman, because it reflects light in the most differentiated way and most clearly makes color nuances visible. Ryman also tried out unusual methods of hanging and attaching pictures.

Another exceptional artist of the time was Gotthard Graubner (1930–2013), who exhibited together with his colleagues from Zero. Graubner tried to enhance the spatial effect of color surfaces with "picture objects." His work impressively illustrates the multifaceted character of artistic expression in monochromy. From 1956 he occupied himself with minimally nuanced, subtly modulated color pitches and color spaces. Cool and warm tonal values alternate. Graubner's subject, the embodiment of color, receives its charge from the contrast between shape and dissolution, and gives rise to the expression "breathing images." To produce these he developed, after 1960, a cushion-like painting platform padded with absorbent cotton wool.[39] Many layers of paint or scumble are used to produce vibrant irregularities and cause the colors to vibrate. The color appears modulated. The desired expression and liveliness is the result of the interaction of the colors and the stimulating effect the colors produce between them. It is only the effect of the color—its elasticity and permeability, its physical heaviness or fogginess—that constitutes its essence. Graubner's paints sink deeply into the carrier of the image. In

1970, Graubner replaced the older designations of his work—"color body" or "cushion picture"—with "color-space body." With the "fog spaces" he developed between 1968 and 1971, and again in 2006–7, he wanted to foster sensitivity in the viewer.[40]

Many artists at that time focused on the materiality of color, its structure and the way it is created, on the characteristics of pigments, reflective behavior, and methods of working with color. When Radical Painting came about in New York in 1978, color resurfaced as the sole subject. Radical Painting had its roots in the crisis of modern art in the 1960s. The characteristics of pictures and objects became more and more ambivalent; the distinction between painting and sculpture blurred. The relationship between color and architecture was further explored, and the problem of the illusion of space within the flat surface of a picture was reexamined again and again. Sometimes pictures were created directly on a wall or on absorbent, reflective, or dampening materials.

The Metal Pictures developed by the painter and Beuys student Blinky Palermo (1943–1977), formerly Peter Heisterkamp, in New York between 1973 and 1976 were painted directly onto aluminum panels. The repeatedly applied acrylic layers, placed in extremely delicate horizontal lines on the reflective aluminum, appear to be floating in front of the wall. The colors are in strong contrast to each other and, to the observing eye, seem to be shimmering. The repeatedly superimposed layers are the result of a change in conceptual intent during the painting process, which Palermo "was not able to conceptualize and imagine at the beginning of the work"[41]; it was in this way that the artist characterized his work in 1975 on the occasion of the eighth Bienal de São Paulo.

The Swiss painter Jean Baier (1932–1999) was interested in the aesthetics of industrial manufacturing. He used a spray gun to apply cellulose paint to hard, plain materials such as metal sheeting, aluminum, and synthetic fabric. His surfaces are metallic, enameled, synthetic.[42] Baier's work is based on his own set of rules, which he established freely and undogmatically. In his view, "experiencing" was of greater value than mathematics. In spite of the structure and order inherent in his work, Baier differentiated himself from the members of the Zurich School with whom he was in friendly contact, even though he was much younger. His work is characterized by strong compositional elements and a great variety of shapes made up of simplified surfaces. In his work, form and color are interwoven in a charged, higher-order overall system that is characterized by homogeneous, rhythmically placed color fields which at times appear to be cut up.

His main oeuvre consists of three-dimensional pieces in the public domain, which enabled him to achieve extraordinarily large dimensions and to create references to architecture and the city. Within the images too, he developed a spatial and sculptural impression; flat forms appear as volumes, and an impression of depth and transparency ensues. Baier worked on the principle of subdividing the picture surface. White shards with pointed angles slide like wedges into the strong, full color tones. This creates the impression of intersections, sliding elements, expansion or

39 Liesbrock 2012, 17.
40 Ibid., 6.
41 Richter 1990, 142.
42 Neubert 2014, 6.

Flat forms appear as volumes, and an impression of depth and transparency ensues.

Jean Baier,
"Composition/Relief", 1987,
cellulose color on metal,
100 × 500 cm, five parts

contraction. His color palette remains limited to blue, red, and yellow in combination with black, gray, and white.

In the 1960s and 1970s, Baier—using ceramic panels—developed artistically designed facades and large murals, which cannot be grasped in an instant but have to be viewed along their entire length as the spectator walks by. In so doing, Baier expanded his work by the factor of time, because with each new movement, new relationships arise. He included this instability in his designs. Color is used to create transitions, ruptures, or vibrations. Everything remains static and dynamic at the same time.

The development from wall painting to space painting can be illustrated clearly by the work of Gerwald Rockenschaub (born 1952). Whereas in 1987 he was still painting oil pictures, he then proceeded to relate his geometrical color compositions directly to the exhibition space.

In this way painting, and hence color, expands into the realm of the entire installation, sometimes including furniture and room surfaces. Analogously to Marcel Duchamp (1887–1968), the artist John M. Armleder (born 1948) integrates "Readymades" (utility articles) and places them in a geometrically abstract overall context (see p. 29).

With the installation *Genter Raum* of 1979–1980, the artist Imi Knoebel (born 1940) also goes far beyond the conventional notion of a painting, working at the interface of sculpture, installation, architecture, and painting. Variably arranged wooden panels were painted by brush on both sides. They lie on the floor, sorted in stacks, giving the impression of material taken apart, and are ordered by color. Further panels hang on the walls like illustrative plates. Knoebel has selected and combined the colors with great care and extends his composition into space. Other sections of wooden panels are stacked in groups on the floor and seem like sculptural blocks (see p. 29).

Painting does not mean coloring shapes, but shaping color. [43]
Henri Matisse

Artists' work on the subject of color appears inexhaustible. The development of painting from the Renaissance to the twentieth century proceeded as artists went into increasing detail in specifying the language of color. When, at the beginning of the twentieth century, color was used in much more intensive ways, as its own motif, the numerous facets of its essence became apparent.

Today it seems unthinkable that, for centuries, color was used purely as a means of coloring, of filling in forms, putting an edge to shapes, or depicting objects. "Painting does not mean coloring shapes, but shaping color."[44] This quote by Henri Matisse aptly characterizes the painter's understanding of color.

The different artistic approaches that opened the way to abstraction, the search for a strong expression, radical principles of composition and structuring, but also the diverse work with color material and all attempts to unfold its three-dimensional effect, gave color an autonomous strength. From the time when color and shape departed from the compulsory representation of reality, all generations of artists have explored the relationships between image content, shape, and color, and used these to formulate their artistic messages, generating completely diverse picture languages. Color is capable of making new statements again and again, and can dissolve our static and defined world of pictures. The desire and search for the essence of color, either as material, space-defining element, or cause of the exalted make it a fascinating medium. Donald Judd, who regarded color as one of the most important elements in his work, considered the interaction with color an inexhaustible process: "Color will always be interpreted in a new way, so that I hardly think my use is final, in fact I think it is a beginning. Infinite change may be its constant nature."[45]

43 Schröder 2013.
44 Ibid.
45 Elger 1999, 115.

Ad Reinhardt,
"Abstract Painting No. 5",
1962, oil on canvas,
60 × 60 cm

Positions
on color
in architecture

Color perception as an individual event

In the presentation of architecture, color is never just a line on the wall. It shows itself as skin, as paint or stain coating, as a film or colored material, with or without visible traces of the person who applied it. Color perception is a momentary snapshot in a context that changes continuously due to lighting and environmental conditions.

The real essence of color unfolds only through the viewing by the spectator or through a design intention, since color cannot be captured by general statements and our sense perception of it is linked with subjective ideas of color. This linking process is renewed again and again; it influences our impression of color and equates to a collection of experiences that we compare with previous observations and memories. These ideas undergo constant change throughout our life. For this reason, color is difficult to grasp and is often perceived as a risky instrument, which all too easily can be manipulated by whims of fashion. As a tectonic means of design it is still subject to debate, and architects often perceive its application in space as indeterminate, arbitrary, and blurred.

Furthermore, it is an extremely imprecise undertaking to try to verbally formulate the appearance of color with its constant variations. Even though our eye is capable of distinguishing over 7.5 million color differences, it is impossible to name these huge numbers of color shades and to differentiate them verbally. This explains the difficulty of communicating color and the ideas of color in words; categorizing and naming color of necessity involves selection and prioritization. It is known that ethnic communities sometimes have numerous different terms for certain colors, whereas other color shades are collectively referred to with one term. Up to now, each society, epoch, and culture has produced its own ideas on color. When the historian Michel Pastoureau speaks of color as a multilayered cultural construct, he refers to the fact that, over time, every society has, in its cultural context, developed its own access to color based on regional possibilities.[1] In this process, throughout thousands of years, color was given symbolic meaning and was semantically charged.

Time and again, artists, scientists, and architects throughout the course of history have tried to establish principles of application and to formulate a systematic approach to color in order to generate a repeatable, reliable, and objective access to color. How well we handle color, however, is not determined by its unequivocal graspability, plannability, and usability, but in the experience and perception of its indeterminability. This is probably what prompted the architect, painter, graphic designer, and sculptor Max Bill (1908–1994) to make the statement that "color has nothing to do in architecture."[2] In contrast to the color applied with coatings, the inherent color of materials appears honest and straightforward, whereas the perception of color and its free application involve subjective, cognitive, and emotional processes that are based on a purely personal view of color.

A historical assessment of how color was used in the art of building

The reticence of many architects to use color in space is not only due to its lack of tangibility but also due to historical reasons. Nicolas Le Camus de Mézières (1721–1789) was one of the first architects to investigate the effects of light, shadow, color, and proportion on the human psyche and on the atmosphere of spaces. In his work *Le Génie de l'architecture, ou L'Analogie de cet art avec nos sensations* dated 1781, he considers not only purely decorative issues and personal taste, but also, for the first time, the interdependencies of synesthetics.

Until the nineteenth century, color in architecture had been determined by decorative considerations, for example in the form of embellishing accoutrements such as heavily ornamented wall hangings, wallpapers, or ornaments, which had a significant influence on the atmosphere of interiors. It was this type of embellishment that completed the building, and the color scheme became a key subject in architecture. Nicolas Le Camus de Mézières held the view that it was the architect who was responsible for the overall appearance in the sense of a holistic room impression, and not the decorative painters hired for the job.[3] Nevertheless, the occupational profile of the *peintre d'impression* included a wide range of tasks such as stuccowork, ornamental painting, and panel and ceiling work, and this was left entirely to the skill of the respective craftsman.

In the same century, the archaeologist Johann Joachim Winckelmann (1717–1768) was one of the first to explore the polychromy of architecture and sculpture in antiquity; at the same time, in his statements, he referred to these artifacts in classic white as representing the ideal of beauty. "As white is the colour which reflects the greatest number of rays of light, and consequently is the most easily perceived, a beautiful body will, accordingly, be the more beautiful the whiter it is."[4]

The impressive white ruins of the ancient sites of Rome and Athens were considered perfect owing to their pure white aesthetics. They were illustrated in the 1873 work *L'Art de bâtir chez les Romains* by the French art historian Auguste Choisy (1841–1909), who researched in depth the construction systems of classical antiquity.[5]

In reality, however, these ancient artifacts were not white, but colored. Sculptors, architects, and painters worked hand in hand. The ancient color schemes did not, however, consist of decorative styling, but were intended to emphasize the real essence and hence the identity of places and objects and to make them merge with the whole. The findings on the polychromy of ancient architecture and sculpture that had been discovered as early as the eighteenth century were not recognized until the end of the nineteenth century; they contradicted the rational, classicistic approach, which was to omit color. Its common idea and architectural language was influenced by the white buildings and sculptures of antiquity and espoused a coolness of color, largely omitting applied color and preferring the colors of stone. The classicists' idea was that buildings should be determined by the monochrome color of the stone only; no external paint should be applied. In the

1   Pastoureau 2013, 7.
2   Archithese, no. 6 (November/December 1994), 46.
3   Le Camus 1780.
4   Winckelmann 1764, in Winckelmann 1849, 38.
5   Choisy 1873.

nineteenth century, this led to a fundamental discourse on the treatment of color in space. Important artists, architects, and scientists took part in the discussion, the point of departure of which was antiquity.

"The frequent abuses so easily made in painting and coloring should not be a reason to ban all color and simply to declare garish everything that is not gray, white or pale earth."[6] Gottfried Semper (1803–1879), one of the leading architects and theorists of the nineteenth century, occupied himself in detail with the subject of polychromy in architecture. With his writings, Semper wanted to overcome the one-sidedness of the rational and cool classicism. When he wrote "Colors are less glaring than the blinding white of our stucco walls," he tried to directly point out the expression of the time and the diminishing reference to nature.[7] Semper published these thoughts in 1834 in "Preliminary notes on painted architecture and sculpture by the ancients," an essay in which he elaborates that polychromy can be natural and necessary. Semper based this on the protection and durability achieved by coating the material. In his discussions on the use of color in ancient architecture, there is already an implied suggestion that color has a sociopolitical dimension. For Semper, polychromy was a consistent component of architecture. In his later writings that became known as his *Bekleidungstheorie* (theory of dressing), he presents the importance of the visible surface as a form of garment that has been draped over the hidden load-bearing structure to create the interior space. He held that "it is certain that the beginning of building coincides with the beginning of textiles."[8] According to this assumption, ornament and color were based on the textiles that originally formed the outside walls and were retained as decorative elements when such components were replaced by solid buildings. Semper was less interested in the material/aesthetic aspect than in the way the load-bearing structure and envelope work together, merging both physically and in our conceptual appreciation.

New developments in the context of color, space, and art

Finally, in the nineteenth century, a change of paradigm occurred in the way color was used. Decorative painters lost their artistic independence because architects accepted comprehensive design commissions, and color, either on the strength of coatings or the color of materials, acquired new relevance in terms of space and architecture. Now color was no longer decoration randomly applied to the wall but part of the spatial composition, in the truest sense of the word constituting and dematerializing space. In particular this can be observed in the interior color design of the Crystal Palace, which was designed by the British gardener and architect Joseph Paxton (1803–1865) for the first Great Exhibition in London in 1851 in the form of a huge construction in iron, glass, and wood. Based on the findings of Michel Eugène Chevreul on simultaneous contrast, the law of multiple proportions by the English chemist George Field (1777–1854), and his own studies on Islamic ornamental art, the architect and designer Owen Jones (1809–1874), also a Briton, developed an abstract color concept that was radical for its time.

William Simpson
Imterior of the Crystal Palace, c. 1851,
watercolor

The watercolor shows the interior of the
Crystal Palace as planned by Josef Paxton with
the color scheme by Owen Jones.

It consisted of simple geometric shapes in the base colors of blue, red, and yellow, supplemented with white, and was intended to enhance the monumental dimension of the building and to structure it at the same time. In accordance with the principles of complementary contrast, from a distance the colors become blurred over the great length of the building, thus neutralizing one another. At the same time, when seen from the middle distance, the impression of light and shadow is emphasized. In the longitudinal view, the iron beams with their light-blue coloring merge with the sky. Beneath the beams there are red stripes that disappear in the shadow and thus reinforce it; they only become visible when looking directly upward. The columns are coated with narrow strips in the base colors, always separated by white lines, in order to avoid them becoming blurred and to enhance their radiance.[9] "With this approach the term of atmospheric color was introduced—over a decade before Impressionists and Neo-Impressionists started to introduce pointillism in painting."[10]

The gigantic dimensions of the Crystal Palace facilitated the concept of optical mixing of colors in the distance and led to a unique diffused blurring, which in contemporary media was compared to the color effect of the paintings of J. M. W. Turner.

In Space, Time and Architecture, Sigfried Giedion described the Crystal Palace as "the realization of a new conception of building, one for which there was no precedent."[11] In both technical and aesthetic terms, the building was deemed a forerunner of modern buildings at a time when, in large parts of Europe, the various types of historicism—based on the search of the middle classes for identity—were the defining styles.

One of the most important architects of that time, Adolf Loos (1870–1933), wanted to counteract historicism with the idea of modern man. In consequence, he developed modern architecture from historicism. He objected to any kind of embellishing, historical decoration, and the imitation of materials. In his architecture and theoretical terms, he adopted Semper's principle of *Bekleidung* and primarily defined the living space via the enclosing surfaces, whereas he disregarded the construction. His functional designs were based on concepts developed from the inside to the outside. Loos combined spatial three-dimensionality with color,

6   Semper 1834
    im Semper 1989, 69–70.
7   Ibid., 70.
8   Semper 1860
    in Semper 2004, 247.
9   Jones 1865, 11
10 Olsson, in Color
    in Art 2010, 121.
11 Giedion 2008, 251.

and used the color to introduce an additional level of perception. Loos combined surfaces such as marble, with its strong color tones, or heavily patterned burl wood with wood elements or wall and floor finishes painted in strong colors.

He objected to color as a pure adjunct; instead, Loos used it for contrast and in order to enhance his idea of a space. For this reason he referred to the strong, pure colors as natural and "real" colors. His wide and very vibrant color palette stood in stark contrast to the muted color shades in common use.

The room surfaces and room delimitations had to follow the principle of dressing; Loos believed that the dressed material must not be confused with the dressing. "This means, for example, wood may be painted any color except one—the color of wood."[12] In this way, Loos took a fundamental stand against *holzfladerei*, that is, the imitation of hardwood with the appropriate paint materials and the application of colors imitating wood. Under no circumstances would he permit cheap materials to be enhanced with paint.

Adolf Loos followed the same principles in the design of his interiors; the seeming absence of embellishment was counteracted with appropriate details, strong color schemes, and expressive materials. In this way he managed to achieve some opulent interiors in prestigious premises such as the Brummel residence in Plseň: a strictly asymmetrical floor plan in which all rooms are connected via a central axis was supplemented with finishes, linings, built-in furniture in heavily grained and strongly colored woods, or stone slabs and textiles in strong colors rather than the conventional decorative ornamental patterns. In the dining room, he used burl wood paneling from Canadian poplar; the living room features paneling of stained oak. Behind the dining room lies the Yellow Room, the study of a later owner. For the construction of seats and built-in cabinets, Loos often used colorfully finished plywood panels.

It was not only Loos who recognized the importance of the color and appearance of the material. At the same time he was building villas and creating interiors, the architect Ludwig Mies van der Rohe (1886–1969), also one of the most important representatives of modernism and director of the Bauhaus, designed the German Pavilion for the 1929 International Exposition in Barcelona.

In this project, van der Rohe used the means of material opulence[13] in order to emphasize context of space and scale. Surfaces are identical to color units, only in this case there is no paint involved; instead, it is the color of the materials, which have been deliberately selected, polished, and treated for their surface properties. In this way, and in accordance with Loos's approach, color became an integral part of the space concept.[14]

Many important architects considered it a matter of principle to rely only on the effect of physical matter as they endeavored to create the color content and value of interiors purely by the use of materials. The Russian theorist Dimitri Alexandrovich Toporkov (1885–1937) saw the justification for the resurgent interest in the material in its underappreciation and misuse

12 Loos 1898
   in Loos 1987.
13 werk, bauen + wohnen,
   no. 6 (June 2016), 9.
14 Mack 2001, 8.
15 Opel 2010, 173.

Green becomes olive green, red becomes red-brown. And in this olive green and red-brown wallpaper gravy we have been floating about for a whole century.[15]
Adolf Loos

Simplify your forms in order to be able to successfully appear colorful.[16]
Fritz Schumacher

in the artistic production of the nineteenth century. He formulated a close connection between the material and the form derived from the material's natural propensity to be formed. "Material must be formed. This stipulation reverses the previous disdain for the material. The material must not be neglected, otherwise we will again fall into the trap of the old tastelessness."[17] He strictly rejected imitations and forms of processing that were borrowed from other materials, such as woven porcelain baskets. "In short, it appears to me that the subject of the material, so topical in our modern times, gives rise to many erroneous developments and wrong turns."[18]

At the same time, new materials such as iron, concrete, and glass, technical inventions, and political change heralded a new era of building. In these conditions, people had to completely revise their perceptions, and art and architecture needed to find new approaches. As a result, the beginning of the twentieth century was characterized by many reform movements.

With the foundation of the Deutsche Werkbund in 1907, there was a coming together of a group of architects, artists, artisans, and entrepreneurs who considered the functional appropriateness of the material to be an important design criterion for creating a new, independent awareness of form and quality. The founding members included Peter Behrens (1868–1940), Theodor Fischer (1862–1938), Wilhelm Kreis (1873–1955), Hermann Muthesius (1861–1927), Joseph Maria Olbrich (1867–1908), Karl Ernst Osthaus (1874–1921), Richard Riemerschmid (1868–1957), Fritz Schumacher (1869–1947), and Henry van de Velde (1863–1957). Muthesius and van de Velde in particular argued about the orientation of the Werkbund as a promoter either of standardized industrial mass production (Muthesius) or of an artistic approach to individually designed objects (van de Velde). In parallel with the discourse amongst the artists and architects, flat ways of painting were becoming more popular, new theoretical concepts were pursued, and a new understanding of space developed on the basis of art. Whereas, at the end of the nineteenth century, the Impressionists had postulated the detachment of color from form (see p. 7–36), a short time later, in Expressionism, a newly defined and abstracted relationship between form, color, and surface led to the development of a strong pictorial dynamic and powerful polychromy. "When the colored areas are so large that there is no optical blending, an effect of visual interaction appears."[19]

Full of conviction, the architect and member of the Werkbund Fritz Schumacher published his still-relevant article "Colorful Architecture" in 1901. In it, he points out the mutual influence of form and color, including John Ruskin's (1819–1900) thoughts on the independence of form and color, in his assessment. In this context, he also points out the possibility of form and color influencing each other negatively.[20]

At the beginning of the twentieth century, a radical new aesthetic appeared in the form of Cubism in particular, which developed from 1907, and through the emphasis on functional and rational criteria in design processes, providing key stimuli to modern architecture. The movement beyond conventional spatial perspective and the discovery of simultaneity in Cubism could not be directly transferred to architecture, but nevertheless inspired artists, theorists, and architects throughout Europe. All previously upheld laws of painting were to be laid aside. The demand was no longer for a representational art, but for an art based on imagination.[21] Cubism was not the only source of new, distinguishable definitions of various positions; the abstract relief constructions by Vladimir Tatlin (1885–1953), for which the term *Constructivism* was used in 1913, or the Suprematism of Kazimir Malevich (1878–1935) are other examples.

16 Schumacher 1907, 116.
17 Toporkov in Rübel
    2005, 292.
18 Ibid., 294.
19 Olsson, in Color
    in Art 2010, 122.
20 Schumacher 1907, 116.
21 Apollinaire
    in Wood 1998, 226.

Wenzel Hablik,
dining room in the Hablik residence,
Itzehohe, Germany, 1923

Wenzel Hablik—Spatial art and painting

The universal artist and Expressionist Wenzel Hablik (1881–1934) was considered one of the most productive individuals in his field, enjoying a rich vein of experimentation. When the architect Bruno Taut founded the Glass Chain in November 1919, one of the most famous chain letters for architects and artists, Hablik maintained a lively discussion with Walter Gropius (1883–1969), Hans Scharoun (1893–1972), and other architects, writers, and painters about utopian visions of space and architecture.

Based on the general enthusiasm for color of the early 1920s, and motivated by the desire to combine architecture, sculpture, and painting in the idea of an overall work of art, Hablik designed impressive space concepts for numerous interiors. His aim was to design spaces as artistic units. Between 1921 and 1928, Hablik worked at the interface between paintings, murals, and space compositions and created his own color cosmos. His designs reveal influences from the Dutch De Stijl group, as well as from the Russian Constructivists.

In 1923 Wenzel Hablik created colorful spatial artwork when he painted walls and ceilings in his own house in Itzehoe. An interlaced image of colorful ribbons is created like a web structure, which, in spite of its asymmetry, appears balanced as a whole. Concave coving between ceiling and wall served to create the basis for a continuous color texture. In spite of the many intense color shades and stripes that are of different widths, change direction, and cross over, the work appears to be based on a compositional order. Contours, areas with denser patterns, and a few areas that are fully colored are used to bring together individual room elements, such as furniture or opening elements, into as consistent a room image as possible and to include the composition. Examples are the golden rectangles on the ceiling that mark the position of the luminaires. But smaller, compacter color elements at the walls are also part of the overall design. With their abstract, architectural appearance, they are reminiscent of the Suprematist artist Kazimir Malevich.[22]

22 Bartel 2007, 26–31.

De Stijl—Abstraction based on color

The increased search by artists in the twentieth century for pure means of expression and new spatial concepts resulted in color, form, material, and space interacting in surprising new combinations. Key figures such as Le Corbusier (1887–1965) and Amédée Ozenfant (1886–1966), Kazimir Malevich, László Moholy-Nagy (1895–1946), Theo van Doesburg (1883–1931), and Piet Mondrian (1872–1944) worked on objects of art that tried to depict the scientific and technical givens of their time.

In 1917 a group of painters, sculptors, and architects around the painter and theorist Theo van Doesburg, the painter Piet Mondrian, and the architect J. J. P. Oud formed the Dutch group De Stijl, for which Van Doesburg issued a magazine of the same title. The name De Stijl was given in reminiscence of Gottfried Semper's incomplete main work *Style in the Technical and Tectonic Arts* (1860–1863), which at that time had been widely discussed. The protagonists pursued their artistic aims with heavily reduced means, without any personal expression, and drew their strength from at times radical simplification. The primary maxims were clarity, facticity, and suitability for purpose. They were convinced that they would be able to derive a universal subject and generally applicable laws from the invention of an abstract, unrestricted system.

The fundamental three-dimensional elements mentioned by Van Doesburg in the *De Stijl* magazine in 1924 were mass, plane, time, space, light, and color. These are used functionally and sparingly while maintaining complete abstraction. The range of permitted means of expression was limited to straight or "gently waving" vertical or horizontal lines in combination with a color spectrum based on the work of Piet Mondrian, which consisted of the complementary colors blue, yellow, and red supplemented by the so-called noncolors black, white, and gray.

In May 1924 Theo van Doesburg published the article "The Significance of Color in Architecture" in the Belgian magazine *La Cité*. In this article, Van Doesburg emphasizes color as the essential element of architecture that was mandatory for establishing the references between object and space. "We have given colour its rightful place in architecture and we assert that painting separated from the architectonic construction (that is, the picture) has no right to exist."[23]

One year later, Theo van Doesburg writes: "The new architecture permits colour organically as a direct means of expressing its relationships within space and time. Without colour these relationships are not real but invisible."[24]

The function of color as a compositional element, the charge and balance between colors and planes, becomes the determining factor. He postulated that color should be recognized as a means of expression equivalent to building materials such as stone, steel, or glass. Van Doesburg makes a distinction between the conventional use of color as coating and the use of color as a space-forming element. On large areas and via strong contrasts, color took on the role of defining the space.

23 De Stijl
   in Conrads 1975, 66.
24 Ibid., 80.

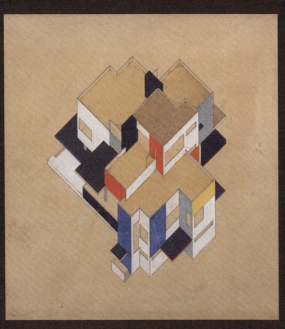

Gerrit Rietveld,
Rietveld–Schröder residence,
Utrecht, The Netherlands, 1924

Theo van Doesburg,
Cornelis van Eesteren,
Maison particulière,
1923, pictorial drawing

Between 1947 and 1958, Jean Albert Gorin produced
artistic works and architectural drawings in
equal measure. He referred to himself as a "painter-
architect." In his space composition of 1930,
he pursued the key idea of De Stijl.

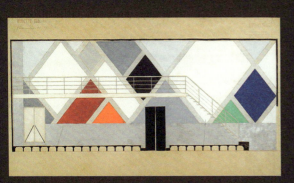

Theo van Doesburg, Café L'Aubette,
Strasbourg, France, 1926
design sketch

Jean Albert Gorin,
"Chromoplastique architecturale", 1930,
ink, gouache, silver paint, and pencil on paper,
50 × 40.5 cm

DE STIJL—ABSTRACTION BASED ON COLOR

In the Maison particulière project, in cooperation with the architect Cornelis van Eesteren (1897–1988), the theories were, for the first time, implemented in space: the principles of painting were transferred to space. Paint no longer took up entire surfaces within a space, but colored areas were deliberately composed with the aim of dissolving these surfaces and confining elements. The color design influences the perception of spatial volumes in such a way that the building appears to be open-plan, even though it was built in accordance with the traditional principles of masonry construction. The result is the abstraction of the space. In 1918 Theo van Doesburg put this effect into words in an article in the *De Stijl* magazine: "Architecture should create a constructed, closed sculpture, which is reopened by the paintwork using unmodulated colors in balanced proportions. The role of the architect is to stabilize, that of the painter is to destabilize."[25]

The Dutchman Gerrit Rietveld (1888–1964), who had joined the De Stijl movement early on, systematically applied the idea that color and form were compositional elements of equal standing in his Schröder residence in Utrecht, completed in 1924. The residence is a spatial color sculpture that can be lived in, detached from any kind of convention. Randomly fitted colored areas and bars form the space; visually, the building dissolves into its individual elements.

The range of colors is limited to white, gray, and black, with occasional highlights of blue, red, and yellow. The building is based on the basic idea of pure construction, formed of rationally joined elements that are independent of one another. The installation of these elements determines a dynamism that arises from the interactive relationship between independence and mutual connectivity.[26]

From 1923 Theo van Doesburg experimented with dynamic diagonals in his *Contra-Composition* pictures. In 1926 he published the "Manifesto of Elementarism" in the *De Stijl* magazine, in which he introduces the dynamic diagonal. Elementarism absorbed ideas of the Dada, of De Stijl, of futurism, Russian Suprematism, and of the "Prouns" of El Lissitzky, with whom Van Doesburg had contact at the Bauhaus in Weimar. Van Doesburg implemented the ideas of Elementarism in the function hall of Café L'Aubette in Strasbourg, which he designed, and about which he said: "The viewer is no longer located in front of the painting, but in it."[27] The project's renunciation of the right angle led to Mondrian's breaking with the De Stijl group of artists.[28] The walls of the function hall are covered by a composition of rectangles arranged diagonally to the edges of the space and worked in the form of reliefs. They are filled with the strong base colors of De Stijl and, in order to prevent color interference, separated from each other by white bands. The space was not to be comprehended at first glance, but was to be experienced spatially through movement.

The representatives of De Stijl superimposed a new interpretation level on architectural space, that is to say, color. All texturing, embellishment, and ornamentation that had hitherto been an essential part of architecture were given up in favor of an interaction with volumes, areas, and spaces. They were searching for a key to truly contemporary architecture and art.

Bauhaus—A total work of art

As a forerunner of classic modernism, the De Stijl group also exerted great influence on the Bauhaus in Weimar that had been cofounded by Walter Gropius in 1919. Gropius was in contact with Theo van Doesburg and invited him to Weimar at the end of 1921. In 1922, Van Doesburg took up an atelier in Weimar and, in private courses and lectures, articulated his Constructivist ideas of design. At the time, this contrasted with the orientation of the Bauhaus toward an interlinking of craft and Expressionist ideas as a primary objective.

In his role as director, Walter Gropius gathered together a group of leading representatives of Expressionism, so-called masters of form and workshop masters, with the aim of linking architecture, as a total work of art and leading genre, with all other arts. This focus on architecture, however, was not necessarily reflected in the teaching program in the initial years: a separate class for architecture was not started until 1927. Teaching at the Bauhaus only developed step by step toward its guiding idea, according to which the arts are to free themselves from isolation and enter into a symbiotic relationship with art, architecture, design, craft, and industry.

Some of the teachers, amongst them Lyonel Feininger, Johannes Itten (1888–1967), Josef Albers, Paul Klee (1879–1940), Wassily Kandinsky, and Oskar Schlemmer (1888–1943), taught very different aesthetic points of view in their courses in relation to form and color. Initially, the teaching and application of color was strongly influenced by the theories of Itten, an important representative of international Constructivism. As a painter, he occupied himself with the interaction between form and color. He allocated certain colors to the basic shapes and associated colors with properties such as temperature or mood. In his courses, students created studies on the juxtaposition of colors and color contrasts; he published his findings in his book *The Art of Color* in 1961.[29]

In the class of the German/American painter and caricaturist Lyonel Feininger, the focus was on using color to create depth in the image composition, amongst other subjects. In addition, there was a separate workshop for wall painting led by the artist Wassily Kandinsky and Master of Form Oskar Schlemmer, where murals were produced at full scale. As part of the foundation course, Kandinsky taught the theory of form, which also included a comprehensive theory of color. He had already developed this in his early writing *Concerning the Spiritual in Art* of 1911.[30] It was the first of his books that dealt with the theory of abstract symbols and was synesthetic in its orientation.

Owing to the study of Theo van Doesburg's theses, and following the departure of Itten in 1923, a more rational attitude began to dominate. Johannes Itten's successor, László Moholy-Nagy, granted color the value of an independent material, the surface of which is formed by the composition of different combinations and concentrations of pigment, binding agent, and additives.

25 Blotkamp 2000, 59.
26 Rüegg 1994, in: Daidalos, no. 51 (1994), 66–77.
27 Blotkamp 2000, 95.
28 Ibid., 89.
29 Itten 1961.
30 Kandinsky 1912.

Work in space was influenced by the ideas of Expressionism and the robust color schemes of rooms in the Biedermeier era in Weimar. Strong colors were allocated to entire individual room surfaces. The grading of different color shades in a room created special spatial impressions; for example, the proportion of rooms was modified by dark ceilings. At the same time, experiments were carried out by applying paint in numerous, almost transparent layers, creating colored surfaces with a particular structure and depth. The Bauhaus student, artist, and architect Andor Weininger (1899–1986) became a member of Kandinsky's wall painting workshop and, at a very early stage, concentrated on the subject of flat plane and three-dimensionality, as well as on the interaction of painting and architecture. Van Doesburg's ideas had a strong influence on Weininger, and he continued the discourse with De Stijl in an independent series of works. His many small-format designs can be transferred to the format used in wall painting, and were fleetingly captured in a series of sketches. The balance between form and space and the conquest of the room with color can be seen as unifying themes running through his work (see p. 98–102).

At the end of 1924, the Staatliche Bauhaus in Weimar opted for a move to Dessau. In response to the new architecture, the buildings constructed there show how color is used as an independent design element capable of modifying the appearance of space and of increasing the effect of the total work of art on the viewer.[31] Under the influence of Hinnerk Scheper (1897–1957), a period started in 1925 in which color was no longer used decoratively but purely in relation to the architecture. In the new Bauhaus building color was used, on the one hand, to differentiate load-bearing and non-load-bearing elements and, on the other hand, with ceilings painted in different colors, as a system of orientation.

In spite of the contemporary discussions on polychromy that took place between Le Corbusier, Fernand Léger (1881–1955), and the De Stijl group, Gropius remained a proponent of white architecture—at least for the exterior envelope of buildings—which for him was a symbol of clarity and purity, and hence of a greater spiritual quality in architecture.[32] The newly constructed houses of the Masters had white facades, but the insides were decorated in color schemes designed by their users, and thereby were an expression of the different personalities. Paul Klee painted his atelier with contrasting black and yellow colors; in Wassily Kandinsky's building, rooms and zones were differentiated by a color palette of more pastel shades, which nevertheless marked off each room as a whole.[33]

In addition to the Bauhaus, important stimuli were created by the Weissenhof Estate in Stuttgart, also known as the Werkbund Estate, which was completed in 1927. The estate was part of the 1927 exhibition *Die Wohnung* (The Home) initiated by the Deutsche Werkbund, which took place in several locations in Stuttgart and included buildings by internationally known architects who had all committed themselves to new building. The designs were produced by the artists J. J. P. Oud and Mart Stam of the De Stijl group, as well as Walter Gropius, Mies van der Rohe, Hans Scharoun, Le Corbusier, and Pierre Jeanneret.

The architects of the De Stijl movement and Le Corbusier in particular created many analogies between art and architecture with their work. Their modern architecture involved the various disciplines in the sense of a synthesis, thus creating a platform and a space for projecting the new ideas. An important connection between color, space, and art was also created via the furniture. Once an overall aesthetic image had been created, the idea was that man's entire environment should undergo complete renewal.

Le Corbusier—From wall painting to space painting

For the young painter and architect Le Corbusier, whose architectural oeuvre was divided into the initial white phase and the later polychrome phase, Auguste Choisy's *L'Art de bâtir chez les Romains*[34] represented an important source of inspiration.[35] As a painter, however, Le Corbusier had, at an early stage, worked with the colors applied to flat surfaces in the style of Cubism and was closely interested in the ideas of the painter Fernand Léger.

During the 1920s, lively discussions took place on painting and architecture and the role of color in space. Le Corbusier quoted the statement of his friend Léger that, like water, color was one of the basic human needs.[36] The two agreed on the point that color was essentially capable of modifying and dissolving space, but whereas Le Corbusier, as an architect, considered this process as part of his creative remit, Léger insisted that only painters were able to implement color concepts in space.

In their article "Le Purisme" on the purist understanding of art— published in 1921 in the magazine *L'Esprit nouveau*—the painter Amédée Ozenfant and Le Corbusier expressed their theories on the application of color in a style they themselves referred to as Purism, which is based on the dependence of color on form. Now color is no longer a decorative element in space, but develops its space-forming quality by supporting the actual geometry of the room. To this end, colored areas always cover entire room elements, similar to the principle of Cubist painting in which objects are abstracted to colored forms. In the same vein, Amédée Ozenfant and Le Corbusier described three series of colors that were based on their observations of the three-dimensional dynamics of individual color shades, and thereby created a solid basis for the use of color in space: Grande Gamme (Grand Color series)—the colors that are constructive and preserve shape, Gamme dynamique (Dynamic series)—the colors that are dynamic and change shape, Gamme de transition (Transition series)—the series of flat colors.

This was to be the beginning of Le Corbusier's preoccupation with color, which in 1931 flowed into his *Polychromie architecturale*, which was extended again in 1959. In his article "Color in Interior Architecture," the architect Alberto Sartoris wrote in 1937 in reference to the ideas of Purism: "But each color will have to respect the wall, its form, volume and purpose."[37]

From the 1920s, Le Corbusier, with the Grande Gamme (Grand Color series), reduced colors to a strictly limited selection of mostly mineral

31 Buether 2013.
32 Wick 1983, 486.
33 Droste 2015, 126f.
34 Choisy 1873.
35 Heer 2009, 129.
36 Léger 1946, quoted from Léger 1971, 118.
37 Sartoris in Circle 1937, 213.

But each color will have to respect the wall, its form, volume and purpose.[38]
Alberto Sartoris

Le Corbusier,
interior of a building at
the Weissenhof Estate,
Stuttgart, Germany, 1927

color pigments. These included the earth colors yellow and red ochre, white, black, ultramarine, and any color shades derivable from these. The characteristics associated with these colors were naturalness, familiarity, restraint, and balance. Their application in space and their characteristic restraint appeared manageable; their seeming neutrality deepened the three-dimensionality of space without manipulating it, deconstructing it, or emotionalizing it too heavily.

In addition to the architecturally static Grand Color series, Le Corbusier compiled the Dynamic series of strong colors, which were produced chemically. The main colors in this group were cobalt blue, Veronese green and lemon yellow, and orange and chromium red. Owing to their strong saturation and color intensity, but also to their sometimes emotionalizing color shade, these colors can lend greater dynamism to the space and modify it, as well as change the proportions with their effect, influence the perspective view, and increase contrast. The series of the more flat colors was used decoratively for surfaces, and includes scumble paints with colors such as emerald green or carmine red.

Le Corbusier more closely explored color in his pictures, in which he—following the tradition of Cubism—applied the principle of dissociation of form and color in the image construction. As described by Stanislaus von Moos,[39] he disengages from the "figurative integrity of form and color." Le Corbusier used color shades in order to control and correct the spatial effect in the dichotomy between the holding and flowing of space.

At the same time, in his writings, Le Corbusier emphasized the importance of the color white. The text "Le Lait de chaux—la loi du Ripolin," which appeared in the 1925 book *L'Art décoratif d'aujourd'hui*, makes an enthusiastic plea for an invented law stipulating that a white coating cover all paints and decorations at all buildings. In this context, the white color symbolizes social change, renewal, and purification. At the same time, white is used as background for colored volumes in space in order to enhance their readability. This white background became the dominant feature of Le Corbusier's buildings in the period between 1922 and 1931, and served as the unifying basis of all his architectural compositions. In front of this white background, colored architectural elements such as fireplaces, ramps, or wall slabs protrude sculpturally. Nevertheless, Le Corbusier emphasizes the importance of these colored elements. He likens a purely white house to a "pot of cream."[40]

Le Corbusier reacted with criticism to the model of the Maison particulière that had been exhibited by Theo van Doesburg and Cornelis van Eesteren in 1923. He emphasized that, in Purism, walls were interpreted as colored units that balanced the space.[41]

Impressed by his theoretical writing, the industrialist Henry Frugès gave Le Corbusier free rein to implement his ideas in order to create standardized, economical apartments for the workers at his sawmill. The outcome was the Frugès Estate in Pessac, built in 1924–1926. The form language and proportions of the houses are determined by the optimized production process. In this example, color is seen as a means of design of equal standing

38 Sartoris in Circle
     1937, 213.
39 Von Moos 1966,
     in Das Werk 53, 413–20.
40 Klinkhammer 2011, 22.
41 Ibid., 23.

with the architecture and is used consciously and deliberately in order to achieve a spatial effect.

Up until then, Le Corbusier had used color primarily in a bid to emphasize the three-dimensionality of the overall form and to unify the prefabrication methods that were still rather basic in construction. At the houses in Pessac, however, it is used in a way that gives it a value equal to that of form. Color is applied flat to a three-dimensional body without creating the impression that the body is inherently colored or even "colored through and through." The selection of colors is governed by careful composition; with its earthy red, sky blue, pale green, and white, his color palette is reminiscent of the paintings of the Purists. In the urban design competition, the different colors are assigned specific tasks. In the street view, white and dark surfaces alternate in order to break the uniformity of the geometry and create seemingly greater depth, which makes the gaps between the houses appear larger. The light and dark color shades meeting at the building corners make the volume of the houses disappear and move the colors on their different surfaces to the foreground.[42]

In the years between 1922 and 1927, Le Corbusier created additional buildings, the color schemes of which were based on the ideas of Purism. Space was reduced to architectural form and color. The entire surfaces of rooms were coated with color in order to enhance the three-dimensionality of the architecture, to underscore the flow of space, and to hold space.

In the layout of Villa La Roche (1923–1925), which is free of load-bearing walls, Le Corbusier used color deliberately as a means of reinforcing the three-dimensionality of his architecture. It guides the eye and places points of emphasis. The color achieves an optical depth and unique materiality through a multilayered, in parts transparent, application of the paint created with pigments and oil or paste. A predominant creamy shade of white forms the background for the play with planes, volumes, and color. In the atrium, the light-colored surfaces are deliberately contrasted with dark surfaces that recede like shadows and become almost invisible. This creates the impression of a three-dimensional sculpture; color leads to a reinforcement of light and shadow. The narrow corridors and passages, however, are expanded with the help of blue surfaces. The colored surfaces influence each other through their reflections, which are reinforced by the strong materiality of the paint.[43]

Following the termination of the cooperation with Ozenfant in 1925, Le Corbusier broke with the principles he had formulated himself and further developed his concepts for the application of color in space. He then looked upon color as an autonomous, space-forming means of design equivalent to the plan layout and section. From then on, color was no longer bound to the surface, but overlaid and varied the rigid load-bearing skeleton of the building, which was based on the dimensions of the modular, with its own rhythm. Like a collage, strong color shades are placed next to untreated material such as fair-faced concrete, which appears like a relief owing to the use of different shuttering materials.

42 Le Corbusier 1927, 58.
43 Trautwein 3/2012.
44 Boesinger 1967, 193.

Le Corbusier,
color concept for the Pessac Estate,
Pessac, France, 1926

The contrasts have been effective. With the use of color and the help of the bricklayer's trowel, the beauty of the raw concrete has become visible.[44]
Le Corbusier

Le Corbusier,
Unité d'Habitation,
Marseille, France, 1947–52

Le Corbusier,
Guiette residence,
Antwerp, Belgium, 1926–27

Le Corbusier,
Monastery of Sainte Marie de La Tourette,
Éveux near Lyon, France, 1956–60

The raw concrete of the large structures of the loggias that is visible from the front seems to dissolve through the overlaying with a sequence of colors when viewed at an angle. The side walls of the balconies are painted with strong colors that, in a complex geometric system independent of the surface, create maximum variation of the otherwise monotonous *brise soleil*. In the corridors of the Unité, a composition of material, color, and daylight breaks up the length and geometry of the space, which Le Corbusier himself described as "an extraordinary and mysterious color symphony."[45]

Inspired by his experience as a painter and sculptor, Le Corbusier worked with the full potential of color as material in space. In the chapel in Ronchamp, which was completed in 1955, the white coating of the interior walls acts as the canvas for the spread of color through reflection. This reflection is further stimulated at only a few places by strongly colored areas that are not directly visible from the nave. Lit by the incoming daylight, a large number of small stained glass panels deeply recessed in the depth of the wall generate a type of visible color fog in the interior, which, over the course of the day and along with the changes in external conditions, creates a constantly changing color impression.[46]

In the crypt of the Sainte Marie de La Tourette monastery, the colored light is enhanced by strongly colored surfaces to form an overall composition in which color, plane, and space sculpture interact. Through three light cannons, the reveals of which are colored in yellow, black, and red, light penetrates, colored by reflection, which gives a distinct radiance to the colored surfaces in the room. The blue color of the ceiling is contrasted with a wall slab coated in the complementary color yellow.

The church itself is a simple geometric building with sparse sources of light but, through the use of light and color, has a certain dynamic and a transcendent poetic quality. The color reinforces the powerful interaction between the volumes placed in the room and their surroundings—something that creates a tangible experience in the room. The text "L'Espace indicible" (The indescribable space) published in 1946 in the magazine *L'Architecture d'aujourd'hui* describes the extraordinary spatial impression.[47]

With his *Claviers de Couleurs*, published in 1931 with the Basel wallpaper company Salubra, Le Corbusier created a working instrument that combines base colors and contrast colors with each other using a slide. It must be said, though, that all seemingly freely available color groups had been predetermined by Le Corbusier.

In 1933 his Swiss student Alfred Roth, who had already taken on the execution and interior fit-out of Le Corbusier's two houses at the Weissenhof Estate, presented a compiled color program of modern architecture to the Congrès internationaux d'architecture moderne (CIAM). For this, Roth categorized the colors of individual artists and architects. He became a committed protagonist of modernism. In 1949 Roth explained in his text "From wall painting to space painting": "So the point is not at all to use color in similar ways as in historic times for purely decorative purposes, primarily on construction elements or in the form of ornaments, but to

45 Klinkhammer 2011, 28.
46 Pauly 1997, 124.
47 Le Corbusier 1946.

afford color its own unfolding that corresponds to its inherent being in the context of the architectural frame in order to clarify, in this way, the architectural ideas and to complete and enhance the overall impression. Wall painting becomes space painting, which represents a new turn in the history of art."[48]

Bruno Taut—Color as an expression of utopia

In the early twentieth century, important changes in the world of work and politics placed new emphasis on social issues and on society as a whole. But these were not the only areas affected: philosophy and psychoanalysis also gained more importance through the efforts of Nietzsche and Freud. Color was no longer regarded as a mere decorative medium, but as a fundamental sensual experience that also affects other areas. Composers such as Alexander Nikolayevich Scriabin and Arnold Schoenberg created the genre of Color-Light-Music.[49] In this environment, Bruno Taut developed a new, different, and unorthodox way of dealing with color.

"In contrast to the conservative building practices at this time, the most progressive architects used color not for the purpose of creating ornamental decoration or in a painterly sense that was often simply added to the completed building form, but as what it is: as color, it was meant to have its own inherent effect, and as such it was assigned a specific task in the context of the building concept."[50] Oskar Putz

The thought that was already behind Semper's ideas in his preoccupation with color in Greek architecture, that is, that there is a sociopolitical dimension to color, also revealed itself in Bruno Taut's buildings and developments in the classic modernist style.

In parallel with Mies van der Rohe's rediscovery of the inherent colorfulness of material, Bruno Taut, influenced by the ideas of Expressionism, used strong color shades in his social housing developments. For him this represented a cost-effective opportunity, particularly in the commercially difficult 1920s, to emulate the material diversity of traditional buildings, and it also made it possible for him to create places with identity and spatial differentiation in his housing estates, which otherwise could tend to be somewhat monotonous due to the modular construction methods. In a context of ubiquitous poverty, color was to be used as a source of cheerfulness to counteract the gray misery of tenements and to alleviate the monotony; the architecture was to be linked to the place directly via color. With his ideas, Taut pioneered the reintroduction of color in urban design and, along with that, sparked controversial discussions.[51]

Bruno Taut's first colorful development was the Falkenberg Estate. Shortly after its opening ceremony in 1913, it was given the nickname Tuschkastensiedlung (Paintbox Estate) due to the strong colors used. A composition consisting of fourteen different color shades that was compiled independently of the arrangement of the building types generated distinct

48 Roth 1949, 56.
49 Brenne 2005, 18.
50 Putz in UmBau8 1984, 37.
51 Putz in UmBau8 1984, 39.
52 Brenne 2005, 59ff.
53 Brenne in conversation with Cornelia Dörries, Dab-online, March 2006.
54 Rüegg in Daidalos, no. 51 (1994), 75.

Bruno Taut,
Horseshoe Estate,
Berlin, Germany, 1925-30,
restored interior,
„Tautes Heim",
Ben Buschfeld and Katrin
Lesser, 2012

urban spaces based on color.[52] In addition to the strong artistic component of this estate, Taut's work also had a social element. He undertook small-scale and large-scale commissions and with these implemented his vision of a more socially minded city.

Another criterion for the selection of color was the orientation toward daylight; in his view, color was charged with energy from the sun and was made to radiate. He arranged colors in accordance with the cardinal directions. Taut used mineral-based colors containing earth pigments that were not pure but which, under the microscope, show a dazzling display of all colors of the spectrum. For this reason, they can reflect sunlight and daylight moods much more vividly.[53]

In his own house in particular, in 1926, he explored the possibilities and extremes of strong color rendering of interiors and related their spatial effect to the changes in daylight. He arranged complementary colors in such a way that the sense of colorfulness generated by a white ghost picture in front of our closed eyes was avoided. The bright red of the living room ceiling, which is in shadow, is contrasted by the green of the surrounding meadow; the chromium yellow of the head wall interacts with the ultramarine blue of the adjacent room. In this case color does not generate an abstract space sculpture but directly relates to the environment and interacts with it and the adjoining color.[54]

Bruno Taut's differentiated and multifaceted use of color once again demonstrates how color can be used to achieve individualization, to generate identity and distinguishability. He structured the color, gave it clear purpose, placed it on details, and subjected it to functional duties. Color is used to provide orientation and, at the same time, has a shaping effect: the volume of the building is clearly delineated; additive elements such as balconies, staircases, or railings are picked out by color. Taut succeeded in putting color on an equal footing with form and material, whether in the urban design context, in neighborhoods, or in interiors.

When, in his 1921 book *Call for Colorful Architecture*, Bruno Taut referred to "a tradition of hundreds of years" of using color in architecture under the heading "The Rainbow"—no doubt influenced by Semper—he brought the historical/cultural dimension of color into play. He held that, because "the purely technical and scientific emphasis killed the enjoyment of the visual senses," "gray-in-gray brick boxes" had been created instead of "colorful and painted houses." Taut argued that the "slackness and inability" to apply, in addition to form, the most important artistic means in building, that is, color, should be replaced by the historically established "courage to embrace color both inside and outside the building."[55] With his understanding of color, Taut detached himself from the rather dogmatic concepts of the Bauhaus and countered purely aesthetically reasoned positions with a new approach to perception and how the senses are affected.

Luis Barragán—Between tradition and magic

The Mexican architect Luis Barragán (1902–1988) brought the expressive use of color and light in space to perfection. His work was strongly marked by regional, traditional influences, but was also inspired by the developments in European modernism. In 1924–1925 Le Corbusier's pavilion for the Exposition internationale des arts décoratifs et industriels modernes in Paris attracted his attention when he visited the exhibition during a trip to Europe. During a stay in New York, Barragán had previously made the acquaintance of the Viennese architect Friedrich Kiesler (1890–1965), through whom he learned more about the architectural debates in Europe, the *Raumplan* by Adolf Loos, the developments of the Bauhaus, and the De Stijl movement.

During his second trip to Europe, Barragán met Le Corbusier in person and visited his buildings. In 1926, following the publication of his work *Vers une architecture*, his theories became a revelation for the young avant-garde in Mexico. From then on, Barragán's architecture was determined by rational room divisions, a simplicity in his language of form, and an absence of all ornamental decoration. After a creative break, light became the key element in his work. He focused on the synthesis of modern architecture and Mexican tradition. Barragán perceived color "as bringing out the full potential of architecture. It helps to enlarge the room or make it smaller; at the same time, it gives a space that touch of magic it needs."[56] The poetic quality of Barragán's spaces impressively reflects the power of

55 Taut in Bauwelt Fundamente 8 2014, 97–98.
56 Daidalos, no. 51 (1994), 29.
57 Carranza 2014, 179.
58 Pauly 1997, 150.
59 Pauly 2008, 46–49.

color. His work clearly shows that color, in addition to its spatial effect, can be the atmospherically determining element in architecture that radiates a strong emotional message.

"I believe in emotional architecture. It is very important for humankind that architecture should move by its beauty; if there are many equally valid technical solutions to a problem, the one which offers the user a message of beauty and emotion, that one is architecture."[57] Luis Barragán

By applying large fields of color, Barragán generated an intense, concentrated power of radiation of the color, which would spread across all other building components over the course of the day. On the one hand, the fact that color is bound to building components or bodies ties it firmly to one place; on the other hand, the effect of light and reflection leads to the dissolution and liberation of color in space. For Barragán, this creates a typical melting composition of space, color, and light, with constantly changing color phenomena. The colors used by Barragán can be found in the context of traditional Mexican culture and are witness to his strong personal connection to his origins. In Mexico, color is an expression of tradition, and the color palette includes relatively few natural shades, which are continually reinterpreted in innumerable nuances. In addition to local earth colors and shades of red, they include strong blue and yellow. Barragán's overall oeuvre displays a very wide color spectrum, which not only comprises the Mexican range of colors of his specific home surroundings but also incorporates European influences. He does not, however, use green, since this is added to the scheme by plants and gardens, which—in addition to mirroring water surfaces that, with movement, generate vibrating images—play a key role in his work. The colors are supported by Mexico's strong white overhead sunlight, which, when it falls directly on surfaces, causes strong colors to fade and casts dark shadows, which cause edges to appear in sharp contrast. For example, textural patterns in plaster become much more pronounced due to the shadow cast at a certain angle. Barragán's colored room surfaces increase this effect; the architecture loses its sculptural quality and dissolves into individual planes.[58]

Barragán's critical reflections on modernism and his trips to Europe led him to an ideal of space that was characterized by sense perception and movement; he aimed to convey a dynamic experience of space defined by its confining elements, by color, and by light. These ideas were in contrast to the developments and tendencies of the time, which aimed to dematerialize built space. Following his discussions with the Bauhaus teachers Johannes Itten and Josef Albers, he proceeded to develop his own color/space experiments, and these led him to new findings in relation to the interaction and three-dimensionality of color.

His approach to interiors was not at all academic, but intuitive: he started by having the shell of the building constructed and then decided, on-site, about the further work, having carefully observed the rooms being created and understood the natural lighting conditions. Rooms developed

During his first trip to Europe (1924–25), Luis Barragán visited Greece, Spain, and Italy and was deeply impressed by the buildings of the Alhambra and by the Generalife garden, one of the oldest remaining Moorish gardens.[59]

Luis Barragán,
Casa Barragán,
Mexico City, Mexico, 1948

slowly; the last step was their completion with color. During this process, Barragán did not hesitate to revise any previous decisions. Colors were initially applied to temporary panels and their effect was examined on-site. They gave dimension to space, arranged the depth of space in the manner of a backdrop, or generated flowing relationships between spaces. Barragán made copious use of sketches and working models in his design process in order to study the direction of the light and how it falls on the surfaces.

Throughout his life, he refused to explain his method of design, but invited viewers to derive their own impressions through detailed observation: "Don't ask me about this building or that one, don't look at what I do, see what I see."[60]

A time of possibilities

All of Europe suffered from the destructive influence of the Third Reich and the World War II. Following their seizure of power, the National Socialists smashed up not only the Bauhaus but all avant-garde movements. This created an intellectual vacuum. When, in the postwar years, the destroyed cities were being rebuilt, the majority of architects wanted to reconnect with modernism.

Promoted by the Ulm School of Design under Max Bill,[61] which was influential at the time, the tradition of the Bauhaus continued insofar as the color of material was considered to have its own inherent value and pure white render was thought to be an expression of new building. In spite of the work carried out by Bruno Taut and other proponents of color, the use of color, considered to be a cheap means of design, remained confined to the niche of social housing. Presumably, one of the reasons for this was the low price at which industrially produced paint was available. But in addition, the use of color appeared risky due to its emotional impact. As a result, the 1960s left behind an initially colorless aesthetic until, a short time later, the burgeoning age of Pop unleashed a veritable frenzy of color.

Advances in industry and science brought about additional valuable stimuli for design. Ever since, in 1856, William Henry Perkin (1838–1907) had accidentally discovered the first synthetic color pigment during his chemical tests aimed at producing quinine, the petrochemical industry had been making huge progress. The number of colors and plastic-based materials, which could be manufactured easily and cheaply in consistent quality, grew rapidly. By the second decade of the twentieth century there were already more than 2,000 synthetically produced paints on the market, and by 1939 over 7,500 color shades were available.[62]

The bonding of color to the material proceeded to dissolve more and more. Further augmented by the increasing use of neon lighting, this development fundamentally changed the intensity of color displayed in the urban context. As a result, color became a much more ubiquitous element of space during the 1960s. Enabled by the progress of industry—not only in the production of synthetic paints and pigments but also in the production of plastics and form materials—strong colors could now be used to cover all

60 Pauly 2008, 21.
61 Archithese, no. 6 (November/December 1994), 46.
62 Batchelor 2014, 35.

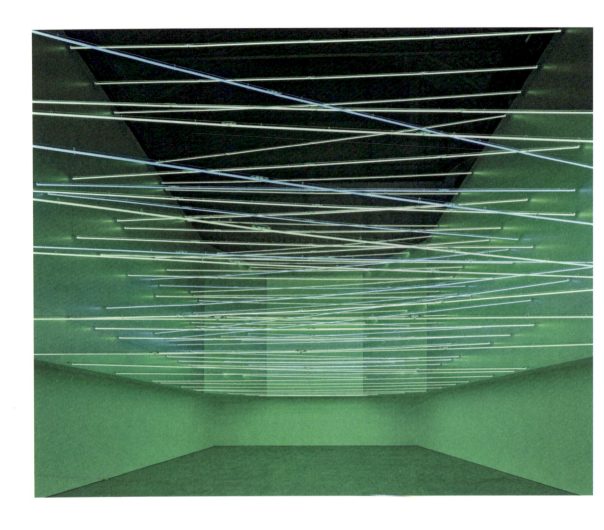

Lucio Fontana, Fonti di energia, Soffitto Al Neon,
space installation for „Italia 61", Turin, 1961,
reconstruction in the Pirelli HangarBicocca,
Milan, Italy, 2017

building surfaces, as well as furniture. Verner Panton (1926–1998) used this development to create artificial space landscapes that, with their cave-like character, anticipated the term *cocooning* and, with their color, involved a painterly concept.

Panton did not use colors in a contrasting manner but constructed color atmospheres in which related colors on all surfaces of a room and all interior fitments work together. This principle of interior design was particularly evident in his concept for the publishing house of *Der Spiegel* magazine in Hamburg. Supplemented by the expressive shapes of luminaires, furniture, and geometric acoustic elements, he created usable three-dimensional room installations. Panton's holistic design approach appears neither brutally functional nor exclusive; his staged living spaces are artificial, colorful, soft, and strong in shape, and correspond to a zeitgeist that stood in opposition to the technical, rational world and to totalitarian political systems.[63]

At the same time, beginning in the mid-1950s, the Zero artists' movement revolutionized the art of the postwar era with a new picture-and-form language. In 1946 Lucio Fontana wrote the *Manifesto bianco*, in which he demanded a dynamic art in which sound, light, and movement are brought together with spatial and colorful design.[64] He felt that a new sensitization of the environment should take place on the basis of the clarity of pure color and the dynamic vibration of light. The group was also influenced by the monochrome pictures of Yves Klein and Piero Manzoni.

Symbolism in architecture and communication in urban space moved more and more to the foreground. At the same time, Pop Art grappled with the phenomenon of mass culture and the interface between art and consumption. This was particularly succinctly described by Robert Venturi and Denise Scott Brown in 1972 in their book *Learning from Las Vegas*, after they observed the urban space of that city with its dominating neon signs and advertising. In reference to a functional building that reveals its function not via the architecture but purely via the embellishment, ornamental decoration, and signage, they coined the term *decorated shed*. Artificial lighting and the commercialization of urban space had consequences for the color design of the exterior space and the city atmosphere. They prompted a completely different perception of space that reflects how contemporary color and material are dealt with. The focus, rather than being on the physical space, was on the effect of the surface, representing primarily the symbols of the consumer and information society.

After 1959, postmodernism developed as a diverse, movable concept that applies to all spheres of life. The movement cannot be clearly defined in terms of design, but it made a succinct break with the formal approaches of the previous classic modernism and stipulated a new architectural language in the spirit of better communication and democracy. In contrast to modernism, the meaning and content of architecture was placed at the same level as the functional criteria, and diversity was accepted. In art, photography and film were recognized as media. The way architecture and also color were handled was more playful, sometimes polemical, and often

63 Brock in Vegesack 2000, 202–10.
64 Fontana 1966.

Verner Panton,
"Der Spiegel" publishing house,
Hamburg, Germany, 1969

Every other generation has a new idea of color. However, this is a generation without ideas.[65]
Donald Judd

anachronistic. The frequently used pastel-type colors, the eye-catching collages made of materials that were obviously applied only as a thin skin, and the embellishment with historical quotes remained on the surface and rarely developed any spatial effect.[66]

In 1993 the American sculptor, furniture designer, and architect Donald Judd stated in a lecture he gave on the occasion of the awarding of the Sikkens Prize: "There is no sign of real color in in present architecture, most of it called post-modern, in which, if there is a little more color, it is small decoration become larger. Color is misused in this architecture, as is its more or less prefabricated construction, the source of the style."[67]

Judd criticized the absence of contemporary theories and attitudes on color; he cited Josef Albers and the De Stijl group as the last artists with their own color philosophy (see p. 7–36). He himself had a critical attitude toward the search for a generally applicable "color language" that had been undertaken by generations of artists, and toward the notion of charging color with emotion. In consequence, he turned to the contemporary colors of the urban environment and implemented color as an unblended, standardized industrial product in accordance with the RAL system. He had his sculptures manufactured industrially to diagrams he had produced in the studio and which showed the number and size of the individual units, as well as the order of the color sequences. He deliberately arranged these

65 Daidalos 51/1994, 49.
66 Ghirardo 1996, 7–28.
67 Daidalos 51/1994, 49.
68 Tempkin 2008, 176.
69 Archithese, no. 6 (November/December 1994), 44.
70 Sauerbruch 2006, 65.

so that they created neither harmony in the classic sense nor dissonance; all colors were to have the same presence.[68] For him, the application of color per se did not necessarily lead to quality. For Judd, establishing and developing positions on the application of color was a fundamental task of art and was never finalized. The quality of color is not released, nor is its versatile impression and appearance enabled, until it interacts with a given situation. For this reason, Judd considered color to be equivalent to material and space, and he criticized any negligent handling of it.

The late twentieth century was characterized by many different approaches and a largely relaxed attitude to dealing with color. It seemed that the often dogmatic and competing color theories of modernism had become a thing of the past. Color became an independent design factor and often played a role that was secondary to architecture. Nevertheless, many architects pleaded for color to be read as part of an independent design concept and for it to be released from its decorative function. Since then, architects have been developing their own independent color approaches and procedures. Often these conceptual considerations are integrated early on, at the design stage, in order to fully benefit from the spatial effect. The concept determines whether building materials are used with their own inherent color or whether the surface is finished with a deliberate color coating or color elements.[69]

Architecture and its connection with art

The architects Matthias Sauerbruch and Louisa Hutton write about their work: "Colour is capable of creating space on a flat surface, such as a screen. The lifelong quest undertaken by Josef Albers is a good example of this. Conversely, it seems possible to dissolve the laws of perspective by using areas of colour in a space where colour and tonality develop their own depths. The interplay of these forces generates a new type of space in which optical and physical space virtually oscillate, the type of space that calls into question both spatial expectations and habitual ways of looking at things."[70]

Sauerbruch and Hutton use color as an equivalent design element analogous to shape and light, and on that basis define their own architectural language. Their colors combine into multifaceted sounds, and their compositions are sensitive and carefully constructed.

In complete contrast is the architect Richard Meier's use of paint. With his white rooms and buildings, he idealizes the immaterial white from the time of the Bauhaus and Walter Gropius. In addition, Meier quotes statements by Le Corbusier, who referred to contemporary architecture as a play between volume and light. For Meier, white represents the fleeting image of constant movement because, even though it is always present, it never appears the same, depending on the surrounding light and reflections.

Beyond this, there are currently various project-related cooperative efforts between architects and artists, an overall concept that was already on the agenda at the time of the Weimar Bauhaus. Concepts for designing

Adolf Krischanitz with
Helmut Federle (color concept),
Neue Welt school and day nursery,
Vienna, Austria, 1994

Helmut Federle,
"Two Side Painting", 1982,
dispersion and tempera
on corrugated cardboard on
wood, 44.5 cm × 62 cm

Color reinforces geometry:
Adolf Krischanitz and Oskar Putz (color concept),
Pilotengasse Estate, Vienna, Austria, 1992

with color are being developed that go far beyond *Kunst am Bau* (art in building), because the cooperation starts at an early design stage. The art historian Philip Ursprung describes the cooperation between the architectural practice Herzog & de Meuron and various artists as follows: "One is tempted to say that an artist such as Rémy Zaugg or a photographer such as Thomas Ruff joined Herzog & de Meuron as a third musical instrument transforms a duo into a trio."[71]

Similarly, the architect Adolf Krischanitz emphasizes in his writing the importance of interdisciplinary cooperation: "In addition to all possible and perhaps all legitimate attempts to bring into play color, as is the case with color psychology, color coding systems or color therapy, what is at work here, the holistic system of color design in the autonomous artistic sense, must be placed at the disposal of the holistic system of architecture. What then happens, not inevitably but logically, is that artistic personalities are brought into the process whose task it is to take part in the concrete, immanent design procedure."[72] In this context, Krischanitz emphasizes what is common to the experience of architecture and art in space, both of which are always seen in relation to each person's own treasure chest of experience and memories. In his view, color should be given more weight in architecture, in addition to its functional and constructive aspects. "Color can play an important role here, because it possesses complex qualities and can intervene with relatively little effort in existing ordering and orientation structures."[73]

To this end, Krischanitz works with various artists in his projects. Very specific concepts are created through dialogue, based on the schedule of functions and the genius loci. In cooperation with the painter Oskar Putz, he developed a color concept inspired by Bruno Taut for the Pilotengasse Estate in Vienna. The urban design form of a curved row of houses is further emphasized by color. The space between the rows is visually widened and defined: On the side with the concave curve, the color is graded from red to yellow, thereby making the lighter center appear to recede farther back. In this case, color and form reinforce each other through their parallelism. In contrast, the houses on the opposite, convexly curved side are strictly separated from each other using the complementary colors blue and yellow, or green and red. This creates the impression of the rows being broken up under tension.[74]

Krischanitz took a very different approach to the color concept for the day nursery and school Neue Welt in Vienna, which was developed in cooperation with the artist Helmut Federle. In response to the surrounding natural environment, the school has been decorated in muted colors that also predominate in the painter's work. The inherent colors of concrete and oak are supplemented by dark gray, black, and a yellow-green for the cross walls at the back that are opposite the large window fronts without parapets. Colorful light reflections are added to the daylight that filters through vegetation. The concept seems to counter the expected colorfulness of a childcare facility, but it generates a calm atmosphere with a strong focus on the surrounding nature.[75]

71 Ursprung 2002, 61–62.
72 Krischanitz, 191.
73 Krischanitz, 193.
74 Rüegg in Steiner 1992.
75 Krischanitz 1994,
    15–25.

For years, the architects Annette Gigon and Mike Guyer have been cooperating with artists on various projects. The continuing cooperation with the artist Adrian Schiess has led to a wide range of color space concepts. "The fascinatingly colourful quality of these projects is the result of the critical openness of all partners, the openness of the painter towards the clearly structured character of the architecture, and the openness of the architects towards the anarchic quality of the colour."[76] For their first jointly produced project, the Davos Sports Center, Adrian Schiess developed a color concept for the interior that assigns a different color to each of the nine different formats of the panels used for lining walls and ceilings. The color tone in space is determined by the rhythm of the sequence in which the panels are fitted. The artist describes the result thus: "A painterly process that is guided by the architectural process and resulted in many a surprise even for the artist."[77]

Quite a different approach was taken for the new building of an underground auditorium at Zurich University. Here, three conceptual approaches are combined for the staging of color in space. From the outside, the auditorium is concealed; only an in situ concrete retaining wall that appears like a watercolor indicates the new building. By adding reduced amounts of pigment to the concrete, layers were created that range from a deep pink at the base to paler shades at the top. The wall terminates in a terrace that has also been paved with fair-faced concrete slabs, in the middle of which a large water pool is a reminder of the space beneath. This pool, which has been painted in a bright pink color, initially irritates the viewer with its color, which is at the opposite end of the scale from the expected green color, and with its deliberate artificiality. It serves to sharpen the viewer's perception of the surroundings. The pool has since been repainted in a yellow-green color, because the original pink proved not to be fadeless.

The interior of the auditorium is also dominated by intense colors. All walls and ceilings are lined with panels that have an acoustic effect and conceal technical elements. High-gloss surfaces in the colors of dark or light pink, as well as blue or gray-green, reflect the light-green furniture of the rows of seating. Reflection and mirroring reinforce and mix the colors into a color space that constantly changes with the effects of the light, and which is further enhanced by the golden reflective glazing of the interpreter booths. Even though the color scheme of this introverted, self-referenced space links up with the polychromy of the existing fabric, it does not present itself as a reference but—in the words of Arthur Rüegg—as "a counterpoint—a 'counterpart'—in the sense of music theory, which comes to life through the authoritative control of harmony and disharmony."[78]

76 Schiess 2004, 15–16.
77 Ibid., 25.
78 Rüegg in:
    Gigon 2012, 317.

Annette Gigon/Mike Guyer
Architects
with Adrian Schiess
(color concept).
Davos Sports Center,
Switzerland, 1996,
refurbishment 2007–9

The painting fits in with the architecture, it merges with it and, in this way, the different media together unfold their effect.[79]
Adrian Schiess

The artist Adrian Schiess works with the space-changing interaction of painting and architecture. In this manner a holistic work of art is created within a contemporary discourse between architecture and art—detached from rigid rules and dogmatism—that can develop in various directions. The artist Oskar Putz summarized his most important theses on the inter-action between color and space in his 1994 article "Fixation and Autonomy of Color in Buildings." He distinguishes between the design unity of color and architecture and the autonomous concept. In the former, the color as active element creates the idea of the building as a whole. It is bound to the architectural form and becomes an essential part of the building's appearance, and thereby an important element of the design idea. Color qualities are assigned to individual elements between which, in turn, reference systems are established. Quite different is the autonomous concept. Here, a dialogue evolves between color and architecture in which either one of the partners can take up the dominant position. "Liberated from the confinement to form, color has the opportunity to unfold freely and to pursue its own theme based on the independence resulting from the process."[80] It no longer follows the guidelines set by space or construction, and is now free to "interpret, analyze, or even parody."

The selection of colors for the implementation of a higher-level concept is completely unfettered by the rigid rules of color ordering schemes or theories on harmony: "On principle, the selection of colors is open. That means any color can be used in buildings. As such, in terms of physics and energy, color cannot be right or wrong. [...] The intended effect to be achieved with the selection of certain colors is the only criterion for judging whether the selection of a color is right or wrong."[81]

79 Schiess in Gigon 2012, 456.
80 Putz in Archithese, no. 6 (November/ December 1994), 46.
81 Putz in Archithese, no. 6 (November/ December 1994), 47.

Annette Gigon/Mike Guyer Architects
with Adrian Schiess (color concept),
Area outside the auditorium and auditorium,
Zurich University, Zurich, Switzerland, 2002

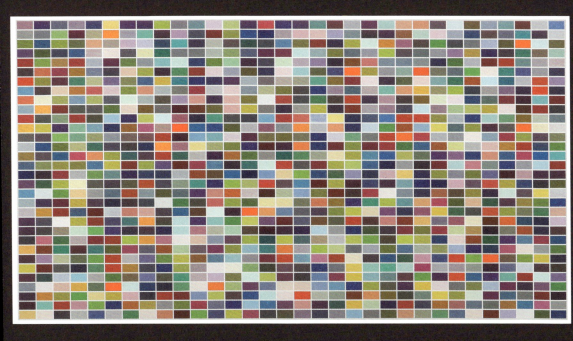

Seeing and categorizing color

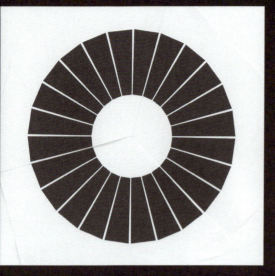

Ólafur Elíasson,
"The grey colour circle" and "The constant colour circle",
in "The colour ciercle series", 2008-9,
polymer gravure print on three sheets, 170 × 175 cm

To be able generally to name a colour, is not the same as being able to copy it exactly. I can perhaps say "There I see a reddish place" and yet I can't mix a colour that I recognize as being exactly the same.[1]
Ludwig Wittgenstein

Seeing color

Many applications of color require a description of the color shades that is as precise as possible. This applies in particular where the design concept and its execution are not in the same hands, that is, in reproduction printing or when color is applied in interiors. The question as to how color shades can be categorized and how one can describe the interactions, harmonies, and contrasts between them has been of great interest to philosophers, artists, and scientists since ancient times.

In theory, a nearly infinite number of color gradations exist; however, the human eye can only reliably distinguish between up to 100,000 color shades. The brain's capacity to recognize color nuances is relatively limited compared with other sense perceptions.[2] Ludwig Wittgenstein wrote about the difficulty of naming color shades precisely: "The indefiniteness in the concept of colour lies, above all, in the indefiniteness of the concept of the sameness of colours, i.e. of the method of comparing colours."[3] A reliable distinction can be made between the base colors of the two types of color mixing: red, blue, yellow, green, as well as black and white; these are also clearly named.[4]

1   Wittgenstein 2007,
    50 (subsection 256).
2   Bollnow 1976, 232f.
3   Wittgenstein 2007,
    27 (subsection 78).
4   Bollnow 1976, 232–33.

In order to understand the phenomenon of color, certain aspects of seeing color are important. Absorption and reflection determine the color in which surfaces are seen because, depending on their characteristics, they absorb different ranges of the visible light spectrum. For example, a surface perceived as white reflects all wavelengths and, due to the mixing of these, appears as white. On the other hand, a blue surface absorbs more of the yellow components of light and reflects blue light.[5] This means that the surface color perceived by the eye has no absolute value, but depends on the ambient light and its fluctuations. Nonluminous colors are created by mixing the base colors of cyan (turquoise), magenta (pink), and yellow, supplemented by black. This CMYK model is used in printing; furthermore, all surface colors used in painting or in the decoration of interiors are based on this model of so-called subtractive color mixing.[6]

In spite of the influence of luminous color, known objects appear in their expected color irrespective of the ambient light; this is due to cultural habit and the personal accumulation of experience. This phenomenon is referred to as *color constancy* or *chromatic adaptation*, and is the result of an adaptive function of our brain. For example, when a lemon is seen at dusk, it still appears as yellow to us; the eye does not detect the green shade of the reflected light until the object is observed more consciously. The Impressionist painters, such as Claude Monet, showed color in their pictures as it is seen, detached from the expectation associated with the object.[7]

The mixing of colored light and the interaction of colored light with colored surfaces follow the rules of additive color mixing. Their base colors are red, green, and blue. This provides the viewer, whose accumulated practical experience is most often based on mixing pigments such as in a paintbox, with a surprise owing to the seemingly unexpected color shades. For example, when green light is laid over red light, the result is yellow-colored light.[8]

In 1867, in his *Manual on Physiological Optics*, Hermann von Helmholtz created the basis for today's understanding of color by proving in his three-color theory, using psychophysical measurements and investigations, that, for human color perception, every color can be generated from the primary spectral colors red, green, and blue by additive mixing. This explained the long-discussed difference between the base colors in additive and subtractive color mixing. In addition, Helmholtz established the distinction of colors using the three values for hue (= color shade), saturation, and lightness, which is still in use today. Nevertheless, the human eye perceives the fourth color yellow also as a pure color.[9]

Today, our understanding of the processes taking place in the eye and brain when we see colors is based on the findings of physiologist Ewald Hering, which he published in 1878 under the title On the *Theory of the Sense of Light*. He defined the four colors blue, yellow, green, and red as so-called physiological base colors. The generation of color impressions relies on neural processes in the brain. He established that the colors red and green, and blue and yellow, are mutually exclusive, which means that, although red can be modified to become bluish or yellowish, it can never be greenish. This observation was also made in many of the early color systems on the arrangement of color shades. Wittgenstein too describes these phenomena: "Someone who is familiar with reddish green should be in a position to produce a colour series which starts with red and ends with green and constitutes for us too a continuous transition between the two. We might then discover that at the point where we perhaps always see the same shade of brown, this person sometimes sees brown and sometimes reddish green."[10]

In 1967 the American biochemist George Wald developed the three-color theory known as "Young Helmholtz theory" that is still valid today, according to which three types of cones are available in the eye for seeing color, namely the colors red, green, and blue. Each type of cone is only responsible for one color; the mixing is performed in a process in the brain. Today, we know that both the Young Helmholtz theory and Hering's observations accurately describe aspects of human color vision, which is a function of light stimuli exciting these cones in combination with neural processes.[11] These processes lead to the phenomenon that, following the observation of his colored squares, Josef Albers describes as follows: "Practical exercises demonstrate through color deception (illusion) the relativity and instability of color. And experience teaches that in visual perception there is a discrepancy between physical fact and psychic effect."[12]

Categorizing color

For better understanding of the categorization of color shades, geometric systems have been established which, as progress takes place, become more and more complex and develop from a simple line to a circular system and on to three-dimensional models. In these, related color shades are arranged close to each other, and complementary color shades are usually placed opposite each other.[13]

As basic characteristics for the determination of colors, the components of hue, such as red, yellow, green, or violet, or the saturation of the color shade, also referred to as intensity or nuance, and lightness have become established. These components can be used to precisely define all color shades and place them into context, which also means that they can be reproduced in print, in photography, or in space. It must be said, however, that these purely physical values do not take into account the uniqueness of character of many natural pigments, the color appearance of which largely depends on how finely the raw material is ground and on what binding agent has been used.[14]

In spite of all efforts to find an overarching system for the categorization and description of color, this has not been achieved to date. Different systems for the exact definition of color shades exist in parallel, with each being particularly useful in the context of certain applications. A selection of systems is presented below.

Today, the RAL system is widely used. It was created during the Weimar Republic beginning in 1925, in a joint initiative of the state and private in-

5   Bachmann 2011, K 09.
6   Bollnow 1976.
7   See p. 13
8   Zwimpfer 2012, 74ff.
9   Welsch 2012, 235.
10 Wittgenstein 2007, 39 (subsection 163).
11 Welsch 2012, 239.
12 Albers 2006, xvi.
13 Meerwein 2007, 34.
14 Bollnow 1976.

dustry, and was introduced with the objective of arriving at a more precise specification of the technical conditions for the supply of goods that were progressively mass-produced. The first RAL color collection comprised forty color shades arranged in a circle, and was later supplemented to become what today is known as the RAL Design System. It corresponds to the worldwide standardized CIELAB system, a color space that was defined in 1976 by the CIE, the International Commission on Illumination, in order to make the connection between human color perception and the physical causes of the color stimulus. To this day, the RAL system is used to define colors that can be produced industrially with common pigments in nearly all technological processes. Many companies, such as Deutsche Bahn or Telekom, use the system in order to precisely define their corporate colors. The current issue of the RAL Design System defines 1,625 colors, which are systematically arranged in accordance with hue (H)—in a circle in the sequence of the spectral colors; lightness (L)—in levels toward white or black—and chroma (C)—concentrically around the neutral gray axis in the center of the circle. The distances between colors were defined mathematically. All color shades are designated with seven-digit numbers from number groups that correspond to the three values. In theory, however, it is possible to place any other color into the system and name it. In this way, the system is capable of responding to color requirements and is well suited to the precise definition of individual color shades.[15]

The Natural Color System (NCS), developed by the Scandinavian Färginstitutet, however, is based on the human perception of the distance between color shades, which is difficult to define mathematically. The system goes back to the first system categorized by aspects of perception, and which was published in 1878 by Ewald Hering. Color shades are arranged by their relative lightness, which means that each color shade—called hue—is allocated a parameter for the proportion of color and the proportion of black. The four pure color shades—yellow, blue, green, and red—together with the intermediate colors, are arranged in a circle and are graded in a double pyramid toward black and white. In the cross section, this creates triangles within which the colors with similar lightness are linked by auxiliary lines. This system also makes it possible to allocate all possible color shades, and nevertheless remains very clear and easy to understand due to its arrangement. The corresponding color atlas comprises 1,950 color shades. Because the system makes it possible to find relationships based on perception also for contrasting colors in the color solid, the NCS system provides a good basis for the composition of color context.[16]

There was a need for additional systems specially devised for specialized digital application areas that are based on additive color mixing, for example the RGB system. At the same time, from 1880, color systems appeared based on the industrial mass production of ready-mixed paints, which manufacturers produced for sale. Most of these were devised purely for the purpose of information, that is, to illustrate the available color shades; therefore, in contrast to the general color systems, they do not follow any compelling logic in their arrangement, even though this may be suggested by their name.[17] Other systems, however, have a justified claim to completeness and a theoretical base, as demonstrated by the cooperation of Le Corbusier with Salubra described in page 53 ff.

Color and world order

Today, the classification of colors in accordance with their type of hue—red, yellow, green, or violet—is common. This system has evolved gradually, as a result of scientific progress in the fields of physics and optics and the development of the modern view of the world. In antiquity and the Middle Ages, an important criterion for classifying color was luminousness, the closest description of which would be lightness and degree of gloss. At the same time, the designation used for individual colors covered a broader range; a term could be applied to whole color families with their intermediate grades.

The first known attempts to make colors comprehensible and calculable took place in antiquity. The late work by the philosopher Plato (428–348 BCE) entitled *Timaios* contains an explanation of colors in a natural philosophy essay on the cosmos written in the form of a dialogue. In this essay, he considers color perception to be based on a "seeing ray" emanating from the eye that interacts with particles coming from the objects. In this context, the base colors black and white play an important role in perception. In the worldview of the Greeks, these colors represent the daily battle between daylight and darkness. The color mixtures derive from a further component he referred to as "something that is glossy" and attributed to the tear liquid in the eye, and from the red of fire. This system, however, is more of the nature of a philosophical treatise than a categorization that is useful in practice.[18] Plato's student Aristotle (384–322 BCE) developed the first traditional color system, which retained its validity as the basis of the known color theories into the seventeenth century. This is a simple linear system in which seven colors link the extremes of white and black that had already been defined by Plato. Aristotle observed light filtered through colored pieces of glass and the change in the color of the light throughout the day. From this he derived the base colors crimson, violet, leek green, deep blue, and yellow, supplemented by the white of daylight and the black of night.

In the early thirteenth century, the Englishman Robert Grosseteste (circa 1168–1253), the first chancellor of Oxford University, occupied himself with Aristotle's writings. He had observed that colors are determined not only by the hue, but also by a component of lightness, which he called *whiteness*. In view of the fact that the resulting multitude of colors with their gradations could no longer be arranged in a purely linear system, he supplemented the color hues that were arranged on a level by a vertically arranged axis between black and white. In this way, he created the first system that could be represented flat and interpreted in three dimensions. Around 1230, he described the system in his book *De colore*.

15 Spillmann 2010, 244.
16 Ibid., 278.
17 Temkin 2008, 16.
18 Stromer 2005.

But this system too had its limitations. At the time of the Renaissance, more complex color systems were created that could be interpreted in space and allowed the representation of a larger range of color shades. Artists were involved in developing suitable systems for mixing colors used for painting. In 1435, in his book on painting, Leon Battista Alberti (1404–1472) described a three-dimensional system based on a flat area on which the colors yellow, green, blue, and red have been arranged. This serves as a base for a double pyramid or cone shape with the achromatic colors black and white at the tips. In spite of his background as a painter, the focus of Alberti's writings is on a theoretical observation of the effect of light and shadow on color. Similarly, Leonardo da Vinci (1452–1519) held that light and shadow were the key optical phenomena, because he did not think that color was suitable for depicting reality due to its tendency to change under the influence of light and surroundings. As a painter, he considered the question of whether the color green, which can be mixed from yellow and blue, should be included in a system as a base color, as Alberti had done. This consideration was based on technical issues associated with the material. As long as painters worked primarily with paints based on natural pigments, mixing colors always involved a loss of brilliance. It was not until oil paints arrived around 1600 that a primary color set was introduced that was valid for painting, consisting of black, white, yellow, and blue, from which all other colors can be mixed. In these paints, the oil film around the pigments prevents any chemical reaction between them and therefore makes it possible to produce more stable colors.

The general assumption that colors are modifications of white light when encountering darkness, and hence the distinction between genuine colors of matter and the apparent colors of light phenomena, remained valid for a long time. In the seventeenth century, the scientific findings of Galileo Galilei (1564–1641) and Johannes Keppler (1571–1630), and the writings of the philosophers Francis Bacon (1561–1626) and René Descartes (1596–1650), laid the foundations for the modern worldview.

Scientific color theory—Isaac Newton

A fundamentally new, mathematically based understanding of the physical properties of color followed the discovery by the physicist Isaac Newton (1642–1726) that, with the help of a glass prism, it is possible to refract daylight into seven different colors and, by using another prism, to reconstitute them to form white light. This was a groundbreaking discovery, because up until then the assumption had been that the colors of the rainbow resulting from the refraction were due to impurities in the glass, and that the pure white light was a "gift from God."[19] Newton's writings marked the beginning of an era in which color was considered a subjective product of seeing or perception. In his 1704 treatise *Opticks*, he arranged the seven colors of the daylight spectrum in the sequence red, orange, yellow, green, cyan blue, ultramarine blue, and violet blue in a circle. This is subdivided into segments, whose size is chosen in proportion to the intensity of the

19 St. Clair 2016, 17.

Aristotle

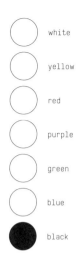

white

yellow

red

purple

green

blue

black

Grosseteste

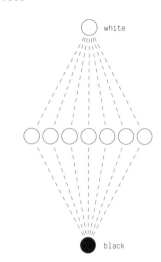

white

black

Alberti

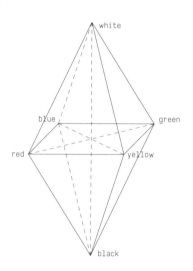

white

blue

green

red

yellow

black

Newton

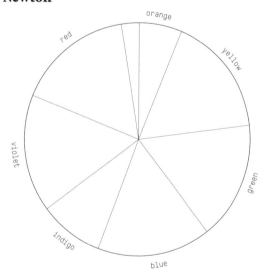

orange

red

yellow

violet

green

indigo

blue

Aristotle: ca. 300 BCE
Robert Grosseteste: ca. 1230
Leon Battista Alberti: 1435
Sir Isaac Newton: 1704

Goethe

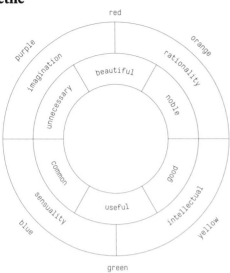

red
orange
purple
rationality
imagination
beautiful
noble
unnecessary
good
common
intellectual
useful
sensuality
yellow
blue
green

Runge

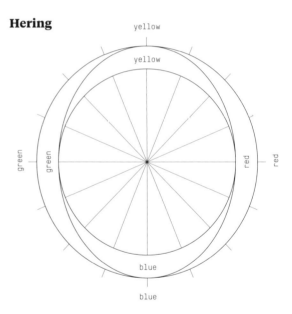

white

green red

black

Chevreul

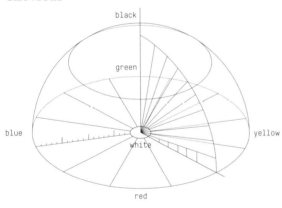

black

green

blue yellow

white

red

Hering

yellow
yellow

green green red red

blue
blue

Johann Wolfgang von Goethe: 1810
Philipp Otto Runge: 1810
Michel Eugène Chevreul: 1839
Ewald Hering: 1878

Munsell

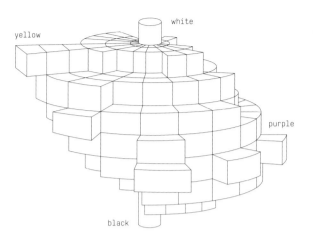

Klee

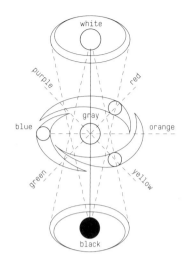

Ostwald

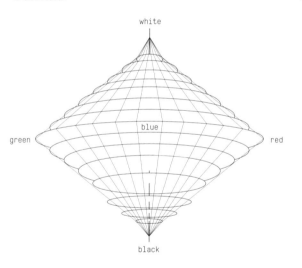

Itten

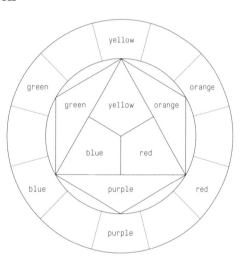

Albert Henry Munsell: 1915
Paul Klee: 1922
Wilhelm Ostwald: 1930
Johannes Itten: 1961

NCS

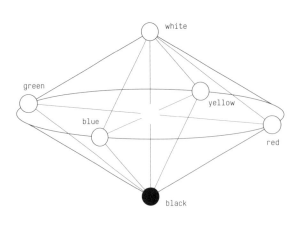

CIE LAB

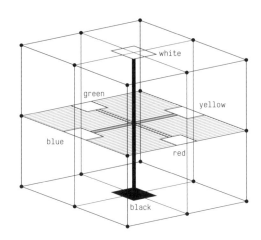

RAL

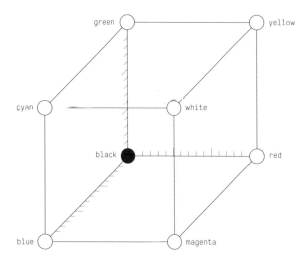

HLS

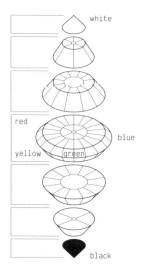

NCS system: 1964
CIE LAB system: 1976
RAL design system: 1993
HLS System: undated

respective color in the spectrum. Furthermore, Newton assigns mathematically definable refraction grades to the colors in accordance with their wavelengths. The radii between the colors rather theoretically marked the transition between the color shades, because Newton had discovered in his experiments that the colors of the light spectrum slowly merge into one another. He arranged the colors in a circle, the empty middle of which is allocated to white because the sum of all included colors is white light. However, this system must be understood purely symbolically, because the range of light and dark values is not considered; black only occurs as a marginal condition in the form of the dark room for the test environment. Newton derived the number of spectral colors from an analogy with the seven tones of the octave in music, and justified this with the rather more philosophical assumption that the harmony of colors can be determined in a similar way to musical harmony; this system is still in use today. Newton viewed all rays in the light spectrum as unmixed, "simple" colors. This was in defiance of the fact that painters can produce all color shades from the colors red, yellow, and blue—a contradiction that was to remain unresolved for the time being.

Color and symbolism

With the aim of considering all branches of the natural sciences and artistic and craft techniques in a systematic classification, Johann Wolfgang von Goethe (1749–1832) took a fundamentally different approach, placing the main emphasis on sense impression. In his attempts to understand Newton's theory, he discovered that when one looks at a white wall through a prism, the expected colors of the prism are in fact not seen, but can only be detected at the edges of the shadow image seen on the wall. From this, Goethe established a color theory that, like the traditional models of Aristotle and Leonardo, with which he was familiar, was based on the incorrect assumption that colors are created at the border between dark and light, through the interaction of light and dark, which he referred to as *Finsternis* (darkness). According to his view, light itself is a pure, original phenomenon that is not made up of individual parts.

In his *Theory of Colors*, published in 1810, Goethe described a theory that had not until then existed, and which was based on the perception of the colors physiologically created by the eye; he supplemented this theory with the component of sense characteristics. Six schematic colors are arranged in the sequence yellow, green, blue, violet, purple (a type of red from today's viewpoint), and orange in a circular diagram, and allocated associated terms. In accordance with their lightness, he arranged the colors in relation to a plus pole (yellow) and a minus pole (blue). He linked the plus pole with positive connotations such as activity, light, strength, heat, and proximity; and the minus pole with connotations such as passivity, shadow, weakness, cold, and others. Together with red, the poles form a triangle in the center. The idea is that harmonious color combinations can be formed by contrasting colors that are located at opposite sides of the circle. With his color circle, Goethe was the first to announce the thesis that colors trigger emotions, and thereby provided a trigger for detaching color from other means of artistic expression.[20] For this reason, his color theory influenced important artists up until the twentieth century, including Johannes Itten, Paul Klee, Josef Albers, and Wassily Kandinsky, who constructed their own color theories on the basis of Goethe's. In spite of its influence, Goethe's color theory was considered somewhat controversial up until the twentieth century. One of its best-known critics was philosopher Ludwig Wittgenstein, who wrote: "Goethe's theory of the constitution of the colours of the spectrum has not proved to be an unsatisfactory theory, rather it really isn't a theory at all. Nothing can be predicted with it."[21]

At the same time, around 1810, Phillipp Otto Runge (1777–1810), who exchanged ideas in letters with Goethe, developed a color sphere that was inspired by the spherical shape of the earth, with the aim of presenting a practical system for describing the mixture of colors. This sphere creates the connection between all colors in terms of proportion, perspective, and space. As a painter, Runge resorted to the three base colors of subtractive color mixing, that is, blue, red, and yellow, and arranged these—supplemented by the mixed colors orange, violet, and green, with their intermediate shades—along the equator. Toward the poles, the colors were toned down with black or white at regular intervals in order to represent the lightness value of the colors in the diagram. In addition to the graded color values that can be graphically arranged, he assigned abstract attributes to the colors; in this scheme, the colors yellow and orange are associated with male and warm qualities and are opposite the blue and violet shades, which he associated with female and cold qualities. Almost one hundred years later, the Expressionists around Franz Marc again focused on the color sphere system, but they reversed the meaning of the abstract attributes, from then on associating blue with male and spiritual qualities.

The color sphere has retained its importance to this day, because it is the precursor of known contemporary theories based on nonluminous colors, even though, according to the current state of knowledge, the purely symmetrical arrangement is outdated.

The interaction of colors

The chemist and director of a Gobelin dye works Michel Eugène Chevreul dedicated himself to the effect of adjacent colors on one another after he discovered that, in a completed tapestry, the impression of a gray veil is visible even though the colors of the yarns used appear brilliant on their own. This effect is the result of the interaction of pigment-based colors adjacent to one another, which, in subtractive mixing of complementary colors, turn dark and become gray or, in the case of a favorable juxtaposition, enhance each other's radiance. Chevreul recognized that the effect had something to do with the fuzziness that is a property of the yarn and makes the boundary between the colors appear blurred.[22] In order to control this in practical application, he developed a system for determining the laws of color contrast in 1839. Like Goethe's color circle, this is based on the three base colors of subtractive color mixing, that is, red, yellow, and blue, which, with intermediate mixed colors, he arranged in a color circle with seventy-two fields. Toward the center of the circle, the colors become lighter, in ten graduations, up to white. The black component is added in a three-dimensional cupola at the top, in which the color shades are darkened in ten graduations. Depending on their lightness, the saturated (= pure) colors are placed at a different position on the radius. For example, a color perceived as light, such as yellow, is placed closer to the center of the circle than blue, which is perceived as darker; in this way, the color shade values are given an appropriate place in the overall system.

This represents the first attempt to deviate from the overall symmetry of a shape in order to be able to allocate color shades an appropriate place. Complementary colors that are at opposite places in the diagram brighten each other, whereas noncomplementary colors next to each other appear "sullied." Chevreul's discoveries had a significant and long-lasting influence on the way artists and architects worked, and provided important stimuli for the new ideas that were developing. Artists such as the painter Eugène Delacroix, who generated his semitones by mixing, not with black, but with complementary colors, and Georges Seurat took up Chevreul's ideas. His theories still resonated in the twentieth century, for example with Van Gogh, who worked with the dynamics of complementary colors, and Robert Delaunay, who experimented with simultaneous contrasts, producing a series of pictures of circles with concentrically arranged color rings, *Disques*. To this day, a color series of counterpairs with maximum simultaneous contrast developed by Chevreul is used as the basis for the twelve colors contained in the school paint box in accordance with DIN 5023.

Color harmonies

One of the most frequently used color systems in North America today has its origin in the psycho-visual experiments carried out by the painter Albert Henry Munsell (1858–1918) around the turn of the last century. He developed a highly differentiated color system based on human perception. He published the tree-like, three-dimensional model in *A Color Notation* in 1905. In this system, the components of type of hue or color shade, lightness or tone value, and saturation or purity are combined in such a way that the different degrees of lightness of the so-called pure color hues can be illustrated.

This approach had already been pursued by Chevreul, but he was unable to illustrate it in the required complexity. In contrast to a mathematical or physical distribution, the colors are differentiated in accordance with "equal distances as perceived by the senses"; in other words, the distance between adjacent color shades is judged to be equal by the human eye. In the Atlas of the *Munsell Color System* published in 1915, the different branches of the system are clearly illustrated as longitudinal or cross sections through the color solid.

20 Glasner 2010, 7.
21 Wittgenstein 2007, 11 (subheading 70).
22 Stromer in Color in Art 2010.

Munsell's color system is based on degrees of lightness and is thus significantly different from the system favored in Germany almost at the same time, which was developed by chemist and philosopher Wilhelm Ostwald (1853–1932), who graded the colors with black. Ostwald, who maintained relationships with the Werkbund and therefore was familiar with the concept of the honesty of material, ordered the colors in accordance with the three variables of color content, black content, and white content. *Die Farbenfibel* (The Color Booklet) was published in 1917 and by 1930 had been reprinted a total of fourteen times. In the autumn of the same year, *Der Farbatlas* (The Color Atlas) was published with 2,500 colors, which was designed to help architects and designers find harmonious color combinations. Ostwald's color theory was most popular in Germany in the 1920s. In several European countries he was involved as a consultant to the paint industry and tried, in cooperation with the industry, to achieve the perfectly pure primary colors. His theories influenced the artists of the De Stijl group around Piet Mondrian, whose idea was that the number of primary colors in the spectrum should be limited.

Following the discovery by the German physicist and psychologist Gustav Theodor Fechner (1801–1887) that there was not an equal but a proportional relationship between stimulus and perception, Ostwald developed triangular scales of color shades composed of changeable proportions of white, black, and one color shade each, with each of the color shades being graded by adding a quantity of black equaling the square of the previous quantity. Together, the triangles of all color shades make up an overall system in the form of a double cone, around the equator of which the saturated colors yellow, orange-red (referred to by Ostwald as *Kress*), red, *Veil*, *Urblau* (original blue), ice blue, sea green, and leaf green are arranged in such a way that, when complementary colors that are located opposite each other are mixed, the result is a neutral gray.

Ostwald's theory of color harmony is based on the assumption that the perception of harmony in color combinations can be described by universal laws. He was of the opinion that only colors with equal amounts of black or white should be combined with each other. When combining colors with different values, it is important to ensure that the grades between the colors in the color cone model are always identical. This makes it possible to find harmonious colors for any color in the color model by comparing the numbers and letter values. Ostwald's is the first color system based on perception and equal distances that makes it possible to define individual colors in a colorimetric manner. In spite of the system being widely used, it was not adopted in any standards.

In the attempt to find laws for the harmony of colors, different approaches have been taken that were repeated over time: color harmonies were determined using the analogy of musical harmonies or they were established through complementary arrangements and tonal values. The subject of color harmonies was important for many artists who, to this day, try to graphically illustrate their personal approach to the subject of color. Many of these systems, however, are far from comprehensive, and instead reflect the theoretical and creative approach of an individual personality. Nevertheless, they have achieved a certain importance and popularity via publications, teaching, and discussions amongst contemporaries.

Subjective color systems

In this respect, the teachers at the Bauhaus in Weimar were particularly productive; they developed color systems and theories of harmony for their lessons and used these to demonstrate their approach. During his time as a teacher at the Bauhaus in Weimar, Johannes Itten published his color theory, which is based on the realization that no absolute generalization is possible, because every person perceives color differently. In 1961 he explained his theories in his book *The Art of Color*. This includes Itten's explanations on the seven color contrasts and the relationship between color and form.

After studying the systems by Goethe and Runge, Wilhelm von Bezold, and Chevreul, and the color circle and contrast theory of his teacher Adolf Hölzel (1853–1934), Itten developed a system in which subjective color perceptions and objective principles are combined. The principles are represented in a color star that develops from the base colors of subtractive color mixing—yellow, blue, and red—arranged in the center. The next level is formed by the resulting mixed colors of green, violet, and orange. The star is completed by color shades, each of which is mixed from two intermediate colors. The system does not include any color, such as brown or olive shades, that is mixed from three base colors. The arrangement stretches from the light yellow tones to the dark blue tones; the connecting lines resulting from the selected geometry are intended to link colors that harmonize particularly well. Itten was of the opinion, however, that the harmony of colors cannot be calculated and can only be detected by a trained eye.

By contrast, Itten's colleague at the Bauhaus, the artist Wassily Kandinsky, developed a color theory based on the principle of synesthesia, the linking of different senses to form a comprehensive whole. Kandinsky established a connection between color and form; he linked the color yellow with the triangle, blue with the circle, and red with the square. This was supplemented by color series that deviate from conventional color arrangements, which are intended to illustrate the spatial behavior of colors, for example a receding effect of yellow and blue and a static effect of red.

Yet another approach was taken by Paul Klee (1879–1940), who formulated his own color philosophy as part of his creative teaching on form at the Bauhaus. After carrying out studies of nature and of the rainbow, he assumed a critical stance toward both Ostwald's eight base colors and the seven-path system defined by Newton, and in contrast resorted to Goethe's and Runge's theories, amongst others. However, he also viewed these critically, and in his writings in 1922 he spoke about the "deficiency of the appearance of the rainbow," the observation-based color spectrum of which he held to include an excessive proportion of blue and violet shades. Furthermore, Klee suspected that the number of colors usually associated with the rainbow, that is, seven, was due to the desire to create an analogy with music.[23]

With the aim of finding a better form of representation in order to depict the "purity of the cosmos,"[24] around 1922, inspired by Ewald Hering's *Theory of the Light Sense* (1920), he sketched a color circle that relies on colors coming to the fore or ebbing away. It must be said, though, that, as a painter and in contrast to Hering, he used the three main colors of subtractive color mixing, that is, blue, red, and yellow, and the secondary main colors green, violet, and orange that result from mixing the main colors. On a vertical axis, he adds the colors black and white, which he considers to be in a constant battle. Their mixture and influence on the color hues, however, was not illustrated in any detail. Like a canon in music, in which an identical melody is sung with a time delay, thus creating an overlay, Klee developed a theoretical idea of how "competing" colors sound together and, like a pendulum, remain in balance due to the movement and countermovement and develop into a circular movement.

With the dissolution of the Bauhaus, the attempt by artists to develop independent, original color harmonies came to an end. Finally, philosophical and experimental considerations were replaced by the attempt to generate a defined and controllable selection from the almost 17 million possible color combinations using color samples. Furthermore, it became more and more important to specify colors so that they would be compatible with different media, for example in color printing, and to pave the way for a worldwide understanding of and communication relating to color. The international success of color systems such as the Pantone Matching System (PMS) is the expression of an era in which cultural differences are gradually disappearing.[25]

Nevertheless, the color fans produced by manufacturers to support sales have a certain fascination. During the 1960s, the painter Gerhard Richter focused on the subject of color in contemporary painting and, in reaction to Pop Art, and in particular the art of Andy Warhol, developed his so-called *Color Chart* paintings. He began with a format that is strongly reminiscent of the aesthetic of the color charts of commercial manufacturers. For a series consisting of four pictures, he developed a system for depicting color shades that can be mixed using the three base colors plus gray. These are further differentiated using the number 4 as a multiplier to produce a total of 1,024 colors; he held that additional possible color shades in the series could no longer be distinguished by the eye. On the one hand, with this work Gerhard Richter explored the number of colors distinguishable in illustration—similar to the classic color systems—and on the other hand, he removed the colors from the logical context expected by the viewer, arranging them in a deliberately random way.

"The arrangement of the colours on the squares was done by a random process, to obtain a diffuse, undifferentiated overall effect, combined with stimulating detail. The rigid grid precludes the generation of figurations, although with an effort these can be detected."[26]

This aspect of artificial naturalism fascinates me—as does the fact that, if I had painted all the possible permutations, light would have taken more than 400 billion years to travel from the first painting to the last.[27]
Gerhard Richter

23 Klee 1922
    in Oswald 2002, 4.
24 Ibid., 4.
25 Tempkin 2008, 18.
26 Richter 2009, 91.
27 Ibid, 91.

Part 2

Color as two-dimensional, structural and spatial element

I have always tried to avoid "colouring forms." I want to create a colour form, not coloured forms.[1]
Bridget Riley

Camille Graeser,
"Three Progressively Moved Color Groups with White Core",
1958, oil on canvas, 32 × 64 cm

The rectangular shapes rotating around the center of the image convey the impression of movement and space. "Two pairs of colors, red/green + yellow/violet, arranged in complementary polar positions, trigger a peripheral movement, whereas two inner pairs of colors move in the opposite direction. From this double movement results a white square space that makes the eccentric energy field of this concretion visible."[2]

Units of color and surface

 Whether in the plane of the two-dimensional surface, on structured substrate, or in three-dimensional contexts, color develops special characteristic effects and qualities. But what is the cause of this, and what intention and method is the respective color application based on? How is a balanced composition of two-dimensional colors created? Are color and form structures overlaid, or does a color idea move into three-dimensionality?

Even on a level surface it is possible to use color to create balanced systems, dynamic processes, or relationships of strength. In order to achieve these results, artists usually base their work on strict ordering schemes, which precisely define the relationship between two-dimensional area and space, form, and color. The relationship between these parameters has an influence on whether two-dimensional areas stabilize and steady each other, whether colors displace each other and create spatial associations, or whether the color space seems to dissolve.

The intended perception when viewing the image is preceded by the artist's systematic color investigations in the form of precise proportional studies and gradation processes. The options for sculptural effects of two-dimensional areas are explored in the same way as the limits of the plannability of color events, using dynamic interactive processes. In spite of defined principles of composition and order, unexpected mechanisms of interaction and color phenomena appear, however much the color is tied to geometric forms of organization.

Josef Albers, Bridget Riley, and other artists challenge viewers' habits of perception by using complex color field or line images to create two-dimensional geometric structures that can be read three-dimensionally. The spatial effect of two-dimensional color areas and lines is based on contrast, parallelism, offsetting, intersections, repetition, interlacing, or inversion, even though there is no "genuine" three-dimensionality.

Despite the sometime strict mathematical constructions, one's perception can change from an irritating to a playful impression. Within the same base structure, a color can displace the adjacent color or even make it appear flat, but it can also make it more radiant or vibrant. The color intensity can be increased to create density and even to generate virtual color solids. Likewise, it is possible to create the illusion of space through graduation of lightness.

The number, type, and size of color units selected within a certain format or area—whether compositions of shapes or lines—determine the image space and create a specific image scale. Within this, the relationship of color to area, and of color to color, is defined by geometric and hierarchical principles of composition and order. The resulting structure and system of the color composition determines the relationships between the colors, and hence a balance of colors and shapes.

Depending on the principle of composition, the picture surface appears calm and balanced, dense and complex, or rhythmical and in movement. Another element that is relevant to the appearance of the color, in

1   Riley 2014, 7.
2   Camille Graeser
    Foundation 2009, 81.

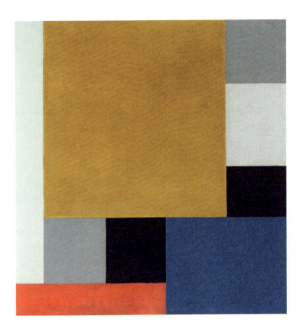

addition to its extent, is the adjacent color, which impacts on their correspondence and the mutual presence of chromaticity.

Relationships of power are created through color alone based on the proportions between them, either numerically or intuitively, and on the increase of color intensity and contrast, and also just between monochrome color fields; the colors enter into a multifaceted exchange with each other and, depending on their position on the surface and the size of the shape, develop great intensity.

The subject of abstract composition, balancing color elements, and making color shapes protrude from the image carrier has been seized upon and debated by numerous artists. Exact proportions and defined relationships of the individual parts with each other are often developed sketchily but precisely on millimeter graph paper before transferring the image to the canvas. Thinking in variations and series, basing the work on numbers and calculations, and changing the scale are features that characterize the works, which consist of many color graduations and contrasts. Above all, however, different approaches and positions exist with respect to the relationship between two-dimensional area and three-dimensionality. The artist Andor Weininger summarized these ideas when he worked in the wall painting class at the Bauhaus, and was influenced by Theo van Doesburg: "I began to ask myself, what is a surface? What is a plane? I began to reflect on two-dimensionality. I thought about this for months. I tried to understand Doesburg's theories."[3]

In the compositions with two-dimensional shapes produced by the De Stijl artists, it is the color rather than the perspective that gives the pictures depth and weight. The group was intent on avoiding three-dimensional interpretation. The task is to use the compositional means, with their different dimensions and color, to create a balance and achieve approximately equal weight. Andor Weininger focused on working on the proportions of two-dimensional forms with respect to each other and on the relationships between colors and between the sizes of shapes. In numerous development series on the subdivision of area, he examined the extent to which the two-dimensionality of the areas is preserved or a three-dimensional illusion is created. Again and again, Weininger tested similar color compositions in different combinations. He also tested the identical colors in alternative systems and arrangements. Later, Weininger developed his strictly two-dimensional compositions into space.

The artist Piet Mondrian defined his approach to pictures and painting as an "art of pure ratios" in the form of his laws of *Neoplasticism* that determine the purely compositional means and their use.[4] The balance in the picture was to be achieved by "a large area of noncolor and a rather smaller area of color or mass." "The equilibrium that neutralizes and cancels out the compositional means is created through the proportional relationships which exist between them and which generate the vibrant rhythm."[5]

In view of the fact that color inherently creates depth of space and three-dimensionality, the allocation of element and color determines space. In addition, the manner of application influences the perceived depth of image and the relationship between shapes and colors. Depending on the intention, the artist creates an image that conveys a sense of depth or a deliberately one-dimensional/flat image, in which elements are at the same level in terms of hierarchy.

In his 1946 work entitled *Bird*, Auguste Herbin deliberately avoided the impression of three-dimensionality and, within the form, tied the color directly to the two-dimensional shape. The image is constructed of four clearly structured parts within a frame. Basic shapes such as circles, squares, and triangles are depicted in radiant base colors, forming an abstract composition within these segments.

Within a clear image structure, Herbin developed a free arrangement without any spatial effect. This led to the symbolic template-like impression that appears evenly balanced without any trace of movement or foreground and background.

Between 1942 and 1944, Herbin developed his key idea, the *alphabet plastique*. In this principle of composition, letters, colors, shapes, and tones are arranged in relation to each other. For example, red is linked with a circle and yellow with a triangle. This self-imposed rule was to be applied in the sense of a retractable allocation of letters, geometrical shapes, and colors, and provided Herbin with a wide range of options for variation. He proceeded to develop numerous new, methodically designed modifications.

3   Svestka 1990, 32.
4   Jaffé 1967, 224.
5   Ibid.

Piet Mondrian,
"Victory Boogie Woogie",
1942–44 (unfinished),
oil and paper on canvas,
127 × 127 cm

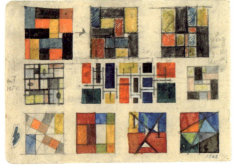

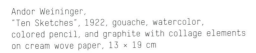

Andor Weininger,
"Ten Sketches", 1922, gouache, watercolor,
colored pencil, and graphite with collage elements
on cream wove paper, 13 × 19 cm

Auguste Herbin,
"Bird", 1946,
gouache,
98.5 × 72 cm

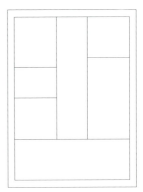

Proportional sketch
for "Bird"

Dynamic two-dimensional compositions

The artist Horst Bartnig developed the allocation of color and shape from algorithms, mostly on the basis of squares, with which he depicted series, which he had designed once, in all variations. Even Bartnig's pure color compositions are based on an exactly calculated system; color and shape combinations are created that appear accidental and put into question the self-imposed system of rules upon which the composition is based. In a series of variations, images are created with complex interactions between structure and color and with a strong visual presence possessing a high dynamic potential.

The *Boogie Woogie* pictures by Piet Mondrian (1942) already had an independent pictorial rhythm in the form of small, seemingly moving, mosaic-type color elements. These dissolve the continuous stripes and cause the eye to move about, thus creating the impression of vibration. The unconscious search for logical content in the image based on repetition and a system causes the eye to glance across the surface of the image and prevents it from being grasped directly.

Using self-adhesive tape, Mondrian had worked with preparatory sketches in order to check the positioning of the primary colors. In contrast to Mondrian's earlier strict compositions, the *Victory Boogie Woogie* image creates the impression of rhythm and movement in analogy with the music. Mondrian had a penchant for American jazz, in particular boogie woogie, which he perceived as pure rhythm. In 1927, Mondrian had published an important article entitled *De jazz en de Neo-plastiek* and was convinced that rhythm, whether optically or musically, is the linking characteristic between life and art.[6]

The visualization of music and sound was also a key interest of artist Camille Graeser throughout his life. He referred to his own work as "a visual expression of painterly sound similar to music."[7] In his "play with dimension and value of color, shape, and line,"[8] Graeser tried to emulate the laws pertaining to music in his pictures, as had already been attempted by Wassily Kandinsky and Paul Klee, who were important influences on him. Max Bill too had compared artistic design and sculptural processes with musical principles, making reference to the fugues of Johann Sebastian Bach.

Graeser arranged his larger and smaller shapes analogously to the intervals of musical notes and, with smaller image elements, provided rhythm to the picture surface. In this way, he emphasized the themes of movement, dynamics, rotation, relation, and rhythm above the intention of creating geometric compositions.

Depending on their content, Graeser arranged his compositions in accordance with a certain principle, for example from the inside to the outside, as in *Eccentric Rotations*. The impression of rotational movement is created by the alternating arrangement of increasingly large vertical and horizontal forms around a white core.

6   Gage 1993, 243.
7   Camille Graeser
     Foundation 2015, 37.
8   Ibid.

Horst Bartnig,
"Variations with Four
Times Four Squares
in Four Colors", 2004,
acrylic on canvas,
180 × 255 cm

The artist Richard Paul Lohse developed a complete system of elements and colors. Lohse's main focus was on working with modular and serial arrangements; he used these to devise a methodology in which the colored shapes take up autonomous positions. Color movement results. Lohse eliminated the difference between color and form. Without his color allocations, the image remains inaccessible and incomprehensible to the viewer. It is only the color that causes the movement in the image space, activating the color elements and making them rotate and move rhythmically. He arranged his image structure on the basis of purely mathematical rules rather than compositional criteria, deliberately focusing on a certain theme. Numerous schemes document his rational and reasoned method of working.

9   Albrecht 1979, 120.
10 Ibid.

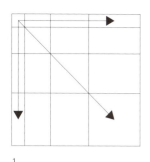 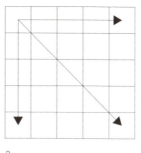 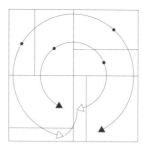 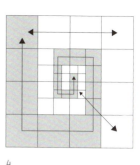

1   2   3   4

Schemes for the design of elements and areas
by Richard Paul Lohse[9]

1 Adding and sequencing an element that remains
   unchanged in vertical and horizontal directions.
   Diagonal forms are the result.
2 Progression/degression of proportions, which
   also cause variation of the element.

3 Rotation and gyration around the central axis while
   at the same time increasing the element width in
   the inner circuit and decreasing it correspondingly
   in the outer circuit. Both directions of rotation
   can be swapped.
4 Combination of a range of different operations.
   Color differentiation is required to make the spiral
   visible.[10]

Richard Paul Lohse,
"Fifteen Systematic Color Series with
five equal Horizontal Rhythms",
1950–62, oil on canvas, 150 × 150 cm

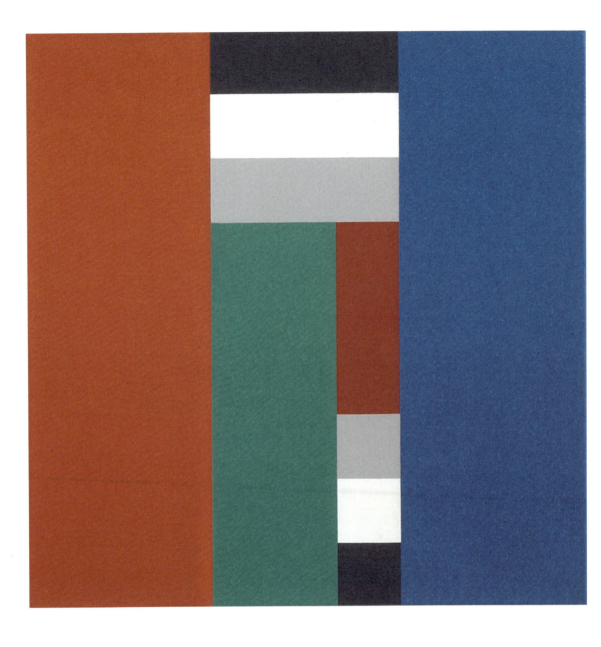

Camille Graeser,
"Rote Dominante", 1957–61,
oil on canvas, 72 × 72 cm

DYNAMIC TWO-DIMENSIONAL COMPOSITIONS

Two-dimensional compositions creating the illusion of depth

In addition to rotating and gyrating movements and rhythmically moved structures, it is possible to construct two-dimensional compositions that, starting out from the two-dimensionality of a surface, develop colored image illusions and even illusory perspectives. Depending on the pictorial arrangement and choice of color, color becomes the means of creating space and depth, unfolding its sculptural dimension. However, reading colored shapes three-dimensionally is more than an effect—it is rather the result of our effort of perception. The artist H. H. Zimmermann focuses on the "hardness and conciseness of color shapes that appear three-dimensional"[11] and, using sparse means, develops ambiguity in perception. Working with space and fiction is the key theme in Zimmermann's oeuvre, which the artist describes as follows: "The fascination of space always arises from the imaginative strength of our own ideas; this strength is much more stimulated by the fictitious, the nonexistent space than by the actual space."[12]

The strength of Zimmermann's work lies in the strict limitation of the means of composition with which, working from the two-dimensional level, he creates an event space. The conflict between the perception of space and two-dimensional form is deliberately provoked. By linking geometry with a certain color selection, three-dimensionality on the plane is created in our imagination. Zimmermann makes a deliberate choice of colors and uses them in relation to his geometric elements. "It is the color that makes spaces appear soft or firm, transparent or opaque. It is the image space in which depth becomes visible, a depth that is only effective here and nowhere else."[13]

With his color interactions, the artist Josef Albers also searched for simple image structures that elucidate the properties and characteristics of color and also produce spatial effects. Albers even went so far as to claim that, within the same color image relationship, several perceptions of space involving perspective were possible.[14] In spite of clearly discernible positioning of shapes and the balance of colors, a deliberate contradiction is created. This phenomenon is particularly apparent in Albers's *Studie zu Tautonym*, about which he himself writes: "The direction changes constantly. Depending on how we look at them, they appear convex or concave—qualities that are not intrinsic to them. It is us who direct them in one direction and then in another one. I like this type of work, which is based on an illusory reality and then leads to something that is illogical and enigmatic. As anybody can see, I do not need any real movement in order to make the painting move."[15]

11 Loskill 2012, 33.
12 Loskill 2012, 140.
13 Ibid., 18.
14 Liesbrock 2010, 29.
15 Ibid., 30.

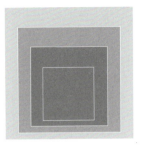

Proportional schemes
of Josef Albers's "Homage to a Square"[16]

Working from an identical proportional grid within identical formats, the perception of depth changes owing
to the different degrees of lightness. When related color
shades are used, the impression of overlaid transparent
layers is created, which generate a spatial effect due to
the apparent transparency.[17]

Josef Albers,
"Homage to the Square",
EK 1a, 1970,
screen print, 35 × 35 cm

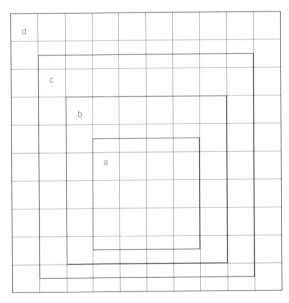

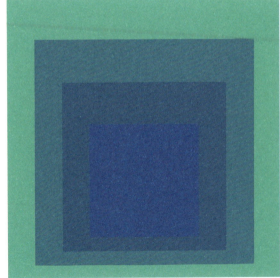

Proportional outline drawing of Josef Albers's "Homage
to the Square"[18]

Through the control and absolute definition of the
composition it is possible to observe the
different effects of adjacent colors and their
influence on the quantity of areas.

16 Albrecht 1974, 88.
17 Ibid., 87.
18 Albrecht 1979, 75.
19 Ibid.

In *Painting on Paper: Josef Albers in America*, Heinz Liesbrock describes the "disparate space construction" in Albers's *Studie zu Tautonym*. "Using five colors, the painter creates a field of adjoining parallelograms that cover the entire width of the painting. The central shapes in gray, azure blue, and pink are repeated, with the colors reversed and with the middle axis of the picture functioning as a hinge between them. Even though the composition of these color shapes at first appears calm, it soon changes in the process of perception into a deeply disparate space construction. The two halves appear to the viewer as something seen from below when looking from the right but, when looking from the left, as something seen from above."[19]

Josef Albers,
"Homage to the Square",
I–S f, 1970, screen print,
34.9 × 34.9 cm

H. H. Zimmermann,
"Between the Planes", 2006, acrylic on canvas,
100 × 100 cm

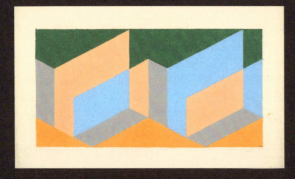

Josef Albers,
"Study for Tautonym", 1944,
oil and pencil on paper,
34.9 × 58.1 cm

Color as structural element

Whereas painting is primarily defined by the fact that it is bound to the level surface of the medium, the relief goes beyond the two-dimensional medium, generating a charge between surface area, structure, and solid. Through this, it acquires both two-dimensional, image-like characteristics as well as three-dimensional, sculptural ones. When color is imposed on the three-dimensionality of the image carrier, the resulting experience is one of continuous instability. Depending on the distance, direction, and angle of view, the color impression changes; in consequence, you can read it in new ways and it brings many different qualities of light to the fore. The interaction between color structure and structure of form leads to a charged dialogue; it creates shadows and makes even monochrome backgrounds appear multicolored. Even when the depth of the relief is small, there is a three-dimensional perception and hence a sculptural effect. Relief works use image layers and include the ambiguity and multiple readability of the image.

Whether the work with color is placed on a two-dimensional surface or a three-dimensional relief-type image carrier is of critical importance also for the perception of the intended effects, because the movement of the viewer comes into play and thus perception is expanded by the factor of time. The depth of the relief structure can be experienced spatially and changes depending on the viewer's position and the light situation.

Many artists have taken the step from the two-dimensional image to a three-dimensional relief structure and have therefore stepped across the threshold to sculpture. The works by artist Ben Muthofer, who has produced innumerous variations of form images and folding sculptures developed from the form of the triangle, unfold an effect that is two-dimensional and three-dimensional at the same time.

Relief works open up potentially charged spaces between the superimposition of foreground and background, density and resolution, movement and rigidity. A wide variety of spaces for imagination are created, ranging from calm compositions of two-dimensional shapes and serial arrangements to vibrant structures that seemingly dissolve the static mode of the image carrier by deepening, layering, or creating greater density. Owing to the different angles of light and the resulting shadow image, it is possible that even surfaces painted in the same color appear different, and thereby lead to a multifaceted color perception.

Relief works consist of two-dimensional or folded media, layered levels, processed carrier plates, serial elements such as slats, spheres, or cubes, or sculptural wall objects. They interact with structures, textures, form, light, and color. The relationships of different surfaces to each other and the multidimensionality of the compositional arrangement create the faint impression of space, without precisely defining it or establishing it.

In his reliefs, the artist Leo Breuer works with series of battens or wood blocks, which he varies and rearranges in their alignment and density. In the course of his work, Breuer departed from the more two-dimensional,

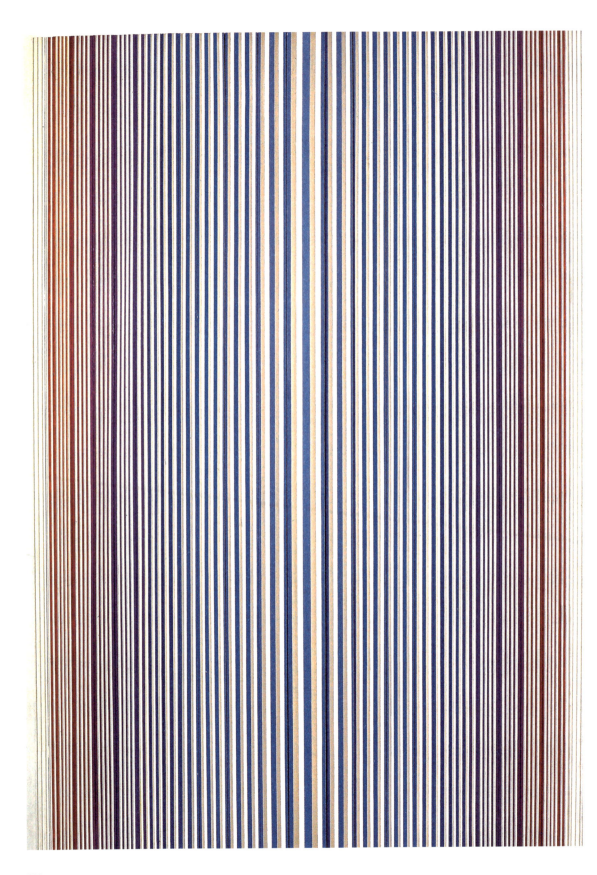

112

Leo Breuer,
"Relief bois, bleu violet
sur blanc, vertical
cinétique virtuel",
1972, acrylic on wood,
180 × 130 × 6.3 cm

field-like units and geometries of his paintings and dismantled these into smaller and smaller shapes, finally ending up with stripes. In this way, the structure in the form of horizontal and vertical superimposition became the determining element of the image rather than the compositional order of the elements on the surface. Rhythm and movement, the central theme of Breuer's work, are developed using colors, lines, and grids. Even during his painting phase, Breuer's interest was in the inherent quality of color that creates three-dimensionality, in color as a "space element" that creates three-dimensionality and movement without the construction of classical perspective.[20] Dynamic color accords alternate with strong contrasts and color perspectives; colors protrude and recede, they "radiate in the second row," revealing a "behind" analogously with a curtain. Figure and ground appear on two levels. The color fabric of the relief resembles a three-dimensional texture. Breuer utilizes the three-dimensional effect of a perspective that is an intrinsic quality of the individual colors. Delicate graduations alternate with sharp contrasts, appear full of movement, and demand that the viewer take up different positions. The intermediate spaces are important for experiencing the three-dimensionality. The idea of the curvature is created by the color only. The red comes to the fore, whereas the blue clearly recedes. The rise and fall from light to dark and vice versa generates a sculptural effect in the image similar to a kinetic effect.

Since the 1980s, the artist Edgar Diehl has also been working, both theoretically and practically, on the subject of color and has been developing correspondences between color and form. Inspired by his research into color, he initially focused on painting on canvas; later he developed his own form of color reliefs, which create a strong reference to space. A flat image carrier of aluminum plates is turned into a relief-type surface, mostly using symmetrical folds, to which a wide variety of color compositions is applied in stripes. The folds create a pronounced break in the surface, which reinforces the sculptural effect. Without applying a rigid color theory, Diehl combines subjectively selected colors of similar weights. Warm and cold colors are placed next to each other, or the effect of simultaneous contrast is deliberately used. Diehl counteracts the calm and two-dimensional geometry of the relief with a strong language of color. This creates a topographical image landscape that, in spite of its identical chromaticity, varies due to the changes in light and the kinks and folds. The same color appears completely different, like an optical illusion. The viewer no longer tends to opt for a correct viewing angle from a central perspective, but is virtually challenged to move in front of the painting.

The sculptural relief work by Sigurd Rompza is characterized by a special, finely nuanced play of color and shape, light and shadow. The different orientation and clear delimitation of the sides of the object create a chromatic sculptural effect of the surface. The precisely applied geometric color shape correlates with the sharp contours of the relief and, through the intersection, leads to a new interpretation.

A ridge forms the boundary between the light and the shadow sides of an object and effectively shows the potential of color as a trigger for

20 Breuer 1992, 32.

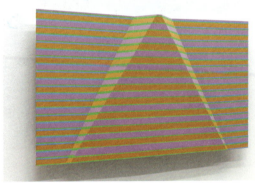

Edgar Diehl,
"Anaxagoras III", 2012,
acrylic on aluminum, 72 × 138 × 14 cm

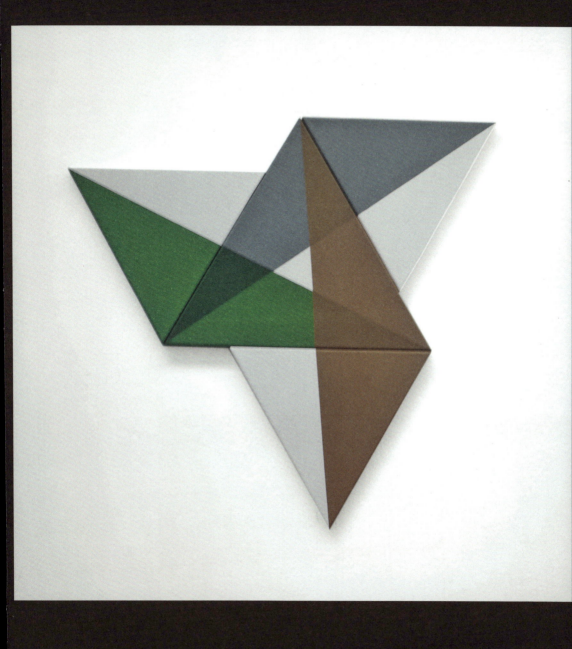

Ben Muthofer,
"m 125, form image, small", 2010,

Sigurd Rompza,
"Farb-Licht-Modulierung",
2004,
relief, acrylic and
lacquer on MDF,
30 × 90 × 4 cm

The color creates a strong three-dimensional effect,
even when the relief is not very deep. The color
shapes define the perceived three-dimensional solid,
irrespective of the actual crease line in the relief.

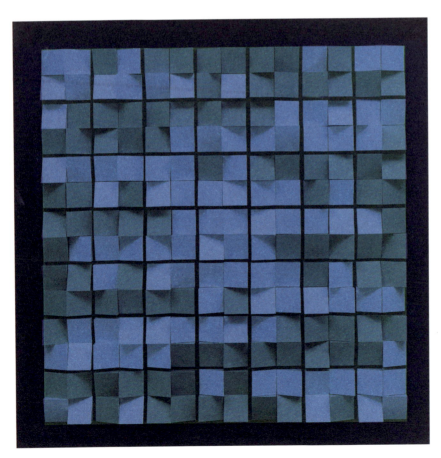

Klaus Staudt,
"CB8 in Cölinblau 602",
1970, polystyrene
and acrylic glass,
71 × 71 × 7 cm

a sculptural-material, three-dimensional, and at the same time sensual perception experience. The incidence of light, lighting intensity, and movement of the viewer cause the appearance to vary and spread the same color into a range of fine nuances and superimpositions, through to optical illusions. "Phenomenologically, the same color on the light side [...] is perceived as lighter than on the shadow side, and also appears changed in terms of color direction and saturation. Two colors, including white, appear as four [...]."[21]

The preoccupation with the viewer is clearly apparent in Rompza's writings on art theory, which were published in several volumes and which elucidate the harmonious relationship between the influences on his work and the corresponding sculptural interpretations. It is also possible to read these as an instruction on "the activation of seeing." In them, Rompza explains, above all, the importance of shadow in his reliefs: "In my reliefs, the shadow is not painted but generated in reality. To that extent, the reliefs are also light instruments. By contrast to many reliefs in Modernism, the shadow on the relief surface is not a cast shadow but a deep shadow."[22]

This effect on the viewer is reinforced by a further variation of the color/light modulations involving matt and shiny colors. With the use of these different color media, the reflection results in an interaction between object and viewer; the viewer becomes part of the art.

In his writings dated February 20 and 21, 2013, Rompza writes: "The shiny lacquer surface in the new wall sculptures reflects objects but you can only catch a faint image of them, not see them clearly as in a mirror. Sometimes—depending on the viewer's position—one only sees colors and light and space. This is what I intend: representation and presentation."[23]

One of the leading representatives of concrete art in Germany, the artist Klaus Staudt, works less from the basis of inclined surfaces and more with the variation of simple space modules. In spite of the recognizable forms and clear grids, his serial elements result in a multifaceted compositional structure. Staudt has produced many works in which he focuses in depth on the color white. Another characteristic of his work is the use of a wide range of material combinations, for example wood with acrylic glass. Making use of the interactions between light, reflection, and material, Staudt creates three-dimensionality similar to topography. In combination with the play of shadow, the image displays a strong sense of depth.

The French-Venezuelan artist Carlos Cruz-Diez uses color as a chromatic event. He is considered one of the most important representatives of optical and kinetic art. Through the interaction with the viewer, an event is created that cannot be planned to the last detail and that takes place under defined conditions; this event can create color nuances depending on the light, chromatic mutations, vibrational effects, or a displacement of image levels with the movement of the viewer. In the work "Physichromie 1455", the applied slatted structures are overlaid with parallel color strips of identical width, and thereby determine the permanently changing reality of the image. Due to the chromatic diversity of the vertical lines, which Cruz-Diez calls "Chromatic Event Modules", the frontal view gives the

21 Rompza 2011, 35–31.
22 Rompza 1981, 36–40.
23 Rompza 2015.

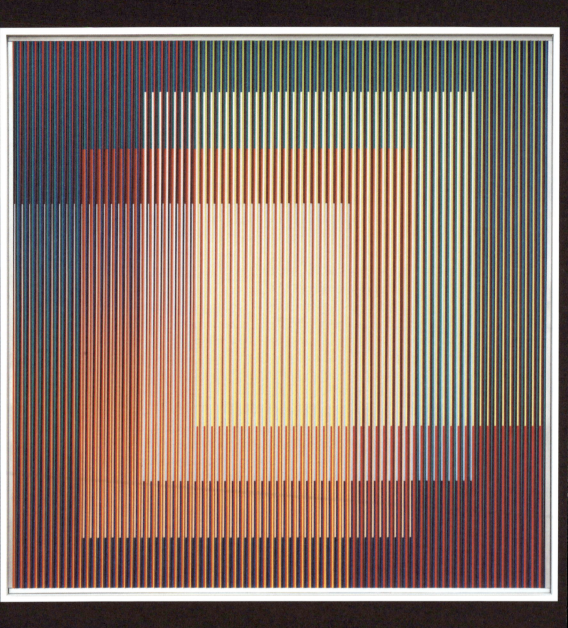

Carlos Cruz-Diez,
"Physichromie 1455", Paris, 2006,
Chromography on aluminium, plastic inserts,
80 × 80 cm,
Collection Museum Ritter, Waldenbuch, Germany

"Physichromies" are structures consisting of different
compartements and other conditions concerning
color. They are the outcome of a complex research by
Carlos Cruz-Diez, in which he investigates the
change of color in relation to the movement of the
viewer and the incidence of light.

impression of several intersecting, layered, and overlaying squares. The slats protruding vertically from the image base consist of semitransparent red plastic. The translucent red of the slats conveys the color to the viewer in its immaterial quality, creating flowing chromatic variations that merge into each other.

With his work, Cruz-Diez intends to launch color into space. "The task of the *Physichromies* is to accentuate the endless sculptural fullness resulting from the sunlight falling on color in nature throughout the day. They also illustrate the possibilities provided by the flexibility of artificial light. I am concerned with finding another 'materiality of color,' another 'propensity of color' that is neither the eternally identical surface painted with pigments, nor the chromaticity of church windows. The *Physichromies* are changeable structures that disperse color into space. They create a color/light atmosphere that changes depending on the intensity and position of the light source and with the position and distance of the viewer."[24]

Scheintrilogie I–III (2007), the work produced by the artist Eckhard Bendin, plays with the interaction mechanism of nonluminous color with chromatic glow or reflection. In contrast to the hard and closed surface of light colors that can be experienced directly in space stands the soft, open, and room-filling color glow. Color perception occurs, on the one hand, through the lightness of the base and, on the other hand, through the formation of color pairs in the foreground and background. Bendin refers to Goethe's observation of the effect of colors on a light or dark background and develops the combination algorithm of relationships of lightness on the basis of a "generative grammar," and hence an ordering principle. This relationship between lightness and color differentiation is illustrated in the relief trilogy. On the basis of the designation of prismatic color pairs (yellow–orange-red, violet-blue–cyan, and magenta–green) and a light (yellow, cyan-blue, and green) or dark (orange-red, violet-blue, and magenta) background, a specific chromaticity is created, the diversity of which is defined in combination with the degrees of lightness (inherent and ambient lightness) and with gradations between white and black. But it is not only the selection of the color that is important; it is also the way the color appears. Whereas the so-called nonluminous color defines clear object and space limits, the chromatic glow of color reflection, also referred to as *space color*, has its effect in a space-enveloping, sensual manner. The perception is not triggered by the nonluminous color; instead, the spherical effect is generated through the iridescent space color that reflects the indirect light.

24 Galerie Denise René
    1973.

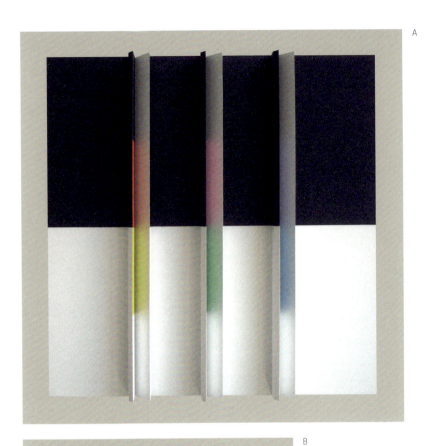

Eckhard Bendin,
A   "Scheintrilogie I", color generation 2/6, 2007,
    relief, acrylic on MDF, 80 × 80 × 8 cm
B   "Scheintrilogie II", color generation 7/6, 2007,
    relief, acrylic on MDF, 80 × 120 × 8 cm

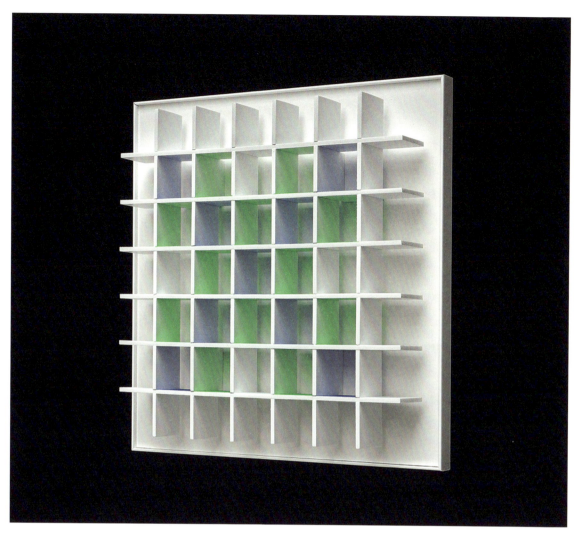

Luis Tomasello,
"Grille chromoplastique C",
2012, relief,
plastic and aluminum,
25.5 × 25.5 × 6 cm

The indirect appearance of color through reflection and the immateriality of color are themes that interest many relief artists, and they form the subject of repeated variations. For his reliefs of the *Grille chromoplastique* series, the artist Luis Tomasello constructs a grid frame that floats above the surface. Within the grid, the entire inner space is filled with a nebulous chromaticity that was applied at the base of the respective segments and develops three-dimensional depth. The color itself cannot be determined in this context, but it develops a strong effect on adjacent surfaces that radiate toward the inside space. This color glow creates color of a high density and concentration. In spite of the openness of the grid toward the picture base, all colors appear as independent and separate from one another. As the viewer changes position, the color, light, and movement merge. Sculpture and picture become one.

Tanja Locke,
composition of flat forms
with three-dimensional illusion,
student assignment at Darmstadt University,
2011, color study

The individual, freely composed color fields interact
with one another and, with the help of the diagonal, create
an impression of space. The white empty space is just
as important as the filled area. The "false" lightness
of the different space units has the effect of elements
protruding from the picture surface, contrasting with the
impression of depth.

Deniz Aldemir,
"Shadow Relief",
student assignment, Darmstadt University, 2011,
relief, wood painted, wood sticks,
100 × 100 × 10 cm

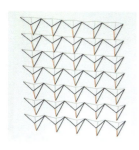

The point of departure of the work is a space structure
consisting of 140 sticks. Only the sticks in a vertical
position are orange, and are arranged on an invisible rectangular grid. They create the reference plane
for the shadows. It is the shadow that makes this grid
visible and places the chromaticity into a new sense
context. When viewed from the front, the three-dimensionality of the relief only becomes apparent through
the permanently changing shadow formations.

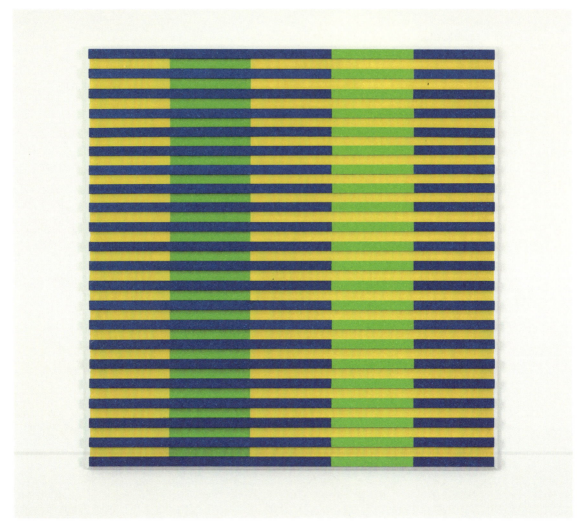

Daniela Ludwig,
"Stabrelief",
student assignment, Darmstadt University,
2011, acrylic on wood,
100 × 100 × 5 cm

A phenomenon that describes the color effect on structured surfaces is referred to as the Bezold Spreading
Effect. It describes the perception of colors in relation
to the surrounding colored areas. The color impression
varies because the difference between adjacent colors is
optically reduced through overlying radiation.
The vertically oriented green fields are identical. Only
their position on two different levels of the wall
relief leads to the perception of different color effects.

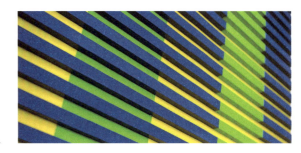

Maria Luisa Kram, Rafael Pfaff,
"Structural Relief",
student assignment, Darmstadt University, 2011,
relief, wood, paper, printed and folded,
100 × 100 × 10 cm

The microstructure created by folding the medium creates
the display of color, which changes when the viewer
changes position. The result is an opalescent image, similar to textile fabric, with numerous intermediate tones.

Color as spatial element

The correspondence between architecture and color starts with the color coating of surfaces in the room and thereby interprets the three-dimensional structure of the environs. The overlaying of color and space can thereby lead to completely new space phenomena. When color is assigned to a place, it can dissolve the space, distort it, or compact it; it can create the illusion of two-dimensionality or highlight three-dimensionality. The colored surfaces applied in a room and corresponding with one another generate their own effective sphere, linking color with architecture.

When colored surfaces or graphic elements seem to query the orientation of the room, when they cut up the structure of the room and rejoin it in a new fashion, the impression of the space is completely alienated, and in an extreme case an abstract image may result. The readability of the room is broken when the delimitations of the colored areas dominate visually and the room contours recede so far into the background that they can no longer be clearly distinguished. The room proportions and the perception of perspective change, which leads to a completely new space impression. Through a deliberate display, the graphic use of color can nearly eliminate the identification of its substrate and the physical laws of the space.

In 1979 the German artist Günter Fruhtrunk in cooperation with the architect Paolo Nestler designed the so-called Quiet Room in the UN headquarters in New York with a decor that is strongly reminiscent of his paintings. Within Fruhtrunk's painting of two-dimensional shapes, his geometrically abstract, nonrepresentational pictures create confusion. Rows of contrasting color patterns seemingly begin to move—an effect that is created in front of the eye through the images of carefully balanced proportions and contrasts. The black/white vector-like diagonal stripes have been arranged in accordance with a strict rhythm and a clearly defined direction. They develop a strong dynamic pattern language in the room. The decor of the Quiet Room comprises a pattern of partly fragmented, also diagonally arranged stripes that are applied to the different surfaces in opposite directions, and creates an effect that explodes the limits of the room and moves the surfaces of the room against each other. The lines, stripes, and shapes overlay the geometry of the room and, through the distortion of perspective, introduce a new level of interpretation.

In her pictures composed of simple elements such as lines and squares and a palette that is reduced to black, white, and a few gray shades, the artist Esther Stocker generates the impression of spatial depth and superimposition through minor interventions. Individual elements turn out of a rigid, given grid, and thereby seem to be located in front of or behind the surface. When Stocker transfers this approach to space, the perspective takes on the function of the interference factor.

In an installation entitled *Abstract/Spatial* at Kunsthalle Krems, Stocker created a strongly fragmented, three-dimensional grid structure with minimal means, using bar elements that delineate parts of cubes.

Esther Stocker,
"Abstract/Spatial", space painting,
Kunsthalle Krems, Austria, 2016

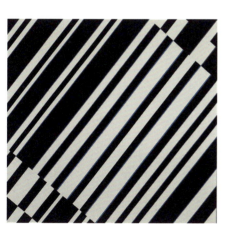

Günter Fruhtrunk,
"Diagonal Progression Black and White (Studie II)",
ca. 1970, acrylic on canvas,
140 × 148.5 cm

Günter Fruhtrunk,
Quiet Room of the Security Council
in the UN headquarters,
New York, USA, 1979

Depending on the viewer's position in the room, new geometric relationships arise. The perspective generates diagonals and crossing lines in the strictly orthogonal system. The artist describes her approach thus: "[...] I return the space to the picture. Albeit a picture that you can walk into. [...] Quite suddenly there is perspective, which previously did not exist in this form and which obviously increased the complexity of the work."[25] At first glance the graphics make the room appear two-dimensional, but then, owing to the possibility of moving within the picture, so to speak, the complexity of the composition increases through the constantly changing viewing angle. Elements that are strictly orthogonal in relation to the room surfaces become diagonals due to the distortion caused by perspective.

The Dutch artist Jan van der Ploeg works at the interface between wall painting and space. Through graphics and strong color contrasts, a dialogue with the space is created. Van der Ploeg explicitly refers to the context and eliminates the boundaries between wall image and architecture. "I'm always working on a good sense for the architecture in which the wall painting will be situated. I strive for different forms of contrast, sometimes regarding form, sometimes regarding color or rhythm [...] how do I choose colors? I think it is very intuitive, there are favored combinations that appear more often [...]."[26]

The abstract wall paintings seize on themes of classic modernism, for example those of De Stijl, by generating a collective entity comprising graphics, wall, room, and architecture through color and form. His work is inspired by the protagonists of minimal art and conceptual art, as well as the American Color Field and hard-edge painting. However, Van der Ploeg's works, whether as commissions or for exhibitions, are always place-specific; they relate to the existing space with its elements and make use of existing visual relationships. The form in Jan van der Ploeg's work remains open; his abstract structures do not begin and end with the delimitation of the surface but can continue into infinity. In *Wall Painting No. 392*, the design continues across the reflective floor and thereby, with its oscillating rhythm of zigzag stripes in bright orange, reaches far into the room. In other wall paintings, colored triangular shapes generate the illusion of a folded plane.

25 Stocker 2015, 90.
26 Wiehager 2916, 236.

Jan van der Ploeg,
"Wall Painting No. 392, Clean", 2014,
acrylic on wall, 320 × 877 cm,
Sarah Cottier Gallery, Sydney, Australia

Jan van der Ploeg,
2008, acrylic on wall, 560 × 2851 cm,
"Wall Painting No. 240, Untitled", 2008,
Aschenbach & Hofland Galleries,
Amsterdam, The Netherlands

Jan van der Ploeg,
"Wall Painting No. 379, Untitled", 2014,
acrylic on wall, 450 × 9000 cm,
MOTI, Breda, The Netherlands

Color in the architectural context

Ricardo Bofill,
Apartment building La Muralla Roja,
Calp, Spain, 1973

Dominique Coulon & associés,
Seniors' care home,
Orbec, France, 2015

Ceiling and walls: white color RAL 9003, red color
LC.32.090—kt.color; floor covering: light gray
linoleum, marbled, type Forbo Marmoleum Fresco—3860
silver shadow

Areas of color
and room surfaces

Colored Surfaces

Attachment of color and linking to space

Color is tied to surfaces and objects in space. Depending on their size, the selection of the color shade, the color density, and the lightness values, colored surfaces change the perceived dimensions of space. This means that there is a close relationship between spatial and chromatic composition. With its tonal values and contrasts, color develops its own rules that are independent of the physical, spatial impression and can counteract or enhance spatial perspective. Colored surfaces can make a space appear narrower, wider, deeper, flatter, larger, or smaller. This means they have an impact on the perceived perspective and proportion of the space.

But changes in color, such as sharp-edged transitions, also have an impact on the perception of space. In John Gage's essay on Mark Rothko, discussing how he influenced colors in order to achieve a different effect and perception, he wrote that the color blue, especially, can be radiant and pushing forward, or can be muted and receding, and that it can be manipulated in order to serve either one or the other function.[1]

Large dark areas that are in contrast to their surroundings usually reduce or blur the perceived dimensions of the space. As part of a color scheme, however, they can generate the impression of a visually difficult-to-fathom depth of space or of an unlimited height. Colors convey the three-dimensional impression through communication with one another, which means a color shade will push forward or recede in terms of perspective depending on the adjacent colors. As a general rule, lighter adjacent colors seem to push forward and the darker ones to recede into the background. When applied in the context of architectural structures, these color effects can be used to create new levels of perception.

The architect Adolf Krischanitz describes the interaction between colored surfaces and space as follows: "The plastic design of the architecture is contrasted to the ordering power of the color surface. From this separation and fusing of the systems a dialogue dependence of the two components develops, which leds to an 'initiating' connection."[2] Planar compositions in space open up a new level of interpretation and readability; similar to a text, the statement, content, and sense is not revealed until it is studied more closely.[3]

The personal accumulation of viewers' experiences determines their expectation of the chromaticity of a space. For example, it is commonly expected that floors appear darker than walls. This can be traced back to the experience of nature, in which, during daytime, the bright sky extends above the landscape.[4] Deviations from the habitual notion of the distribution of colored areas in space lead to a brief irritation, from which arises a changed space perception.

Architectural space is formed by building elements that enclose the space or structure it. The interaction of its surfaces makes it possible for the viewer to experience the space as such. Architect Hans van der Laan describes it this way: "We look at the things around us, and have the power to convey them to our imagination: we see the shaped walls, and can

1   Gage 1998, 252.
2   Krischanitz 2010, 195.
3   Albrecht 1974, 114.
4   Lorenzini 2015, 42–45.

thereby construct a certain image of the space they mark out. We consider the inside, no longer as a space we move within, but as one that becomes visible through the form of the wall."[5]

Working with colored room surfaces creates visual highlights; as a result, the existing room structures are ordered, zoned, and given a certain rhythm. Color can enhance the idea of the plan layout or overlay it, creating new contexts. Where color is used in a monochrome application, it has a homogenizing character and unifies spaces of similar function and characteristics independently of their layout. A continuous colored area at the level of the floor merges the boundaries of the spaces and creates overarching zones in the layout. By contrast, changes in color have the effect of creating a threshold, setting a clear boundary.

In the Niederglatt gymnasium, colored room surfaces were used by L3P Architects as a means of orientation, as well as room-defining elements. Within the different functional areas, the colored floor extends without threshold or interruption through all associated rooms. It becomes an element denoting an area, makes room boundaries appear more diffuse, and links the associated rooms into one unit. In the form of a chromatic, two-component polyurethane surface finish, it is used not only on the floor but also on the wall to which the sanitary appliances are fitted. By including the entire room surface, the color is no longer just functional, but radically changes the entire space. Due to reflections on the untreated fair-faced concrete of the remaining areas, the entire room is affected, and the visual focus shifts. In this way, a defined area for coat hooks and changing seats is created in front of the untreated in situ concrete wall without any further separation.

The impression created by colored surfaces in a room changes depending on which parts of the room are colored. If, instead of the floor, the ceiling is coated in color in combination with the wall surfaces, a completely different impression of the space is created. Depending on the proportions of the space, a dark ceiling will have a flattening effect on the space or, in combination with light reference points such as luminaires suspended from the ceiling, will have a similar depth to the night sky. This can create the impression of a larger expanse lying behind, which is not perceived due to the darkness.

Nefa Architects used this motif for the design of the offices of Optimedia in an existing industrial building. This simple device created space that can be furnished in many different ways and has a high recognition value. The floor, furniture, luminaires, and side walls with windows are finished in white. The contrasting blue ceiling and back wall recede into the background like parts of the night sky. All technical installations beneath the ceiling remain visible but are not perceived thanks to the homogenizing effect of the blue color and the arrangement of dark and light elements.

5   Van der Laan 1983, 32.

Nefa Architects,
Optimedia Media Agency Office, Moscow, Russia, 2015,
Wall and ceiling: latex paint, matt on gypsum
panels and brick, color shade: light blue NCS S 2065-R90B

L3P Architects,
Extension to multipurpose twofold gymnasium,
Eichi Niederglatt, Switzerland, 2010,
Floor and wall: polyurethane coating, blue

Color can enhance the idea of the plan layout or overlay it, creating new contexts.

The architect Luis Barragán composed the interaction of colored surfaces in space in such a way that they seem to become detached from the built volume and develop a completely independent atmosphere. Barragán used the radiant property of color in relation to architecture while at the same time modifying the visual effect of the architectural elements. The seemingly monumental effect of the large areas is counterbalanced by subtle light reflections and diverse color nuances. On the roof terrace of his own studio building in Mexico City, walls of different heights that appear as pure areas due to their chromaticity define an abstract space. The result is a place of reflection that is completely introverted and detached from its surroundings.[6]

The staggered, colored walls in the stables of San Cristóbal appear reduced to the form of a two-dimensional backdrop. The purely functional facility for horses, which has been optimized for this use, becomes a poetic place through the use of precisely composed wall areas, turning them into abstract colored surfaces. The water of the horse trough serves as a mirror and further increases the complexity of the composition.

In the dining room of Casa Gilardi, which had originally been designed for two bachelors as a place of festivities, the mirroring water surface within the interior color composition plays an important role. Half of the room is taken up by a water basin, the rear corner of which ends at two blue wall surfaces that seemingly support the roof light above. In addition, a red wall slab is placed in the water basin; this does not, however, have a load-bearing function but was introduced by Barragán in order to complete the composition. Through the mirror image and its invisible, indeterminate end in the roof light, the colored areas are extended into infinity. When the water surface is agitated by a slight movement of air, a pulsating, shimmering effect becomes visible; the floor of the room loses its materiality at the water surface.[7]

A similar dialogue between surfaces and color was developed by the artist Peter Roesch together with Gmür & Gschwentner Architects for the extension of the Scherr school complex, with his color concept for the circulation areas. The corridors leading from a central hall are arranged like city spaces and, with their intense chromaticity, contrast with the calm classrooms finished in neutral shades of gray. Strong pink, orange, yellow, and blue colors give the building a specific identity in the circulation areas and shared facilities and create a distinction from the teaching rooms. The rooms have been divided into a three-dimensional puzzle of colored areas. However, when looked at from close up, it becomes apparent that the colored areas are always applied to entire room surfaces and join these together to form unexpected new colored solids, sometimes around corners. The color structure corresponds to the room structure, but overlays the three-dimensional space with a new level of interpretation.[8]

The strong intensity of the colors has been achieved, as in a painting, by the application of several layers; acrylic-based artist's paints were put on in horizontal strokes with brushes on in situ concrete that was primed in white using the same technique. The visible pattern of the shuttering

6   Barragán 2008, 113.
7   Ibid., 19.
8   Adam 2003, 21.

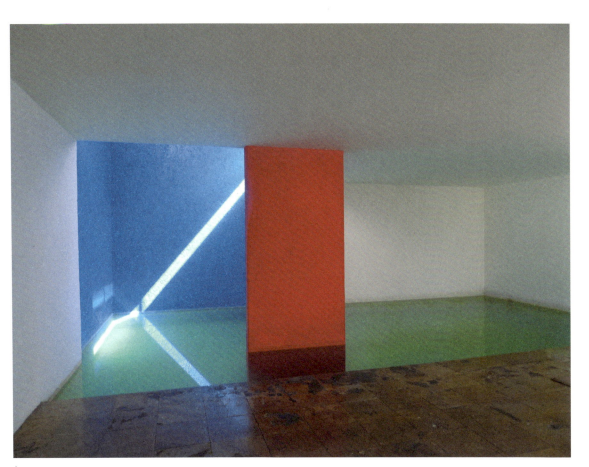

A

B

Luis Barragán,
A   Casa Gilardi,
    1976, Mexico City,
    Mexico
B   Cuadra San Cristóbal,
    1968, Mexico City,
    Mexico

I produce a kind of musical score, which then, in a manner of speaking, is interpreted by a painter.[9]
Peter Roesch

Gmür & Geschwentner Architekten AG
with Peter Roesch (color concept),
Scherr school complex, Zurich, Switzerland, 2002,
Colored surfaces: acrylic-based artist's paints
on in situ concrete with white primer,
color shades: pink, orange, yellow, and blue

boards increases this effect, resulting in an image that looks as if it were applied with brushstrokes on a canvas. The picturesque effect is further enhanced by streaks of light coming in through roof lights. The play of daylight and artificial light dynamically changes the color shades throughout the day and with the changing seasons.[10]

When colored surfaces do not coincide with the geometry of room surfaces, they develop a spatial autonomy; a new web of relationships is created within the space geometry. This happens, in particular, when the color composition seen by the eye has a stronger effect than the physical edges of the room. But likewise, the overlaying of colors instead of a homogeneous monochrome application generates a special, more apparent three-dimensional depth of space or seemingly shortened dimensions.

A space decorated with stripes ranging from white to black will produce a completely different visual effect depending on which end it is viewed from. When the prospect goes from light to dark, the space appears enclosed and dense; when viewed from the opposite end, the space appears wider and the light back wall visually increases the depth of the space.

The three-dimensional effect of a staggered color range is even more complex. In addition to the extending and compacting effect, visual points of emphasis are created around the areas of the base colors, which seem to expand the space. In the House of Bols in Amsterdam, the designers of the Staat Amsterdam Creative Agency use a staggered color range in order to provide a visual experience and thereby enhance the stations aligned along a long corridor that offer samples of olfactory stimuli. Every second color stripe is occupied by a sampling station. This graphic design supplements the spatial quality with a pictorial reference relating to the liqueur manufacturer's brand statement "mixing and combining."

Differentiated color shades create a clear distinction between areas and volumes and can increase the impression of spatial depth through deliberately used tonal values, similar to a stage set. In the design of the outside areas of Sotogrande Legorreta House in Cádiz, Spain, the architect used a strong color finish, which clearly separates the sculptural shapes of staircases and wall slabs from each other and, when seen from above, emphasizes their three-dimensional depth in combination with the bright sunlight.

9   Stadler 2007, 3.
10 Esch 2003, 5–10.

...,staat,
House of Bols,
Amsterdam, The Netherlands, 2007

Ricardo Legorreta,
Sotogrande Legorreta House,
Sotogrande, Spain, 2004

Monochromatic spaces

Combining different elements with the same color can help orientation if the color is used to distinguish one area from another. The color creates an affiliation with a certain function or arrangement.[11] When the surfaces in a room and all objects, installations, and fitments visible in that room are finished in the same color shade, the objects visually disappear through the homogenizing effect of the color. The opposite effect could be achieved by picking out individual elements with a deliberately contrasting chromaticity. The color and geometry of a space are emphasized in our perception; monochrome surroundings prompt us to concentrate on what is essential, similar to a black-and-white photograph. This effect comes to bear at all scales. For example, in Villa La Roche, Le Corbusier applied a monochrome finish to the more personal rooms in contrast to the colorful rendering of the circulation areas, with their sculptural effect. The bright rosé shade of the dining room is used for all the room's surfaces, thereby creating an intimate, concentrated atmosphere for conversation.

In an unexpected manner, the designers of Marques Architekten AG in cooperation with the artist Jörg Niederberger created a highly focused learning atmosphere at the Hinter Gärten School in Riehen by applying monochrome color schemes in the rooms. A single color was assigned to each type of room, and it was used systematically for all surfaces, furniture, and fitments, including washbasins and towel dispensers. Classrooms are a pale yellow, the gymnasium is orange, corridors are blue, and stairwells and sanitary facilities have been finished in shades of green. The rooms appear to have an inherent radiance, not unlike colored light; the color seems to become detached from the walls and lie "in the air like powdery material."[12] The completely monochrome ambiance affects the surroundings; the color shines on all objects and surfaces, and colors these.[13]

The effect of monochromatic rooms on the user's perception was investigated by the artist Ólafur Elíasson in his work. When one enters the room, the monochrome color is perceived very strongly. After a short phase of adaptation, the room seems to disengage from the surroundings due to a shift in perception and create a completely inverted, concentrated atmosphere. After a while, the effect of the color subsides owing to the cognitive processes involved in seeing, in which the afterimages, with their complementary colors, play an important balancing role. The brain now looks at "the color as the new 'white,' and considers all other seen colors in relation to this."[14] Asked whether the chromaticity of the Hinter Gärten School has a distorting effect, a teacher replied: "You are simply somewhere else."[15]

11 Meerwein 2007, 74–5.
12 Bachmann 2007, 55.
13 Lorenzini 2015, 42–45.
14 Elíasson 2006.
15 Bachmann 2007, 55.

Daniele Marques, Marques Architekten AG
with Jörg Niederberger (color concept),
Hinter Gärten primary school, Riehen, Switzerland, 2006

Interaction of the corridor and
classroom color spaces

Color space classroom

Anne-Françoise Jumeau + Emmanuelle Marin
+ David Trottin,
L'Autre Canal, Nancy, France, 2007

Emmanuelle Marin + David Trottin/
Périphériques architectes,
Espace culturel de la Hague,
Beaumont-Hague, France, 2015,
Perforated aluminum panels, anodized in color

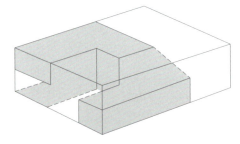

When several spaces are painted in monochrome colors, the spaces adjacent to one another interact with their colors at the interfaces. At internal windows and doors, the blue of the corridors and the yellow of the classrooms combine to create shades of green that vary depending on the daylight situation. Jörg Niederberger calls the use of color at the Hinter Gärten School "a merger of the artist's approach with the architectural intention";[16] in this case, color is a space-forming design device of equal standing.

However, a homogenizing effect is not only achieved by color. A monochrome color rendering will no longer appear uniform in the interaction with light and shadow; instead, it will appear expressive, as demonstrated by the auditorium of the Agora Theater in Lelystad designed by UNStudio. Determined by the room acoustics, the walls have a complex geometry, which is emphasized by light sources fitted in the folds of the surface material. The homogeneous dark red of all elements in the auditorium makes it possible for the form to develop its maximum effect.

A color concept using the opposite principle can be equally effective: in the Casa das Artes in Miranda do Corvo, Portugal, the auditorium, a rectangular space completely finished in black, is deliberately underplayed so that all the attention is focused on the events on the stage. Dramatic chromaticism, combined with an expressive form enhanced by the casting of shadows, can be seen from the outside. The building stands as a landmark at the interface between a rural area and the city in the form of a clearly visible volume that seems abstract in its entirely red coloring.

In the Espace culturel de la Hague cultural center, Périphériques Architectes treated all publicly usable areas as monochromatic space that permeates the entire building.

The archictects had already used the same principle in the building L'Autre Canal in Nancy. Here the public spaces are readable as a "red thread." Depending on the respective function of the space, different shapes are applied, but, owing to the prominent red color scheme, all room surfaces are perceived as contiguous. The room surfaces in the café are smooth and a coving at the edges of the room makes its contours appear blurred. Here the red color is used for the purpose of homogenizing. Revision panels with technical installations form part of the ceiling surface; even the furniture is kept in the color of the room so that this becomes the stage of the users.

16 Bachmann 2007, 56.

A monochrome color rendering will no longer appear uniform in the interaction with light and shadow, for example on folded surfaces; instead, it will appear expressive.

FAT—Future Architecture Thinking,
Casa das Artes, Miranda do Corvo, Portugal, 2013,
Exterior envelope: paint coating on plaster,
auditorium: acoustically effective panels made
of through-colored wood material

UNStudio,
Agora Theater,
Lelystad, The Netherlands, 2007

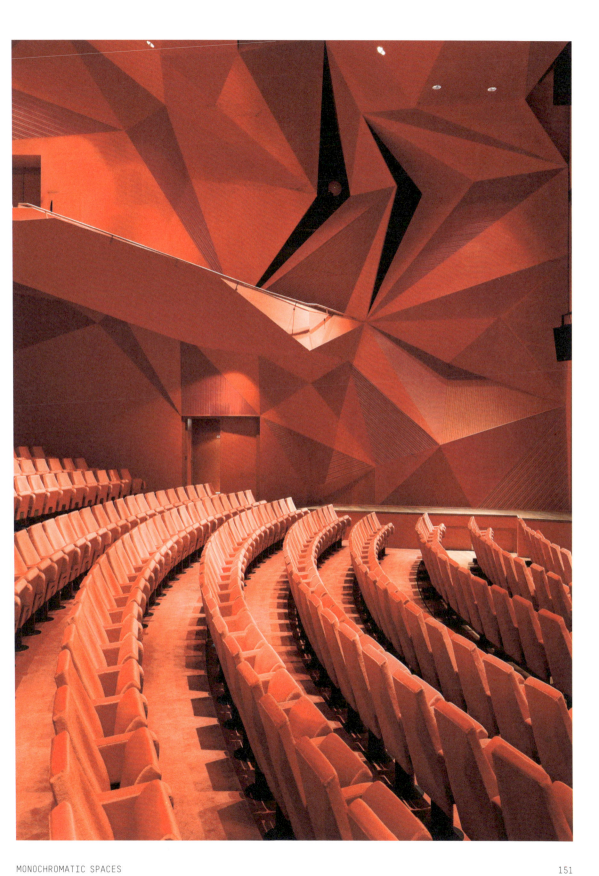

Color niches

In niches, recesses, through-passages, and windows, the depth of a wall, which otherwise is seen only as a surface, can be experienced. Niches with a colorful rendering attract special attention and highlight their function. They can be experienced as an independent color space, and the experience can be significantly different from the remainder of the room. At the same time, they form a retreat space and a type of stage. When the finish of the niche deviates significantly from the wall surface in terms of color and material, the resulting impression is one of a layering in the sense of revealing the room surfaces.

In a large school for 1,200 pupils from form one to form nine in Frederikshavn, Denmark, Arkitema Architects made the shared circulation zones usable by providing color niches in different primary colors. The niches vary in their features, and thus create retreat places for the children of the different age groups. At the same time, they contribute with their chromaticity to identification and orientation in the building. The architectural practice MVRDV used this principle extensively in its offices in a former industrial building. Separate cells of different sizes, which are used as meeting and staff rooms, were stacked three-dimensionally like glass cabinets and were clearly distinguished by the use of the base colors green, blue, and red.

Even without the color scheme, the strong contrast between light and dark directs the focus to a niche in a bank branch in Montpellier, France, by Bigoni Mortemard. By the integration of a completely white counter in a wall finished with dark-gray tiles, the counter gives the visual impression of floating in space. Due to the noticeable difference in lightness between niche and surroundings, the focus of attention is drawn to the lightest point. Depending on the concept, niches can be perceived as part of the room or part of the wall. Since, as a rule, only one of the surfaces is geometrically shared with the room, a niche can easily be separated temporarily by the use of sliding or folding doors. This provides the option of radically changing the chromaticity of a room by opening and closing the niche doors. In a historic residence in Belgium, dmvA Architects have inserted an interior shell of white paneling in deference to the original wood paneling. When closed, the white walls and ceilings enclose a room with a red floor. When the panels are opened, the interior behind the space-concealing wall is revealed, showing a kitchen niche with storage space colored completely in red. The color image is now reversed: the dominant areas, that is, the floor and the visible wall ahead, are now red.

The Splitterwerk architects' group incorporated the concept of niches differentiated by color in pure form in a monochrome, flexible shell in the Schwarzer Laubfrosch (black frog) project. Here too, the work consisted of converting an existing building, a former residence with a fire brigade garage attached that was subdivided into several housing units. These differ radically in their layout and interior design from more common typologies. Each apartment is an experiment in creating an absolutely

Bigoni Mortemard Architectes,
Bank counter, Crédit Maritime,
Montpellier, France, 2010,
Wall cladding: dark gray tiles; niche: acoustic panels
and white-coated wood material panels

MVRDV,
MVRDV House, Rotterdam, The Netherlands, 2016,
Green room: NCS S1070-G40Y;
red room: RAL 3020 traffic red;
blue room: RAL 5010 gentian blue

Arkitema Architects, Nordstjerneskolen,
Frederikshavn, Denmark, 2012,
Colors: Green s1070-G50Y, high-gloss paint coating
on sanded drywall construction

compact space and, through the chromaticism and graphics, becomes unique. Once again, a wall that conceals space behind it was inserted in each apartment in the existing building. This wall creates an empty space in the center and, in the form of niches, integrates purpose-designed wall cabinets that accommodate all functions required for living that in a traditionally designed apartment would each occupy a dedicated room. These cabinet-like rooms contain items such as a row of kitchen furniture, a fold-out bed, movable living room furniture, or bathroom fittings. When the niches are opened, the function merges into the central, empty space that is neutral in terms of function and is referred to by the architect as a "multi-incident envelope." Windows, roof lights, and doors are treated in the same manner—as functions that can be selected.

Depending on the cardinal direction and the external light conditions, which vary in the building depending on the position, the central empty space was finished in cool color shades such as gray or pure white (in the apartments facing south) or in warm ivory shades (in the apartments facing north). In the apartments in the middle zone, which receive only scant natural light, strong colors such as red/blue or yellow/orange were used. The artificial lighting has also been accommodated in the functional niches and, like the windows, roof lights, and doors, is considered a selectable function. In this way, the color scheme of the niches spills over into the space through reflection.[17]

Strong chromatic colors or those contrasting with the surroundings are likely to attract visual attention to the extent that colored areas appear as volumes in the form of niches, even when they are geometrically only built as galleries or corner situations. In the foyer of the Hamer Hall concert hall in Melbourne, Australia, ARM Architecture placed the ticket counter beneath a gallery. The curved balcony projecting into the space with a point has been finished in signal yellow on the underside and on the back wall, and is retraced as a colored shadow on the floor. This creates a protected but easily located spot for the sale of tickets. Due to the superimposition, the interlacing of colored areas and space creates visually effective zones and niches that would not result from the pure space geometry.

The French architect Dominique Coulon uses the power of color to generate places in multiple ways. The school in Colombes, France, demonstrates how color can break up any kind of repetition in the building and create places and spatial experiences on large open areas, such as the outside space on the roof. Parts of the floor, the wall, and the cantilevering roof were finished in bright orange, which was used in parts in the manner of a niche and in other parts across larger areas. In this way, the color connects the interior with the outside space and translates the sculptural architectural language into a completely new color context. In its interaction with form, color has the potential to introduce another level of three-dimensional complexity.

17 Elser 2004, 30–32.

Splitterwerk,
Schwarzer Laubfrosch, residence,
Bad Waltersdorf, Austria, 2004,
Monochromatic space,
colored niches define functional areas

COLOR NICHES

dmvA Architects,
House DM2, Mechelen, Belgium, 2006,
Kitchen in colored niche

ARM Architecture,
Hamer Hall, Melbourne, Australia, 2012

The yellow color shades were selected to ensure that, in spite of different surfaces, materials, and textures, they appear the same to the eye: Terrazzo floor: R230 G215 B22; wall and ceiling: C11 M0 Y95 K0; foil coating on furniture elements, high gloss: R236 G194 B0

Studio Niels & BroekBakema,
Chemelot Campus, Building 24,
Sittard-Geleen, The Netherlands, 2014,
Polyurethane acrylic paint, orange RAL 2010 on MDF

Color islands

Color islands are places in space that are defined on the strength of the color, without clear spatial delimitation. There is no clear-cut distinction between a niche and an island. Color islands can be created in a number of ways—using colored areas, with a combination of colored areas and colored solids, or by highlighting a shape using color. Maat architettura defined the dining area within a large, multifunctionally used main room of a Wilhelminian-style apartment using a lemon-yellow color. By coating just two wall surfaces and a defined area of floor, they created a chromatic space that has the power to take precedence over the multicolored, ornamental tiled floor.

At the seniors' care home in Pont-sur-Yonne, France, the architect Dominique Coulon has designed the circulation routes as an inviting concourse in which to take a stroll. At the corner points, colored areas on walls and ceilings, with a spectrum ranging from bright pink to a strong red, create places for communication and casual encounters. Colored volumes shaped as objects for sitting on or leaning against supplement the areas.

Even without involving walls, clearly defined spaces can be created that develop a high recognition value, for example in the Combiwerk in Delft, the Netherlands, a social training center for people with psychological or mental disabilities. The uniform gray of the office carpet tiles across the large hall floor is interrupted by numerous monochrome islands in different colors. These are formed by carpet tiles in variations of red, green, blue, and yellow color shades that combine like pixels in a picture. The furnishing replicates the color nuances in the floor finish. With this concept, the interior designers of i29 have succeeded in enlivening the economically constructed area with its monochrome gray hall. The design can also be read as a symbol of the diversity and individuality of the users. In order to create extra height for a mezzanine floor in the conversion of a former garage to create a residence, DoepelStrijkers sank the kitchen to a level below the floor. Seating steps leading down to this level were finished with a bright-orange polyurethane coating, thus creating a place for rest and conversation. The shiny surface of the polycarbonate light box fitted above generates strong color reflections and spreads the color in the space. The lower floor level is part of a three-dimensional space sequence that leads from the road, also somewhat lower, to the private garden.

The color island in the library of the Nordstjerneskolen School in Frederikshavn, Denmark, appears as a sculptural object projecting into the space. The multistory color landmark is located in the center of the star-shaped layout plan and, owing to its volume and conspicuous color—orange—can be seen from all areas of the school. The stepped, pyramid-shaped form invites you to sit and develops a strong presence and identity in the large hall.

i29 interior architects,
Combiwerk Delft, social workspace,
Delft, The Netherlands, 2012

Arkitema Architects,
Nordstjerneskolen, Frederikshavn, Denmark, 2012,
Color: Red, s1580-Y90R,
high-gloss paint on sanded drywall construction

maat architettura, Apartment,
Turin, Italy, 2006,
Epoxy resin coating on floor and wall, satin finish,
color code: SIKKENS G8.30.85 (4041 color concept)

Dominique Coulon & associés,
Seniors' care home, Pont-sur-Yonne, France, 2014,
Color shades walls and ceiling: white RAL 9003;
color shades walls and ceiling of island:
light pink Sikkens F8.11.75 or dark pink Sikkens A8.20.60

Following pages:
Duzan Doepel, Eline Strijkers with Stefan Meyer,
Arjan Pit in cooperation with Lex Architects,
Parksite, apartment, Rotterdam, The Netherlands, 2008,
Paint: epoxy resin coating, color shade orange

Color solids

"Architecture is an interplay between mass and cavity, full and empty, body/mass and space. Bodies/masses are perceptible only when they stand out against unformed space."[18] Owing to their contrast with the surroundings, color solids create a focus in the space. They are the opposite of space; they are three-dimensional and can be experienced from all sides. Their effect depends on the size of the other elements of space and their color. A monochrome solid will appear as part of the surrounding room surfaces, whereas color contrast reinforces the individual shape of the object. Depending on scale and positioning, solids divide and structure space, or create space, and facilitate the differentiation of functions. They can accommodate clearly distinguished or separate rooms with special conditions or requirements. Through the color's recognition value, they direct the focus to their purpose and facilitate orientation in space, including across several levels in a building.

Small colored volumes in space can be clearly read as additive elements. They leave their surroundings unaffected while adding useful functions, such as in the former mechanical engineering hall of Darmstadt Technical University, which used to accommodate a culture project called 603qm as an interim function. Various volumes that look like building blocks and were adjusted to the dimensions of the human body are here placed freely in space. With their signal yellow (RAL 1003) color finish that was selected to evoke the danger marking on building sites, they stand out clearly from the fair-faced concrete and rough surfaces that dominate the space. All functions necessary for the operation of the space, such as cloakroom, bar, seating, lounge, and stage elements, can be produced by combining the yellow-colored solids in different variations. They can be moved about in the space at will and be put together in new combinations depending on requirements. A larger, prefabricated steel box in the facade has also been finished in signal yellow and accommodates the entrance, indicating the new use to the outside. The architecture of the hall, with its rough industrial style, remains untouched, and yet the intervention is clear and confident due to the unifying color used throughout the corporate design.

When converting an old school to an information center in Paredes, Portugal, the architects of spaceworkers worked with a strong black/white contrast. The interior of the existing building was completely coated with white paint, thus reducing it to the concise geometric shape of the double-pitch roof. All new functions, such as the shop, counter, projection room, and ancillary rooms, are housed in an almost room-filling, deep-black volume that follows the geometry of the existing building. Only a narrow gap is kept free between the colored solid and the envelope, making it possible to walk around the structure. An empty space in the center of the room serves as reception area. Visually and mentally, this is associated with the dark volume due to its continuous black floor covering.

18 Janson 2014, 293.

Owing to their contrast with the surroundings, color solids create a focus in the space.

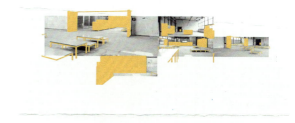

Daniel Dolder with John Lau and Michel Müller,
603qm, interim use of a former mechanical
engineering hall at Darmstadt Technical University,
Darmstadt, Germany, 2003–13,
Color shade: RAL 1003, signal yellow

spaceworkers,
Conversion of a former school into an information center,
Centro de Informação da Rota do Românico,
Paredes, Portugal, 2012,
Black: RAL 9011; silk matt, white: RAL 9010;
silk matt, floor: polyurethane coating

Precisely placed objects can unfold their zoning effect, particularly in generous spatial situations. If they are arranged vertically through several levels, repeating points or orientation are created in the three-dimensional space—in particular when their extent and sculptural shape can be seen through a void. When the color of solids is adapted to the surroundings, they will recede. When the color of a solid stands out, it will emphasize the object's formal independence. Light and the associated shadow reinforce an object's three-dimensionality.

In his Duplex Tibbaut project in Barcelona, the architect Raúl Sánchez uses two solids with a square footprint that are turned 45 degrees against the longitudinal direction of the space in order to create an open residential layout with clearly defined functional areas. One of the objects contains those functions that require privacy, such as the bathroom and bedroom, while the other has the possibility of vertical circulation. The high-gloss surface of the objects features gold particles and creates a contrast to the homogeneous white surfaces of the existing building. The cube shapes stand firmly on the floor without a visible plinth, but seemingly finish just beneath the existing ceiling. This emphasizes their volume and independence even though they are actually connected with the ceiling, by a slightly recessed joint that is coated white like the surfaces of the room.

It is not always necessary to have fully closed surfaces for a volume to appear as a color solid. When the color shade clearly contrasts with the surroundings, objects consisting of individual elements or shapes and forms are visually combined into a colored solid. Rashid Ali of RA Projects London combines the levels in an apartment by using a blue-color solid consisting of different shapes and forms. Here too, the object has an important zoning function in the layout but allows views across the entire width of the space due to its construction with rather closed shelf elements and areas that are made up of narrow slats.

Rashid Ali/RA Projects,
FinHouse, London, Great Britain, 2015

Raúl Sánchez Architects, Duplex Tibbaut,
duplex apartment, Barcelona, Spain, 2017,
Color: gold

Anish Kapoor,
"At the Edge of the World", 1998,
fiberglass and pigment,
500 × 800 × 800 cm

Color volume

Color volumes cannot be detected from the outside surface but fill the interior volume of a space. Owing to their homogeneity, they appear as solid and physically tangible. In his space installation *Green House*, the artist Kyung Woo worked with these phenomena. Here, the color is perceived as a volume; like a water surface, it seems to fill the space as if it were a physical substance. The lower half of an exhibition space is covered in a lighter blue-green and, in combination with suspended items of furniture folded along an imaginary mirror line, is perceived as a water-filled volume on which the fitments seem to float.

A similar effect is created in the stairwell of Casa da Severa in Lisbon by the steps and wall surfaces that are finished in the same shade of red. When he was asked to transform a former residence into a cultural center, the architect José Adrião completely stripped out the building and replaced the interior with two colored volumes. The first floor, which accommodates the ancillary rooms and kitchen, appears to be steeped in red. Visitors enter the white volume of the restaurant on the second floor via a staircase. The contrast between spatial closeness and expanse is further enhanced by the contrast between strong red and bright white.

The artist Anish Kapoor investigates the power of color pigments to form volumes. In his work, indentations are partly painted with mostly unmixed, full-color pigment; these tend to irritate the viewer as they seem to alternate between colored surface and deep space. In other words, the color-filled volumes lose their perceivable physical boundaries.[19] In the installation entitled *At the Edge of the World*, a large red cupola with a diameter of eight meters and a depth of five meters is suspended above the heads of the viewers. "Red encloses the view, limiting it by a red horizon. But after a while the cupola seems to start flowing; the actual height can hardly be ascertained, instead the red starts to adopt immaterial formations of rain or of clouds, that is, one automatically understands the cupola above as a celestial phenomenon, as a red sky."[20] The homogeneous colored volume develops its own dynamic that dissolves the strictly geometric, static space. The artist describes the effect of the color: "The task is to dissolve something out of the volume and to change it into something that would be immaterial."[21]

19 Zschocke 2004, 176ff.
20 Drahten 2004, 140ff.
21 Ibid.

José Adrião,
Casa da Severa,
Lisbon, Portugal, 2012

172

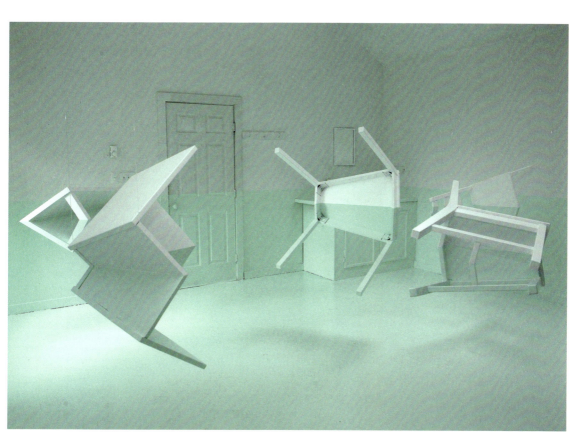

Han Kyung Woo,
"Green House" at the Corporation of
Yaddo Artist Residency program,
New York, USA, 2009,
Color shade white: matt white;
color shade green: Behr Paint P390-1

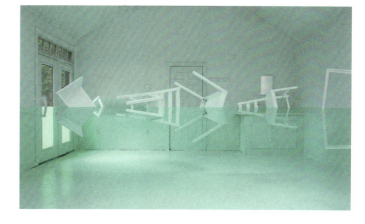

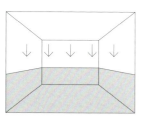

Fabio Novembre,
TDM5: Grafica Italiana, exhibition design,
Triennale Design Museum,
Milan, Italy, 2012-13

Autonomous
color strategies

Friederike Tebbe and Müller Reimann Architekten,
Interior design, legal and economic sciences faculty,
Goethe University, Frankfurt am Main, Germany, 2008,
Faculty Club, color shade: violet/"matter"

Design as artistic intent

Color schemes that relate directly to the surfaces of the room respect the basic geometry of that room. The change is a subtle one; even though the color alters the weight of the surfaces in the room and creates new contexts, it is still subordinate to the architectural configuration of the space. The artist Friederike Tebbe studies human habits of seeing in space and the options for communicating via color. She makes use of her training in painting techniques and also of the findings on the physiological processes of seeing as a basis for her cooperation with architects. She emphasizes the associative power of color: "Color is omnipresent; the world we see is primarily a color world. As a key feature of perception and an emotionally charged medium, color shapes us and our surroundings, guiding us through them. Each person has different ideas, associations, preferences, and reservations that correspond to different colors."[1] Early on in the design process, a decision has to be made regarding the material and surface. However, ideally the final position and coloring of the surfaces is not determined until the space can be physically experienced, because it is not possible to completely simulate visual relationships, light conditions, and atmosphere.

In an architectural context, color can support the space and its uses. For example, when devising a color scheme for the rooms of the legal and economic sciences faculty at Goethe University in Frankfurt (in cooperation with Müller Reimann Architects), Tebbe used color and material in such a way that a coherent overall image has been created in the existing context of materials. Taking into account the strong inherent colors of the granite and wood floor covering, she defined six color shades, of which four are from the green spectrum, one is a greenish gray, and one a strong violet. These color shades were used in accordance with the different functions of the rooms, both as a means of covering the room surfaces and also independently of the building components. In the Faculty Club, a rectangular form in a strong violet—referred to by Tebbe as "matter"—was applied a short distance above the high plinth at the lower part of the wall surface, extending through the corners in order to create an intimate atmosphere in a room with very high ceilings. This creates a zone for conversation while seated. In contrast, in the cafeteria a fully painted dark-green wall surface reflects its color into the room, thereby creating a distinct atmosphere.

In a color installation entitled *murals* in the Framework Gallery in Berlin, the artist proceeded in a different way. Not bound by any functional briefing, Tebbe applied color stripes and fields along a series of walls in order to influence the way the room is perceived. A composition of horizontal, narrow rectangular bands and rhythmically changing, vertical, large rectangles between these bands is applied across the room surfaces. The bands negate the room corners. The change in chromaticity, the size of the elements in relation to the room, and the gaps between them, which have the effect of interruptions, result in a rhythm that appears to alter the geometry of the room. By separating the colors with white space, they

1   Tebbe 2009, 13.

Friederike Tebbe,
"murals", color installation,
Framework Gallery, Berlin, Germany, 2004

visually remain on the wall surface; any effect of protruding and receding is avoided. Owing to its extent, the graphic cannot be comprehended at a glance. As viewers traverse the room, they become aware of regularities, sequences, and cycles. All shapes are clearly distinct from one another on the neutral white background that separates the individual elements, so that each color exerts its influence unaffected by the others and, at the same time, the background binds the composition together.

When this visible background is omitted, the colors begin to interact and create their own three-dimensionality, which can produce a relief-like visual depth.[2] Two-dimensional elements, for example rectangles, have a more static effect. By dissecting the surfaces in the room, rectangles can reduce the perceived size of a volume and create a different sense of scale. By placing color shades directly next to one another, it is possible to create mosaic-type impressions, which give an illusion of spatial depth when applied in space. The architect Alan Chu used an abstract composition of rectangles of different sizes in order to change the volume of a simple cube into a recognizable space for selling tea that is designed to match the tea brand. When closed, neither the graphic nor the volume reveals its function. However, behind the eye-catching graphic there are functional elements that have been integrated into the design scheme. Tied to the geometry of the colored areas, various doors and flaps can be opened, which expose the sales area to the outside and reveal a view to the interior of the volume.

2   See p. 107–110.

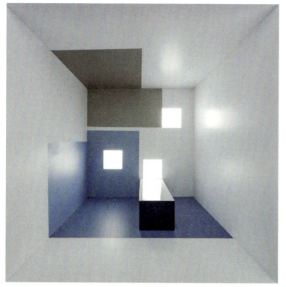
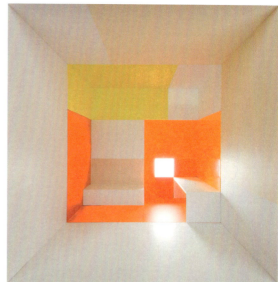

Models of color spaces,
results of workshops in cooperation with
Prof. Esther Hagenlocher, University of Oregon,
and students of h_da: Melissa Kellner,
Peter Fendrich, Vichard Vong, Jennifer Fruth,
Tina Rothenburg, Dorothee Lahr, and Irina Schiebelbein,
Darmstadt, Germany, 2014

DESIGN AS ARTISTIC INTENT

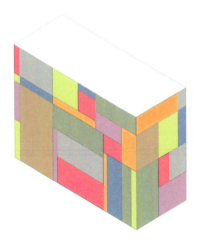

Alan Chu,
Kiosk for the sale of tea,
The Gourmet Tea—Cidade Jardim,
São Paulo, Brazil, 2012

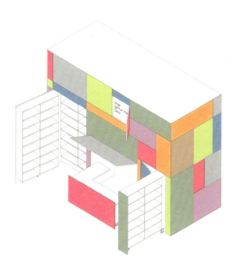

Dominique Coulon & associés,
Day nursery,
Buhl, France, 2015

Color shades floor: Sikkens Z3.37.43, Z8.18.63, Z8.11.75,
A0.20.60; color shades ceiling: dark-pink, high-gloss
paint Sikkens Z2.06.81, light-pink matt Sikkens Z2.06.81;
color shades walls: red and pink shades Sikkens
A9.30.50, A0.20.60, Z3.37.43, Z6.23.60, Z8.11.75, Z8.18.63

Following pages:
SelgasCano, Office,
La Florida, Madrid, Spain, 2008,
Floor and wall: wood planks and concrete
with two-component epoxy resin coating,
white and yellow

In the central hall of the day nursery in Buhl, France, Dominique Coulon developed a subtle, three-dimensional differentiation despite the strong color scheme. Owing to its unattractive location, the building is very introverted and focused on a central space that is lit by roof lights. The surfaces of this space were subdivided into numerous individual rectangles that are colored in many red and pink shades with varying degrees of gloss. This has created smaller subareas, the scale of which is matched to that of the children. A three-dimensional object suspended above part of the area defines a zone with a reduced room height. The high-gloss, dark-pink finish of the underside of this object increases the color reflections in the space. All surfaces above this are white and reflect the bright daylight, which causes the color shades to radiate and, as a result, to interact with one another. Overall, the room appears to be immersed in a warm color hue. The colors were chosen from a group of closely related hues, which in space creates an impression that oscillates ambivalently between homogeneity and fragmentation.

When colored areas do not match the given structure of surfaces in a room, they create their own dynamic in that space. The architects of SelgasCano use this effect in a small office space that has been half-sunk into the ground in order to link it with the surrounding nature. The room surfaces are divided in longitudinal direction, the resulting geometry is colored in white, yellow, and green. The area between the solid part of the wall, belowground, and the roof has been glazed throughout the length of the structure. In the elongated room, a windmill-type rotation develops that directs the view outside, to the treetops. The edges of the room are rounded toward the roof and reinforce the rotational movement.

Interlocking Color elements

"Liberated from the confinement to form, color has the opportunity to unfold freely and to pursue its own theme based on the independence resulting from the process. Color and the architectural components, such as floors, walls, ceiling, piers, can enter into a partnership; parts can be isolated or jointed together without having to defer to the architecture. It can also interpret, analyze, and even parody."[3] This is how the painter Oskar Putz describes the effect that is produced when colored areas are no longer congruent with the room surfaces. When the color composition is more strongly perceived by the eye than the geometric edges of the room, the perception of the space changes. The result can be optical illusions or three-dimensional distortions. Colored forms extending beyond the geometric confines and reaching into other room surfaces create new spatial relationships and contexts because they suggest a new canon of form. The scale of the shapes determines the effect: depending on the size of the colored forms in relation to the geometric surfaces that confine the room, the edges are dissolved or completely new volumes are defined.

Heinz Bienefeld, and his son Nikolaus, used color in the interior of the Kortmann residence in Cologne, Germany, as a means of changing the impression of space. A composition of different, interlaced, colored forms which negate openings and building components result in a spatial weave originated in color. This causes an interaction between the color shades, which produces a sensation of depth. Strong-colored forms in contrasting orange and violet were supplemented by a gentle pink that had been achieved using marble dust. The color was applied in several translucent layers; for this purpose, the architects specified the tools and direction of working. The brushstroke became a material with its own surface characteristics and created great depth and liveliness in interaction with the daylight. The paint was no longer just a thin covering layer, becoming an independent material in its own right. A neutral background was provided with the white ceilings and a matt metal floor. As viewers move about, the perception of space is subject to constant change.

In the Kortmann residence, the overlapping colored forms generate an expressive sense of space. However, they can also be used to create zoning and orientation in an otherwise undefined space, as has been demonstrated by raumkontor in the corridor of the Manus Clinic in Krefeld. Collage-like, overlaid rectangular colored forms provide points of emphasis in the monotonous layout through the grouping of similar color shades, helping with the accentuation and orientation. The individual, carefully placed colored areas extend into one another, creating a uniform whole. In this way, the color develops an independence that is free from the restrictions of the wall surfaces.

In areas of increasing complexity and diversity, and depending on clear and succinct or convoluted room structures, it is possible to create an illusion in space by using the device of overlapping color. The painter Oskar Putz, a representative of concrete art, transfers his painting concepts

3   Putz 1994, 47.

raumkontor interior
designers,
Manus Clinic,
Krefeld, Germany, 2012

Heinz and Nikolaus Bienefeld,
conversion of Kortmann residence,
Cologne, Germany, 1995

INTERLOCKING COLOR ELEMENTS

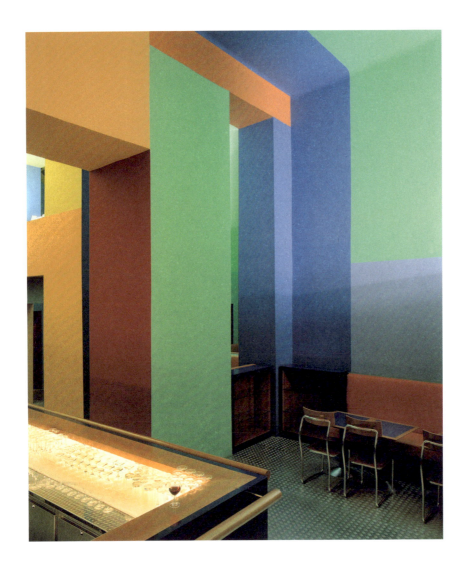

The intended effect to be achieved with the selection of certain colors is the only criterion for judging whether the selection of a color is right or wrong.[4]
Oskar Putz

Oskar Putz,
Kix Bar,
Vienna, Austria, 1987

to space. In the interior design of the Kix Bar in Vienna, he developed a completely autonomous color concept, the weight of which is equal to the existing three-dimensional objects and in parts imposes its own form. Some building components are joined together by the color; others are highlighted, divided, and newly combined.

Putz regards color as a "very active element of architectural design,"[5] which, used correctly, can reinforce the concepts and ideas of the built structure. He detaches the color from the form and treats all color shades as equals and as possible neighbors. He organizes the colors independently of the room surfaces; the objective is a pure pictorial effect.

At doors and windows, the coloring at the Kix Bar emphasizes the function of the construction; different colors are applied to load-bearing and non-load-bearing components. In other places Putz used color fields that extend beyond the geometric edges of the room in order to overlay colored forms; together with an orange-painted wall, the ceiling in the same color no longer appears as a flat surface topping the room but becomes part of a three-dimensional volume. The artist placed an orthogonal beam structure into a shallow niche with an arched top at the rear of the premises; on the one hand this negates the architectural form, and on the other hand it simulates depth through its chromaticity. At first glance it is not clear whether the color emphasizes genuine elements or creates a three-dimensional impression. The spatial effect of the color shades creates this ambivalence, because the red seems to jump forward whereas a dark blue suggests depth and shadow. This creates a charged dialogue between color and space.[6]

The Dutch installation artist Krijn de Koning writes on this significance of color: "All these things create what we call space. And if you alter it or build onto it, then it is suddenly something completely different—even with just a small intervention, for example applying a color or placing a statue in the space. I think it is an interesting fact that the addition of an object not only focuses attention on the object itself, but also brings about an awareness of the surrounding space."[7]

With the introduction of color, the perception of the surrounding surfaces changes. In his space installation entitled *Dick Bruna Huis*, a homage to the Dutch graphic designer Dick Bruna, de Koning used a selection of strong colors that was inspired by the limited color palette in the work of the Dutch illustrator. Even though de Koning followed the geometric givens of a house-like, three-dimensional system, he used color to add an additional, freer level of interpretation and continued to develop the design of the three-dimensional structures. Changes of color on a surface, precisely at the axes and the extension of edges, create the visual illusion of additional edges. The contrasting arrangement of complementary colors such as blue and yellow or red and green next to each other reinforces the effect of edges, and hence the effect of the three-dimensional interweaving of fragmented forms.

4   Putz 1994, 47.
5   Putz 1994, 46.
6   Putz 1992.
7   Koning 2002, 56.

Sauerbruch Hutton,
color concept for the exhibition
of photographs by
Ola Kolehmainen, Haus am Waldsee,
Berlin, Germany, 2014

In the galleries of Haus am Waldsee, Berlin, the Sauerbruch Hutton practice used color to rearrange not only surfaces but entire room volumes as part of the design for the exhibition of Ola Kolehmainen's large architectural photographs. The color segmentation of the exhibition space made reference to the exhibited work. Kolehmainen's photographs are collages of individual parts that were photographed from a slightly offset angle of view. The architects contrasted the photographs by very large colored forms, some of them filling entire parts of the room. The color forms created new spatial contexts and cut through the existing volumes by extending beyond walls and room-confining elements. Owing to the abrupt changes in color, which were always arranged directly behind the exhibited photographs, the pictures no longer seemed to be connected to the wall but appeared to protrude to a level in front of the wall. Strongly contrasting color shades or lightnesses were placed next to one another, thus reinforcing one another in accordance with the rules of simultaneous contrast. The three-dimensional space became abstract, whereas the pictures had a stronger spatial effect due to the contrasts in the background. The color shades were devised in accordance with the plan for hanging the pictures so that they enforced the respective motifs through contrast or color harmony.[8] As the architects described their design: "The three-dimensionality of the images and the graphic qualities of the spaces thus interact and enter into a dialogue that gradually extends real space into imaginary space—and vice-versa—to the point that the observer is present in both, the line between art and architecture dissolves."[9]

8   Wilson 2014.
9   Sauerbruch 2016, 324.

The interweaving of space and surface with equal weight adds a new dimension of simultaneity of the pictorial and spatial effect.

Krijn de Koning,
"Dick Bruna Huis", art installation, Central Museum,
Utrecht, The Netherlands, 1999–2005

Dazzle painting,
camouflaged ship
"USS West Mahomet",
USA, 1918

Tobias Rehberger,
New York Bar Oppenheimer,
New York, USA, 2013

The graphic was digitally printed on matt wallpaper
and the floor covering. Colors: orange Pantone 151,
red Pantone 032, light gray Pantone 428, dark gray Pantone 430, pure black

Graphical superimposition

When colored forms or linear graphics cut through the tectonics of architectural space and merge it into a new shape, the graphical display of color has a similar effect to camouflaging strategies in nature and in military contexts. Strong color contrasts generate visual irritation when they are used independently of their background and based on a logic that does not correspond to that of the object or space. Areas and contours that cannot be allocated distort the reality and lead to fragmentation of the overall image. In World War I, the British naval forces made use of this phenomenon. Since it was practically impossible to camouflage warships and commercial vessels using conventional camouflage methods, upon the suggestion of the illustrator Norman Wilkinson they were painted with large graphical patterns in strong contrasting colors in order to blur the ship's contours, actual size, and direction of travel when viewed through the periscope of a submarine. This strategy was aimed more at confusing the optical senses of the opponent than at actually hiding the vessels. Some of the patterns were developed by artists who were representatives of Vorticism, an English art movement related to Cubism that had its heyday shortly before World War I. The Vorticists aimed to find an artistic language for the forms of the mechanical era; they were opposed to depictions that are close to reality and tried to capture movement, reducing objects to bold lines and graphical elements. For the camouflage strategy that was called *dazzle painting*, different color schemes and scales of pattern were tested on ship models until the best possible blurring effect had been created. The effectiveness of the color patterns remained debatable, however, since in good weather a vessel's direction of travel could be detected through a periscope even from a great distance.

This principle has been transferred to space by the contemporary artist Tobias Rehberger. He uses the method of dazzle painting in order to transform the perception of spaces. The two-dimensional patterns developed by him completely change the appearance of three-dimensional space. Graphically dominant structures of stripes in the contrasting colors black and white, applied at pointed angles and supplemented with orange cover walls, furniture, and sculptures, melting them into one unit. The result is an optical flickering that obliterates the geometric edges and space-confining surfaces. Lines and two-dimensional patterns create nonexistent new edges and folds in space that obscure the true size of the room. The image is further distorted by mirrors.

For the Frieze Art Show in New York, Rehberger had his favorite Frankfurt bar rebuilt as a 1:1 scale, fully working model at the Hôtel Americano, installing exactly the same equipment and fixtures. This bar is distinguished from the Frankfurt original, however, by the completely new interpretation of all surfaces and furniture using patterns inspired by the dazzle painting principle, which is intended to express the function of the bar as a catalyst for creativity and change.

A

B

C

The influence of colored areas on spatial effect:
student assignment at h_da, Darmstadt, Germany, 2009
The influence of color contrast and two-dimensional
area was investigated in longitudinal rectangular model
rooms at a scale of 1:50.

A   Line structure
B   Area structure
C   Light reflection on area structure

Dominant black-and-white patterns constructed using segments of a circle and their intersection dominate the office spaces of AgoraTIC, a company offering digital training. In this way, the architect Stéphane Malka gave expression to an open, multifunctional structure that had been stipulated by the user, in which it is possible to carry out classic office work and hold training events and meetings in rooms of different sizes. The graphical design directly responds to the flexible divisibility of the spaces using a system of movable suspended wall elements. Their axes of rotation lie on the grid points of a chessboard pattern in the colors black and white, which, in addition, is overlaid by the pattern of the rotational radii of the individual elements in the respective contrasting color. Mirrors extend the three-dimensional system into infinity and create a labyrinthine impression of space in a room with a simple rectangular layout. Depending on the position of the movable elements, the room seems to visually expand or contract.

Playing with the ascertainability of a space and its contours was also a theme in the design of the showroom for the Berlin fashion label Smeiline-ner by the Fingerle & Woeste practice. In a former apartment of the Wilhelminian era with high stucco ceilings, structuring volumes were placed into the room to accommodate counters, changing rooms, and podiums. Precisely arranged forms in contrasting colors spread across these elements as a graphical layer independent of the architectural geometry. They cause objects, walls, and floor to melt into a fragmented puzzle by introducing an additional, illusory level of interpreting space: based on the graphical design, space seems to develop into three-dimensional colored solids. A room-changing play between two- and three-dimensionality arises.

A similar objective is pursued in the graphic design of a parking garage beneath a residence in Sydney carried out by the Craig & Karl artists' collective. The central element is a "space ribbon" that runs as central axis from the entrance through the space to the garden outside. In the center, the color design takes over the space completely; it breaks up into a fragmented pattern designed in yellow and green shades. The "nonplace" parking garage becomes a place of experience through the superimposition.

Malka Architecture, La Nouvelle Héloïse,
flexibly usable office and
training rooms for AgoraTIC,
Paris, France, 2016

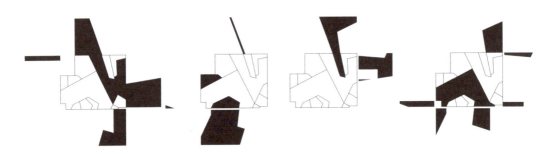

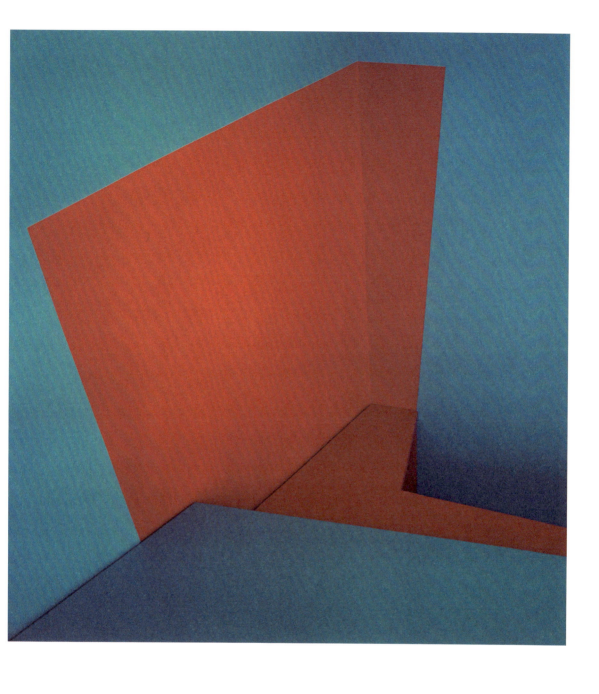

Fingerle & Woeste,
Smeilinener fashion showroom & studio,
Berlin, Germany, 2007

Following pages:
Craig & Karl,
72DP, parking lot,
Sydney, Australia, 2011

GRAPHICAL SUPERIMPOSITION

Two-dimensional or three-dimensional patterns—either as camouflage or with a graphical intent—also influence spaces in their geometric expanse.

Kazuyasu Kochi,
Residence,
Chiba, Japan, 2014

Using a radical intervention of color and geometric shapes, the Japanese architect Kazuyasu Kochi developed a residence for a family that combines great spatial density with ample diversification of atmospheres and spaces. In the existing building, with its traditional timber construction, a charged correspondence is created between construction, space structure, and color structure. A central hollow space was created in the existing building, with triangular or rectangular cutouts placed at random in the grid of the load-bearing structure, at the edges of which the plywood structure of the existing building is exposed. Each of the cut sections was painted in a different blue, yellow, or pink shade. The colors zone and combine, whereas the cutouts permit staggered views. The interior was given an abstract quality; a composition of form and color overlays the space. The architect compares the implementation of his concept to the transformation of Cubist painting into space.

The principle of superimposing graphic designs is effective regardless of the size of the surface area and the scale. Color and pattern have the potential to change the perceived reality also in an urban context. On Mimers Plads plaza in Copenhagen, the designers of Topotek 1, BIG, and Superflex have created what they call a "city lounge" by using a black floor with white lines as combining and ordering element. Various seating elements, barbecue sites, a Moroccan fountain, and a playground have been integrated into the floor graphics. The white lines mark out footpaths and a main cycle route, bypassing the street furniture elements and plants, and running straight across the artificial topography. By virtue of their pattern, like contour lines on a map, they generate illusory cambers in the surface finish and create an artificial viewing mound as part of the overall surface.

When color is added as an additional component in the graphic design, not only are the edges and geometries eliminated, but optical effects are created that are a direct result of the process by which we see color. The representatives of Op Art and Color Field painting of the 1960s occupied themselves intensely with these phenomena.[10] At that time, the American painter Gene Davis focused exclusively on the mutually impacting effect of long colored stripes and their effect on space. In 1972 he created a large-scale piece of work entitled Franklin's Footpath (see p. 207), in which he used about 126 meter-long stripes along the road in front of the Philadelphia Museum of Art; these stripes were pointed at the museum and drew visitors in as if they were being sucked in. He justified his choice of motif by saying that the elementary shape of the stripes "create a simple matrix as carrier of the color and do not distract the eye too much through formal adventures."[11]

Petersen Architects applied the principle of stripes to a built object. The large abstract cube of the BER_AIRPORT Hotel in Berlin is located in the as yet undeveloped commercial precinct around the new airport. The architects responded to the absence of any meaningful surroundings with a flexible, homogenizing concept of horizontal stripes that are adjusted to the dimensions of the windows. This created more an image of a facade than a comprehensible building envelope. The exterior provides no clues

10 See p. 7–36.
11 Gage 1993, 266.

as to the use of the building. For the color composition, the architects relied on the manufacturers' standard colors, which they supplemented with only three special colors. The surface of the steel-coated panels is finished matt in order to avoid reflection and to allow the strong colors to be seen in all light conditions.

The artist Carlos Cruz-Diez added another layer of complexity, using stripes as what he calls "Chromatic Event Modules". In this way, he provokes further interaction between color and surface. He defined his own understanding of color based on studies in physics and chemistry, on the physiology of seeing and optics, on philosophical and humanist writings on color perception, and on work by the Impressionists and other representatives of color theories in art. In his view, the perception of color changes constantly and depends heavily on external influences and contemporary historical circumstances. With his research on the *Inductions Chromatiques*, Cruz-Diez wants to make visible the changeability of color, which he refers to as a chromatic event, by splitting it up into individual elements. Some of these works are at the scale of urban space, where they unfold their effect over large areas independently of the viewer's perspective and entice viewers to interact directly with the art.

On the footpaths leading to the stadium of the Miami Marlins by the architects of Populous, stripes were installed at regular intervals on an area measuring 1,672 square meters using innumerable ceramic tiles in the colors blue, green, and orange, superimposed with black stripes, which were applied at varying distances. As spectators move along, this irregularity creates varying color effects the artist refers to as "double-frequency Chromatic Induction." The colors are arranged in a critical relationship to each other that makes them interact. Spectators in Miami perceive yellow and pink shades that are not used on the surface. This phenomenon is known as simultaneous contrast and refers to the interaction of colors placed adjacent to one another. The process involves a physiological correction in our seeing organ, in which the color seen by the eye changes depending on its neighboring color because of an increase in the complementary nuance on the adjacent color.

Topotek 1, BIG and Superflex,
design of Superkilen,
Mimers Plads, Copenhagen, Denmark, 2013

Petersen Architects,
BERLIN_AIRPORT Hotel Berlin,
Berlin, Germany, 2012,
Facade: steel sheet panels, matt coated,
manufacturer's standard colors plus
three special colors

A   B   C

Carlos Cruz-Diez,
"Chromatic Induction in a Double Frequency",
Walkways at the Marlins Ballpark Stadium,
Miami, USA, 2011–2012

Diagram for laying the tiles
A   Colored stripes: blue, green, and orange
B   Black stripes arranged with varying distances
C   Chromatic effect as a result of the superimposition

Stripes "create a simple matrix as carrier of the color and do not distract the eye too much through formal adventures.[12]
Gene Davis

12 Gage 1993, 266.

Gene Davis,
"Franklin's Footpath",
Paint on asphalt,
Philadelphia, USA, 1972

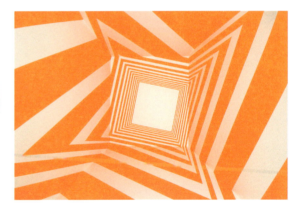

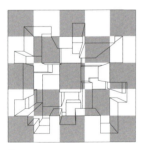

A

B

The installation investigates the effect of different qualities of space and color perception. A graphic design applied with paint that creates the illusion of space can be switched on and off by illumination. The distorted pattern appears to tilt the rectangular room when seen from the entrance. When an additional red light is switched on, the true room edges can be seen again. The space changes between different color intensities and readabilities owing to the phenomenon of color metamerism.

A   Aylin Güllüoglu and Asli Filiz Gün,
    "Chessboard Pattern in Craggy Space",
    student assignment at h_da, Darmstadt, Germany, 2011
B   Florian Siegel and Thomas Heyne,
    "Twisting Room", walk-in space installation,
    student assignment at h_da, Darmstadt, Germany, 2010

Anamorphosis

Pictures that can only be recognized when seen from a certain angle are referred to as anamorphic. The term is derived from the ancient Greek word for "changing shape". On a flat surface, this impression is created, for example, by strong longitudinal distortion; in space, the image can also be split into individual parts. Seen from the correct viewpoint, the eye will correctly put the individual parts together. Often, anamorphic images in paintings from the Middle Ages were used to hide encoded content. In the Renaissance, the technique was used in illusory ceiling paintings to balance vaults and special building features such that a contiguous image was created for viewers looking at the painting from the ground. In contemporary art, anamorphosis has been transposed to space.

In his three-dimensional work, the artist Georges Rousse makes the borders between painting, photography, and space blur. What in the photographic image and from a precisely defined viewpoint is perceived as a flat image becomes three-dimensional in space when the viewer changes position. Rousse implements his works in real spaces on a temporary basis. Often these are abandoned, dilapidated, and vacant structures with a previous industrial or military use. The works of art only persist in the photographic documentation. The complex manual and analog installation depends on a close relationship with the light and the local conditions, and requires a precisely calculated configuration of the image.

The two-dimensional whole that is seen from the camera position and is recognizable as a clear geometric image conceals, in the depth of space, a staggered, in parts distorted, painting. Space and two-dimensional image merge seamlessly with each other. Through the deviation from perception and imagination, illusion and truth, reality and substantiveness are questioned; the role of photography as a medium for precise recording of images is also thrown into doubt. The images in space are initially constructed as sketches that Rousse then transfers to the focusing screen of his large-format camera. This image provides the blueprint for the implementation in space; the arrangement of border lines and colored forms is continually controlled via the camera, while the design is translated into individual elements in space in small steps. The seemingly arbitrarily placed colored forms join to form a contiguous image only from one viewpoint. They seem to float in space as if on a foil.[13]

13 Rousse 2010, 95–100.

In the former Magasin aux Vivres in Metz, France, the artist has painted existing space-confining surfaces and load-bearing building components entirely without additional projections, changes, or installations in the room, creating the impression of a flat image plane floating free in space. The selection of colors was tested in sketches and finalized on-site. The color shades are well-balanced to ensure that no individual color dominates, and there are no two identical color fields next to each other.

One of the characteristics of anamorphosis is that, as viewers move through space, they can perceive the complete image from a certain point, but as they move along, the image splits up again. This aspect was used by the architect Dominique Coulon in the Orbec seniors' care home in France as part of his interior design for the common areas. The idea was to create interesting spaces in the corridors where the residents would walk about and meet up. The color highlights existing niches, accentuates volumes, forms spaces, or deconstructs them in other places. When you approach one of the larger spaces, a geometric form seems to float in the air but then splits up again into colored forms used to structure the space. The experience of the space changes as one walks through it.[14]

14 Magrou 216, 128.

Georges Rousse,
photograph of a temporary installation
in a former bunker, Le Magasin aux Vivres,
Metz, France, 1994

ANAMORPHOSIS

VOX Architects,
Optimedia, offices,
Moscow, Russia, 2017

Anamorphoses have a focusing effect and draw attention due to the spectator's tendency to want to find out the cause of the visual irritation. In a loft office with an open-plan layout, the architect Stéphane Malka created a point of calmness and focus by inserting a centrally placed anamorphosis. He used the existing structural elements in the space, changing them with color in order to economically define zones for flexible uses and to exemplify the transformation-based company philosophy of the users, who work in the Internet and networking industry. Viewed from a central perspective, a series of golden-yellow cube frames becomes visible, between which light enters from roof lights. Mathematically determined forms in two yellow tones precisely applied to the sea-blue floor, the ceiling, and an existing row of columns create this illusion in space, which blurs the boundary between reality and image-based abstraction. Prompted by the conspicuous scenario, the adjoining work zones are obliterated by the eye. Quite a different effect is achieved by the anamorphosis in the reception space of Optimedia in Moscow that has been designed by VOX Architects. Here, it forms a conspicuous interior with high recognition value. Upon entering the space, a bright-blue, seemingly floating square lays itself over building components and interior furnishings like a transparent foil. When the visitor moves closer to the area, it breaks up into its individual parts, which cover all visible surfaces. Using the airbrush method, the graphic design was precisely applied to furniture made of Corian, the PVC floor, the gypsum plaster of the walls, and the technical services lines.

In the *Unbuilding Walls* installation created for the 2018 Architecture Biennale in Venice, Graft Architects address the subject of a wall that dissolves into individual slabs as visitors change their viewing point. When entering the pavilion, visitors first perceive a contiguous black wall surface which, as they come closer, disintegrates into a number of display boards distributed throughout the room. The reverse is used to exhibit projects that have been created on the border strip between the former East and West Germany.

Dominique Coulon & associés,
Seniors' care home,
Orbec, France, 2015

Ceiling and walls: white color RAL 9003,
red color LC.32.090—kt.color;
floor covering: light gray linoleum, marbled,
type Forbo Marmoleum Fresco—3860 silver shadow

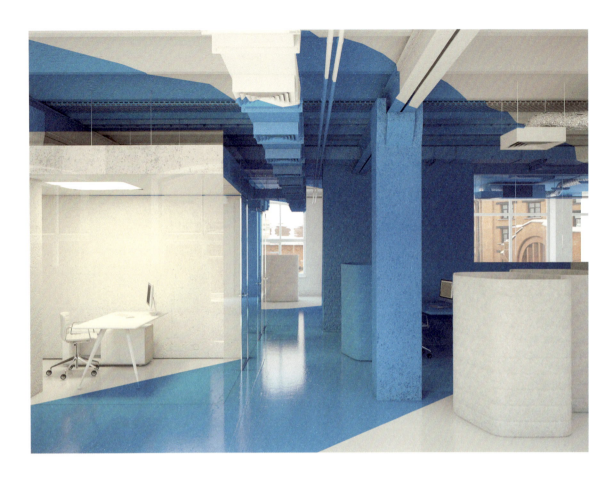

VOX Architects,
Optimedia, Offices,
Moskow, Russia, 2017

GRAFT,
"Unbuilding Walls",
Exhibition in the German pavillon
for the Architecture Biennale,
Venice, Italy, 2018

ANAMORPHOSIS

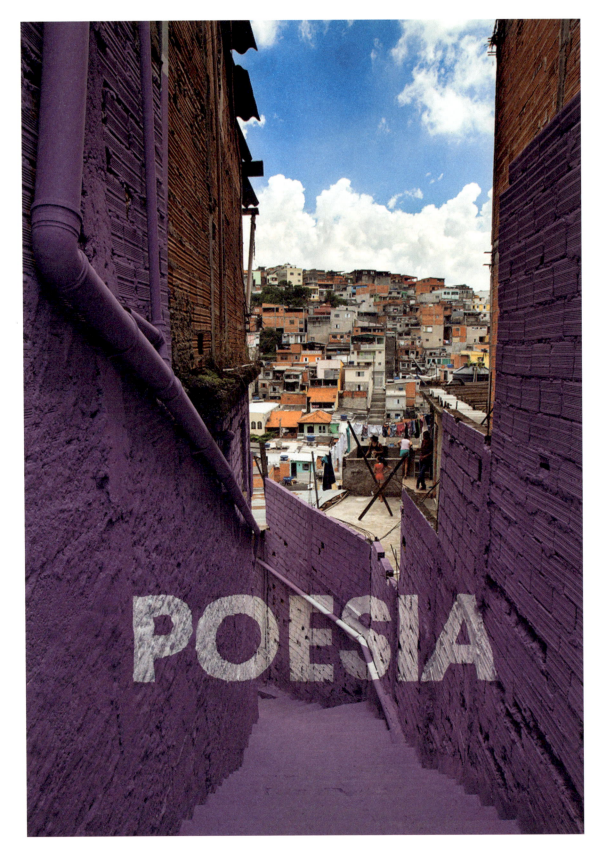

Boa Mistura,
"Poesia" from the
Luz nas Vielas art project,
Vila Brasilândia,
São Paulo, Brazil, 2017

The potential of anamorphosis, when realized on a large scale, can also be exploited in an urban context. The artists of the collective Boa Mistura use this style device in their street art to direct attention to socially underprivileged neighborhoods and slums. In close cooperation with the local residents, colors and words are selected that are then jointly applied throughout entire streets. The color is applied in a homogenizing way across all surfaces, badly maintained pathways, and alleys. Improvised buildings and structures are painted with the help of the group. With the radiance of the color and positive messages such as Peace, Light, or Poetry (to name but a few), the collectives create places with identity. Here too the message can only be read from a certain viewing point, and as one moves through the picture, it blurs into a graphically abstract pattern.

The artist Felice Varini works in similar dimensions but with a formally aesthetic intent. He too uses existing architecture and public spaces as background. His largest projects involve entire mountain villages or fortresses. From a specific vantage point a geometric form appears, for example two bright-red circles above the facades of the Salon de Provence near Marseille, France. As one walks through the landscape or village, one can see fragments that seemingly do not make sense out of the overall context. When working with landscape, the artist appreciates the fact that it influences the geometric shape to the extent that it becomes almost unrecognizable: "If you draw a circle on a flat canvas it will always look the same. The drawn circle will retain the flatness of the canvas. This kind of working is very limiting to me, so I project a circle onto spaces, onto walls or mountain sides, and then the circle's shape is altered naturally because the 'canvas' is not flat. A mountain side has curves that affect the circle, and change the circle's geometry. So, I do not need to portray complicated forms in my paintings. I can just use the simplicity of forms, because the reality out there distorts forms in any case, and creates variations on its own accord."[15]

15 Dekel 2008.

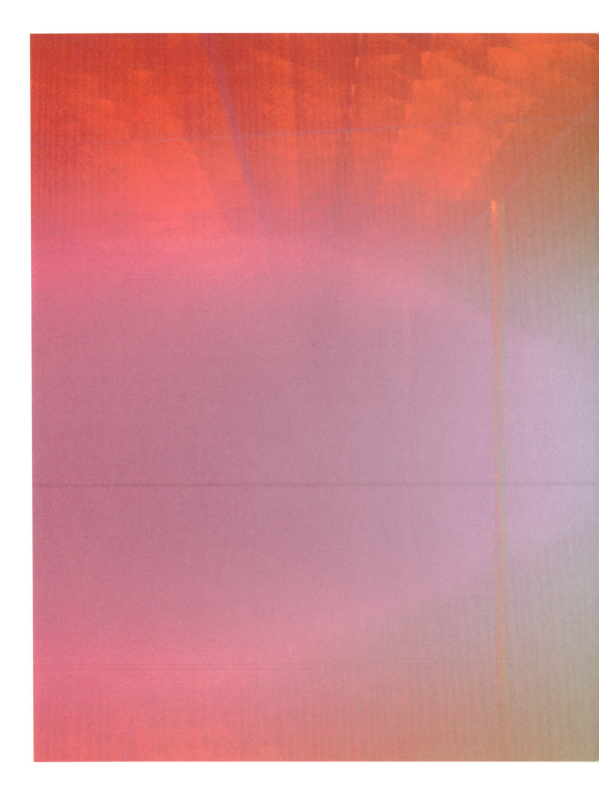

Ólafur Elíasson,
"Your atmospheric colour atlas", 2009,
21st Century Museum of Contemporary Art,
Kanazawa, Japan, 2009

Diffusivity, color reflection, and colored light

Phenomena of light and color

The chromatic appearance of a surface is defined by the chromaticity of its microstructure, like the impression of color in a painting, which is determined by brushstrokes or pixels (see p. 7–36), or by the chromaticity of textiles, which is formed by the individual threads in the weaving process. The eye is not able to separately perceive light stimuli that follow one another very quickly or that are too close together; in the overlapping area, a visual shimmering effect arises. Whether microstructures merge into one or can be perceived separately is determined by the actual size relative to the distance from which they are viewed; the visual impression is determined by the scale. For example, the appearance of a surface can change radically as the distance from the vantage point increases—structures blur and colors blend into new shades. This phenomenon is also used in four-color printing, wherein the chromatic effect of the images is based on the blending of microscopically small grid points in the colors Cyan, Magenta and Yellow, which depending on their size and density are seen as various mixed colors. The rule is: the finer the grid, the more differentiated the color rendering.[1] In addition, as mentioned on p. 90–91, the phenomenon of the reinforcing or graying effect of individual color shades on one another, explored by Michel Eugène Chevreul, comes into play.

Color gradients and color mixes

The architects of blauraum use small, pixel-like units to create a color-mixing effect at the facade of the Bergedorf district school in Hamburg. Tiles in four subtly changing green and blue tones blend in the eye's perception to create an image of a continuous color gradient. In certain light conditions the volume of the building seems to lose its materiality as its color appears to merge with the sky.

Likewise, the interweaving of many divergent color shades generates a homogeneous, almost tender color impression when the individual elements are appropriately dimensioned. In the Immanuel Church in Cologne, Germany, the architects of Sauerbruch Hutton have created a slightly shimmering colored wall behind the altar. When seen from up close, its individual elements appear like the threads of a piece of fabric and consist of contrasting colors. The 10.6-meter-high wall surface, which is perforated to allow the sounds of the organ behind it to emerge, was formed from slightly conically shaped wood slats arranged in eighteen slightly intersecting, overlapping rows. Twenty-six color shades from the blue, green, and brown spectrum are supplemented with individual, bright-red highlights of different degrees of saturation. Due to the arrangement of the colors, a gradation of lightness is created toward the top; this impression is reinforced by the light coming in from the roof light above or, during the hours of darkness, by light from concealed artificial light sources. In spite of the polychromy of the individual elements, they form an achromatic overall picture when seen from farther away, that is to say, from the nave

1 Zwimpfer 2012, 262.
2 Tietz 2016.

Emmanuelle Moureaux,
100 colors no.18 "Forest of Numbers",
NACT 10th anniversary,
National Art Center, Tokyo, Japan, 2017

Color sequence from 60,000 figures arranged in a regular grid in 100 color shades.

of the church. The picture blends well with the calm interior created by the white, waxed wood surfaces of Finnish birch, with its distinct grain.[2] This demonstrates that Chevreul's observations can also be applied at a larger scale.

When the contrast between the colors of the elements and the chosen scale is greater, the individual colors remain visible. For example, oversized colored ash wood parquet boards measuring 20 by 60 centimeters have been used by Tham & Videgård Arkitekter to create distinct zones in an apartment in Stockholm. The uniform floor and the intersecting colors link the rooms to form a unit. Groups of colors create new three-dimensional contexts and link similar functions. A transition to the next zone is indicated by the intersection with a contrasting color.

Sauerbruch Hutton,
altar wall,
Immanuel Church, Cologne, Germany, 2013

wooden slats in 26 different muted colors supplemented
with individual bright-red highlights

blauraum,
Bergedorf district school,
Hamburg, Germany, 2015

Tiles in four colors on a composite thermal
insulation system: NCS S 2050-G60Y, NCS S 2030-G40Y,
NCS S 2030-B40G, NCS S 2030-B10G

Tham & Videgård Arkitekter,
Humlegården apartment,
Stockholm, Sweden, 2008

colored wood parquet sealed
with transparent lacquer

Andreas von Ow,
"Bob's Service", Wuppertal,
Germany, 2013,
bricks of the filling
station in Wuppertal,
acrylic binder at the rear
wall of the building,
approx. 2.5 × 11 m

UNStudio,
La Defense office complex,
Almere, The Netherlands,
2004,
Dichroic films in glazing

Interference colors are created when light is reflected
from thin, transparent layers within a material. When
the light is reflected from the top and bottom of the
layer, the reflected light waves are superimposed and can
reinforce each other or cancel each other out, depending
on the wavelength. The wavelength of the reflected light
also depends on the thickness of the layer, such that
different parts of the light spectrum are absorbed or
reflected. Interference colors characteristically have an
extremely strong brilliancy and opalescence, depending on
the viewing angle. This arises as a result of the increase
in the distance traveled by the light within the transparent material, which causes the reflected wavelength
to change when the incidence of the light is at an angle.[3]

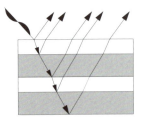

Scheme for a dichroic
film: reflection
of individual colors

Color layering and interference

The three-dimensional effects created by the application of several layers of colored paint in space cause the depth to be increased or seemingly reduced. At the same time, and depending on the saturation, diffuse or compressed color phenomena appear that suggest closeness, dispersion, solidity, or density.

Different effects are achieved by layering color, similar to the effects resulting from the layering of materials, depending on their transparency, the distance between the layers, and the type of material. Perforated, fine-meshed, or translucent materials place a veil of color on the substrate behind; with increasing density, the contours, edges, and boundaries become blurred. Colors blend and optical interferences appear.

In his work, the artist Andreas von Ow creates a multicolored effect from just one color shade by applying the paint in layers. He produces the paints for his pictures himself, not relying on traditional recipes but experimenting with pigment from found objects, dust, or fruit, which he mixes with binder. Often the base material originates from the place of execution, such as in *Bob's Service* in Wuppertal, Germany; here the pigment came from the dust of bricks in the walls. The paint obtained in this way is applied by von Ow layer by layer; the color becomes increasingly saturated and dense—the process and the generation of the depth of the color only being detectable at the edges, due to the inaccurate edges of the various layers. The area with the strongest saturation is at the center of the image; here the color acquires an almost three-dimensional depth.[4] "The layering helps each picture become a plane in which the color reacts with itself."[5] In the case of *Bob's Service*, the artist places three color fields with different numbers of layers next to one another; in spite of there being just one color/paint, the color fields radiate in three different shades. When the number of layers is increased, interference of color is created, including completely new color shades such as red in blue. "In both cases, saturation and interference, the color begins to multiply; although the principle seems to be simple, the corresponding perceivable color effect is diverse and complex."[6]

A color effect that is also based on the principle of interference and is dissolved down to absolute diffusivity was used by the architects of UNStudio in the inner courtyards of the La Defense office complex in Almere, the Netherlands. The facades in the courtyard are extremely colorful, but the colors are not tangible—they continuously change, in a kaleidoscopic display, depending on the light, surrounding colors, and the angle of viewing. This effect is created by dichroic film in the gap between the glass panes. The film is made up of as many as two hundred optical interference layers, each of which is permeable for a certain wavelength of the visible spectrum and reflects others. As the angle of viewing or the ambient light changes, different reflections become visible. At the same time, the complete system is permeable for daylight, so that the rooms inside are lit by neutral light. The dimensions of the filter layers are such that UV light is reflected and

3   Welsch 2012, 302ff.
4   Schlereth 2016, 1.
5   Schlereth 2012.
6   Ibid.

the heat gain from sunlight is reduced.[7] In this project the functional interior that has been designed for office use is deliberately contrasted with a facade that has a seemingly nonstatic character, challenging the optical reference system of the viewer with its continuously changing colors.

Layering and transparency

When the layers have a greater degree of transparency, the overlaying of the colored areas results in direct mixing. The visible layering creates an impression of three-dimensional depth. In a series of epoxy resin pictures and room installations, the artist Peter Zimmermann worked with the effects of overlaying epoxy resin colored with pigments. Under the title *Schule von Freiburg*, he created a colored room installation in the Freiburg Museum of Modern Art in 2016 that extends across the floors of several rooms. Seven layers of colored lacquer flow like puddles of paint through the rooms, filling these completely. The contours of the fluid shapes are clearly delimited; the color spectrum changes from room to room, and yet an impression of great indeterminateness is created. The reflective surfaces give the floor a nonexistent depth, the transparent color layers mix with one another, and, through reflection, the color spreads to the surrounding room surfaces and viewers, immersing them in its color hue. Suddenly the precise edges appear blurred.

Color mixtures can also be generated with transparent layers of paint when applied three-dimensionally. The architects of People's Architecture Office generated a color sequence covering the entire color spectrum by layering laminated glass panes in the three primary colors red, blue, and yellow. The large colored panes were installed at right angles to the direction of flow in the circulation zones of a Chinese confectionery firm's offices. Arranged in sequence, they modify the image of the corridor, appearing like colored film laid on a picture surface. All other surfaces are kept in white and gray and serve as background for the mixing of the colors. When sunlight comes in through the roof light, the reflection of the colors makes them spread farther in the space.

When the transparency diminishes and, for example, one looks through a perforated panel or a surface that has been imprinted with a grid, this will lay like a veil in front of the background, blurring the contours. Even though this creates a mixing of colors between the two levels, it does not have the same brilliance as direct mixing. In a large former room of the University of Ghent, the architects Kersten Geers and David Van Severen installed a furniture-like fixture that can be closed with a skin of movable perforated metal elements that are finished with a strong turquoise-colored coating. This skin generates a homogeneous space that can hide its secondary use as a library behind a colored veil. In this way details are blurred without hiding the implanted use. This has created a spatial situation that accommodates alternating functions, such as events and concentrated work.

7   See baunetzwissen.de.

The overlaying of transparent colored layers results in direct mixing, intensification, and the impression of three-dimensional depth.

OFFICE Kersten Geers David Van Severen,
University library,
Ghent, Belgium, 2014

Layering scheme in the
Brandhorst Museum

a   Wall
b   Substructure
c   Folded sheet metal
d   Ceramic Bars

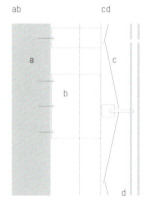

Sauerbruch Hutton,
Brandhorst Museum, Munich, Germany, 2009

36,000 ceramic bars made of four different colors of clay
fragments with 23 different translucent glazes.

A specific material thickness in the semitransparent front layer in combination with the movement of the viewer, the geometries, and the partial translucence of layers generates a lively interplay. Edges and solids lose their distinct shape, and change constantly under the influence of light, shadow, the angle of viewing, and distance. The appearance can no longer be clearly described, but becomes diffuse.

The phenomena described in the section on relief works can be transferred to architecture when the scale is adjusted accordingly.[8] An example of this is the facade of the Brandhorst Museum that has been designed by the Sauerbruch Hutton practice. In this facade the colors of a two-layered microstructure complement each other, creating a stronger color effect or eliminating each other to produce a gray shade. All building volumes are clad with the same facade of a fine texture that is formed of 3,600 slender, vertically arranged ceramic bars measuring 110 by 4 by 4 centimeters. The bars were fired from four kinds of clay with different colors and coated with a transparent glaze in twenty-three different color shades. The resulting possible combinations produce a very wide spectrum of finely nuanced color shades.

The three building volumes were differentiated by using light, medium, and dark color groups. Within the color groups, the colors were deliberately distributed irregularly in order to avoid the repetition of patterns. The image is rounded off by a background layer of finely perforated, horizontally folded metal sheeting with applied colored bands that reduces the reflected sound from the roads. When viewed from the front and due to the distances between the bars, the horizontal bands of the metal sheets dominate, whereas when seen at an angle, the fine vertical texture of the bars at the front stands out.

Owing to the shimmering range of colors, the eye and the lens of the camera do not have any fixed points to focus on; the substance of the building begins to vibrate and to dissolve toward the edges. Seen from close up, the diffuse color intensity is strong, but it decreases with the viewer's increasing distance due to the mixing in the eye. From a great distance the red and green shades of the head building melt into a gray shade; other surfaces come close to the shades of ochre that dominate in the surroundings. Due to the fact that the three-dimensionally interwoven effect of the colors cannot be simulated in drawings, the colors were selected and their composition was designed with the help of a large-format model at a scale of 1:70 and tested on-site with numerous 1:1 scale patterns. Even so, these design tools are only suitable for an approximation because the actual effect on-site can only unfold in the context of the total area.[9]

8   See p. 111–125.
9   Sauerbruch 2016,
    76–77.

Peter Zimmermann,
"Freiburg School", Museum für Neue Kunst,
Freiburg, Germany, 2016,
Epoxy resin in seven layers,
colored with pigments

People's Architecture Office,
21 Cake Headquarters,
Beijing, China, 2012

With their layering along the main routes,
the glass panes in the primary colors red,
yellow, and blue result in a broad color spectrum
when one walks through the spaces.

Light is therefore color, and shadow the privation of it.[10]
William Turner

Interaction between color and light

The three-dimensional perception of space requires contrast, which is created by differences in lightness between light and shadow. Color and material can make surfaces appear textured or smooth. Through the difference between lightness and darkness, reflectiveness and dullness, it is possible to highlight special points in space. A naturally lit room changes all the time because the spectral composition of daylight is subject to natural fluctuations during the course of the day, due to changes in the weather and the seasons. As the intensity of light diminishes, red shades change to brown and yellow shades to olive green. By contrast, artificial light makes it possible to achieve a precisely controllable, switchable effect if daylight is not admitted.

In reflection there is a close relationship between the color shade, the color intensity, and the surface. Color/light reflections bring color to surfaces that are inherently not colored. Is it a case of a direct depiction on a mirroring surface or of a color shadow on a matt wall? Smooth, even mirroring surfaces reflect light and color potentially in multiple ways, which causes the light and color to spread into space far beyond their source. Matt and absorbing surfaces will diminish or even suppress such reflection. Surfaces upon which light falls directly highlight the respective parts of the space; if it is directed, dispersed, or reflected, it can fill a room completely, separate defined areas, or, as diffuse light with constant brightness, lead to the edges of the room disappearing.

Fine artists experiment with colored light in its pure form as a medium that forms space or dissolves space; they explore the workings of optical design and visual perception, and thereby discover the limits of what is possible. Such spaces offer visitors an experience that is shielded from the multiple stimuli of the urban environment and focused purely on visual perception. Under the right conditions, colored light can have the effect of a formable substance—similar to a material that can be tangibly grasped and experienced three-dimensionally.[11]

10 Gage 1969, 206.
11 Böhme 1997, 27ff.

Erin O'Keefe,
"Silver Paper",
photograph, 2012

INTERACTION BETWEEN COLOR AND LIGHT

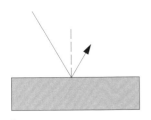
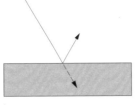
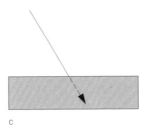
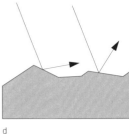

a   b   c   d

a   Mirroring
b   Absorption
c   Partial reflection
d   Reflection on uneven
     surface

The Purkinje effect, so called after physiologist Johann Evangelist Purkinje (1787–1869), refers to the phenomenon by which colors change as the intensity of light decreases. This effect is due to the fact that the human eye has different cells for seeing during the day and at night. During daylight hours, it is primarily the cones that are activated; these are also used for seeing color. During the hours of darkness, however, the seeing process involves the rods, which can also convert very weak light stimuli into signals. The latter facilitate monochromatic, light/dark seeing, because they only react to light from a certain range of wavelengths.[12]

Basic principles of the physics of light

For designing with colored light, some knowledge of the basic principles of the physics of light is required, which are briefly touched upon below. Light is the visible part of the electromagnetic wave spectrum. In order to be able to describe the phenomena of light in interaction with solids and surfaces, particle optics has established the simplified model of the linear propagation of light rays. Changes in direction are caused by reflection, refraction, or scattering when light rays hit a surface. Mirroring surfaces reflect the largest proportion of light, with the angle of reflection being equal to the angle of incidence. Matt surfaces disperse the light depending on the size of the surface grain. Textured surfaces appear darker due to the shadow effect. Furthermore, light surfaces reflect more light than dark ones since the latter absorb part of the light rays, with the energy being converted into more long-wave thermal energy. This process can be clearly felt when dark surfaces heat up more quickly and more thoroughly when exposed to solar irradiation.[13]

     Analog film media in photography also capture changes in color via light unless the photographer controls these deliberately, whereas in neutral light, digital cameras can capture an image that approximates the material color through what is called white balance.
The mixing of colored light and the interaction of colored light with colored surfaces follow the rules of additive color mixing. This provides the viewer, whose accumulated practical experience is most often based on mixing pigments on a palette, with a surprise owing to the seemingly unexpected color shades. For example, when green light is laid over red light, the result is yellow-colored light.[14]

Mirroring

The direct reflection of color and light from mirroring surfaces leads to a specific change in the perceived room dimensions because the distortion of proportions causes the room edges to be extended and the space-confining surfaces to move. When the viewer moves through space, new forms of perspective are constantly perceived; reality and perception blur. Together with the multiplication from the mirror effect, the room is newly constructed as an image.

This complex three-dimensional play with illusion and reality was used by the artist Daniel Buren in his exhibition *Allegro Vivace* in the premises of Kunsthalle Baden-Baden. For his installation entitled *Eight Colors and Their Mirror Image for Four Rooms*, he subdivided a large room with centrally placed crosswise-arranged walls covered with mirrors and applied strong colors to the existing wall surfaces of the room. The real and mirrored colored areas and wall edges stood next to each other with equal weight. As visitors moved through the room, continuously changing combinations of colors created a range of images and room fragments. Mirrored room edges extended the space. After the exhibition, only the photographs remained as souvenirs of the work.

Such an interaction of color, noncolor, and mirroring that builds up an abstract space image was also used by the interior designers of i29 for the exhibition stand of the Dutch magazine *Eigen Huis & Interieur*. The space-defining wall planes and floor areas were covered in strong colors on one half and in matt white on the other. These elements were supplemented with mirroring solids, which accommodated the actual exhibits and functions inside them. The mirror effect influenced the room edges, manipulated the perspective, and generated new solids in space. Rectangular colored forms split into dynamic shapes and, through reflection and mirroring, "populated" the achromatic part of the exhibition stand. The illusion of three-dimensional perception offered visitors new perspectives at every step and at the same time, through its abstraction, created a space of visual calm within the plenitude of products in the exhibition halls.

12 Welsch 2012, 229.
13 Zwimpfer 2012, 51–66.
14 Ibid., 74–79.

Daniel Buren,
"Eight Colors and Their Mirror Image for Four Rooms",
in situ work, in "Allegro Vivace",
Kunsthalle Baden-Baden, Germany, 2011

Mirror film and acrylic paint, applied to walls
in dry construction with brush and roller,
colors Caillebotte yellow and Banyuls red.

i29 interior architects,
Exhibition stand for the
"Eigen Huis & Interieur" magazine,
RAI Amsterdam, The Netherlands, 2015

MIRRORING

Steven Holl Architects,
Chapel of Saint Ignatius,
Seattle, USA, 1997

Reflections make it possible for color to "migrate" through space.

Reflection

Deliberately placed strong-colored areas in combination with reflective surfaces and the incidence of light increase the intensity of colors even without direct mirroring. Reflected color causes white surfaces to assume a colorful glow or, on colored surfaces, mixes the color into a new shade. Reflections make it possible for color to "migrate" through space.

The architect Steven Holl uses colored light and its reflections as an independent medium that constitutes space. He makes use of colored light projections to create a space that is completely detached from the surroundings. In the Chapel of Saint Ignatius light, color, and texture interplay. "7 bottles of light," as the volumes are called by the architect, whose skylights are oriented toward different directions, project colored light into the interior of the church via hidden colored surfaces. A white shell is pierced by deliberately placed rectangular openings and cutouts. It conceals daylight-admitting openings and niches for luminaires, both of which are invisible to the spectator. Color is used only on the concealed surfaces and at the rear, and becomes visible only through the colored reflection of daylight and additional artificial light. Depending on the daylight, the color spectrum of bright colors such as fluorescent green/yellow and orange results in projected colors of different saturations and brilliance that settle into the wall niches like a fog and are carried farther into the room via the black mirroring floor.

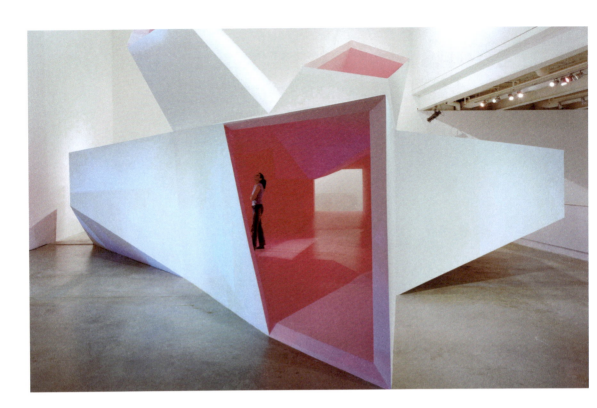

When color reflections spread uninhibited, their luminosity and color intensity can no longer be distinguished from those of a "genuine" colored area.

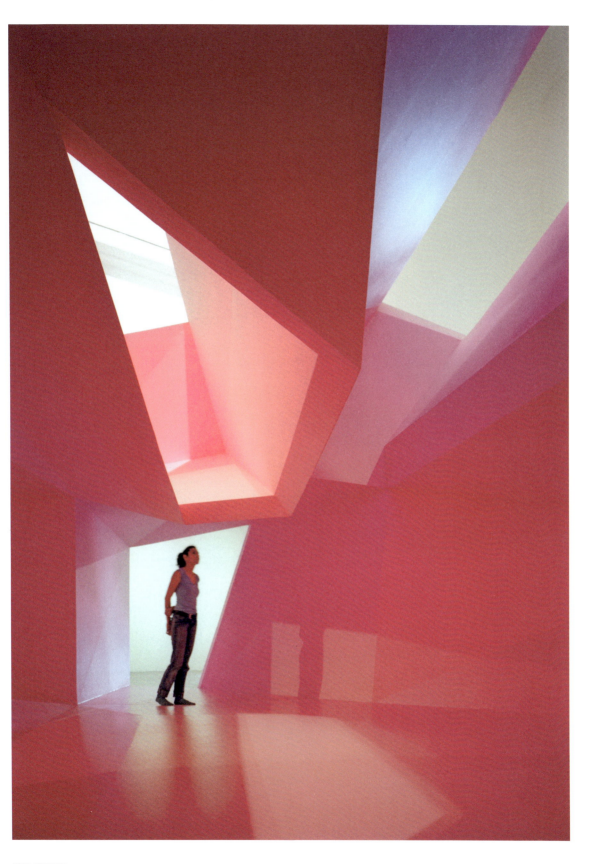

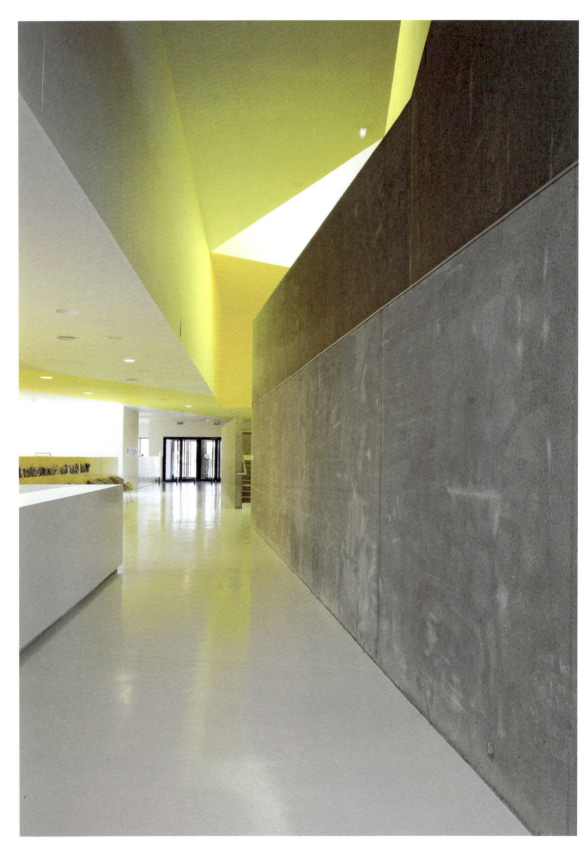

In a space installation entitled *The Holiday Home*, UNStudio combined light, color, and folded surfaces that are developed from an archetypal house volume by extrusion and torsion. This procedure created an impressive space that questions the usual sense of proportion. The spatial irritation was reinforced by numerous light sources that cast multiple shadows on the faceted surfaces and gave the impression of great depth and vibrancy. Multiple reflections from the very smooth folded surface filled the room with intense color, which spread across all surfaces and no longer had a clear visible source. The knowledge gained from this spatial experience was used by the architects and applied to functional spaces in larger projects, for example in the strongly colored vertical foyer spaces of the Agora Theater in Lelystad, the Netherlands.[15]

Color reflection carries color far into space; it moves out of the two-dimensional plane to other building components and thereby becomes visible at other places where there is no direct viewing connection to the colored surfaces. In his cultural center in Isbergues, France, Dominique Coulon uses this radiating effect from strong-colored surfaces onto highly polished surfaces to help with orientation in the building. A yellow space ribbon defines the circulation areas. Through reflection, it develops a strong brilliance that, in spatially confined situations such as corridors or the stairwell, imparts its colors to all surrounding surfaces and thereby becomes visible from other places in the building.

15   ICA and Murphy.

Dominique Coulon et associés,
Multicultural center,
Isbergues, France, 2013

Marlene Oswald,
Tina Spinnler,
model, student assignment
at h_da, Darmstadt,
Germany, 2010, gypsum
board, lacquer, paint, and
artificial light,
60 × 60 × 60 cm

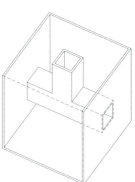

Hannah Hein, relief, student assignment at h_da,
Darmstadt, Germany, 2014, cardboard and colored paper,
50 × 50 × 10 cm

Cubes arranged on an even grid were color-coated on
two sides. When looked at from an angle, a colored
picture is seen from all sides, either owing to the
actual colored surfaces or, when turning 180 degrees,
owing to pure reflection.

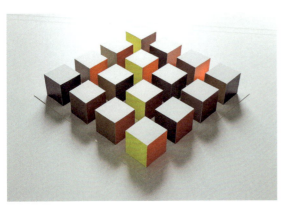

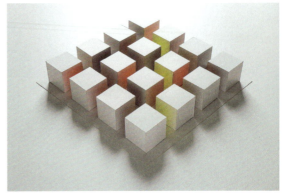

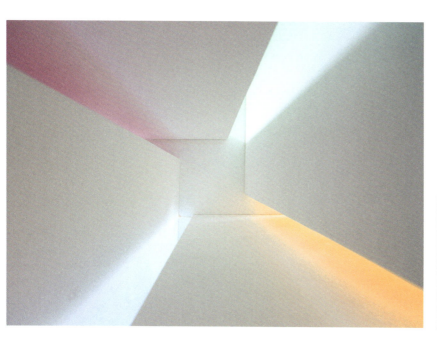

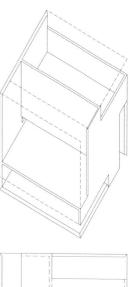

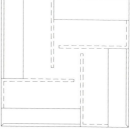

Cekic Fatih, Rahel Yackob, Azieb Debrom,
model, student assignment at h_da, Darmstadt, Germany,
2010, MDF and paint, 60 × 60 × 60 cm

Colored space is created by the reflection from a colored wall to the surroundings. Depending on the color shade and light, the strength of the reflection and the intensity of the colorful atmosphere change.

Erin O'Keefe,
"Things As They Are",
photograph, 2015

Otto Piene,
Foyer roof, University
of Konstanz,
Konstanz, Germany,
1970, renovation 2005

Projection and color filters

Projected light filtered through colored glass has a long tradition in the history of building. In Gothic cathedrals, the light flooding through stained glass windows was deliberately used as an artistic device. The slender and delicate load-bearing structure of Gothic cathedrals, which at the time was revolutionary, for the first time enabled the extensive use of light and color as room-changing elements by means of the projected colored light and color reflections that filled the interior. The carefully planned light event produced a transcendent atmosphere.[16]

Colored glass or glass laminated with colored film permanently changes the color of daylight. This creates a vibrant-colored light that varies with the daily increases and decreases in daylight and—as shown in the following examples—covers surfaces and objects with its projection or fills entire rooms with color. The effect of such glass is similar to that of the historic stained glass window. Glass can either be laminated with film that covers the entire area without joints, which results in a shimmering image of intersecting colored light areas in the projection, or it can be framed to produce an effect similar to leaded lights. In the latter case the shadow cast by the frame becomes a graphical element of the color projection; the individual areas remain clearly defined.

16   Böhme 1997, 29.

When the filtering glass areas are larger or colored monochromatically, the quality of the colored light coming in changes. It develops an almost tangible materiality in the room, affecting it far beyond the surface. The architect Alejandro Muñoz Miranda turned the corridors of a day nursery in Granada into rooms filled with intense colorfulness that vibrates with slight variations in light. He achieved this with the help of large windows, the glass panes of which were turned into filters by the colored film laminated in the gap between the panes. When exposed to sunlight, the color in the space resembles a mist, the pigments of which are almost tangible; when the sky is overcast, the effect is more muted. Different color compositions on the various levels help with orientation in the building.

Whereas for Alejandro Muñoz Miranda the objective is to filter the light as it moves from the outside to the inside, Ólafur Elíasson plays with the effect of colored glass on the physiological processes of color perception in his walk-in installation *Your rainbow panorama* on the roof of Aarhus Art Museum. Visitors enter a circular, completely glazed passageway. The glass panes were colored by applying layers of up to six colored films between two toughened safety glass panes, resulting in fifty-eight finely tuned nuances from the complete color spectrum. This gives the impression of walking on the inside of a rainbow.

The glass panes divide the city into color zones and, through this deviation from the usual outlook, lead to unexpected changes in the panorama and to a questioning of what is seen. When the passageway is traversed quickly, the impression of changing color prevails. If, however, the visitor focuses on one place or color exclusively, he or she will notice several visual events after extended observation: Looking through the red glass panes, contrast is reinforced, an effect that is similar to the use of red filters in front of the camera lens in black-and-white photography. By contrast, the light color shades have the effect of softening the image of the city panorama. In each color zone, a completely different afterimage is seen in the complementary color when the eyes are closed. When one remains for a longer period in a colored area, the color at that point seems to fade; the brain cuts out the change, whereas the colors at the edges of the range of vision become more intense.[17]

17 Crary 2005.

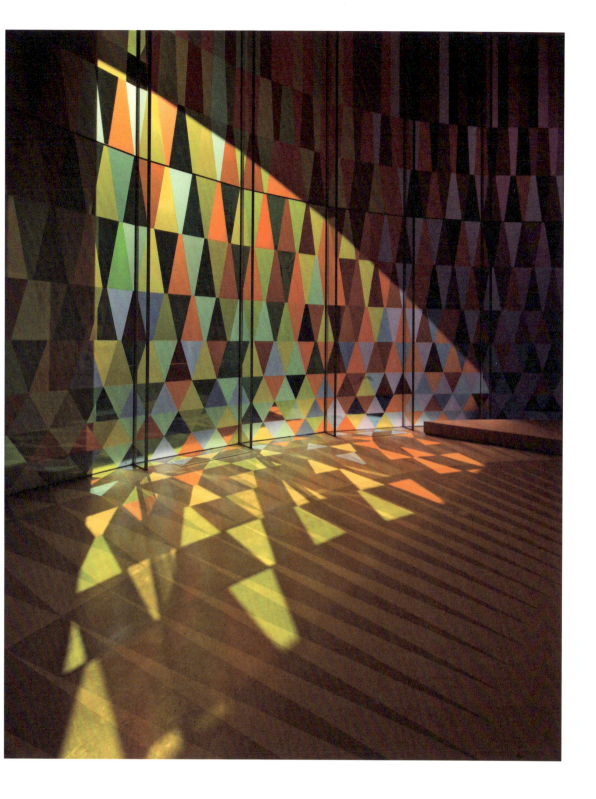

COORDINATION ASIA,
Rainbow Chapel,
Shanghai, China, 2015

Alejandro Muñoz Miranda,
Day nursery, El Chaparral,
Albolote, Spain, 2011

Ólafur Elíasson,
"Your rainbow panorama", art installation,
ARos Aarhus Art Museum,
Aarhus, Denmark, 2011

That effect of colour has real power ... So much power that, in certain lights it seems to become a substance. Once when I found myself in the chapel, I saw on the ground a red of such materiality that I had the feeling the colour was not the effect of light falling through the window, but that it belonged to some substance.[18]
Henri Matisse

18 Matisse 1888
    in Gage 1993, 212.

Colored light

When colored light is generated from artificial light sources, it is possible to precisely define the light intensity, its dispersal, and its color. The available color spectrum of artificial light is greater than that of daylight and can be used to change the color of material to the extent that it looks completely different. The quality of the color rendering of artificial light is determined by the light source, the color temperature of which is stated in Kelvin. The red/orange/yellow light spectrum, which is perceived as warm, ranges from about 1,500 to about 3,300 Kelvin; a spectrum from 3,300 to 5,000 Kelvin is perceived as neutral white light, with typical artificial light character; whereas the blue light spectrum from 5,000 to 9,000 Kelvin, which is perceived as cold, is similar to the light from the sun at its zenith. Depending on the color of the light, every luminaire can be assigned a color rendering index (Ra value) in a range from 1 to 100, whereby all values above 80 Ra can be classed as good color rendering.[19]

Nicolas Dorval-Bory Architects used the visible color difference between luminaires with different color temperatures to provide zoning in a loft apartment. The extended living area is kept in neutral light. At one end of the room lies an area in which all surfaces and objects seem to be immersed in a radiant, warm, yellow-colored mist. All wall areas and surfaces of the apartment are, however, kept in matt and neutral white (RAL 9010) and only serve as background for the materialization of the luminous color. Fluorescent lamps with a color temperature of 4,000 Kelvin, which is perceived as neutral, light the main room. The bedroom and bathroom are turned into radiant-color rooms using low-pressure sodium lamps with a color temperature of 1,800 Kelvin and a wavelength of 589 nanometers, the luminous color of which is in the yellow range of the spectrum. This type of luminaire is usually only used to light areas in which color rendering is not important, for example external pedestrian pathways. A freestanding wall plane on which the different types of luminaires are installed seems to abruptly stop the color mist.

19   Meerwein 2007, 43.

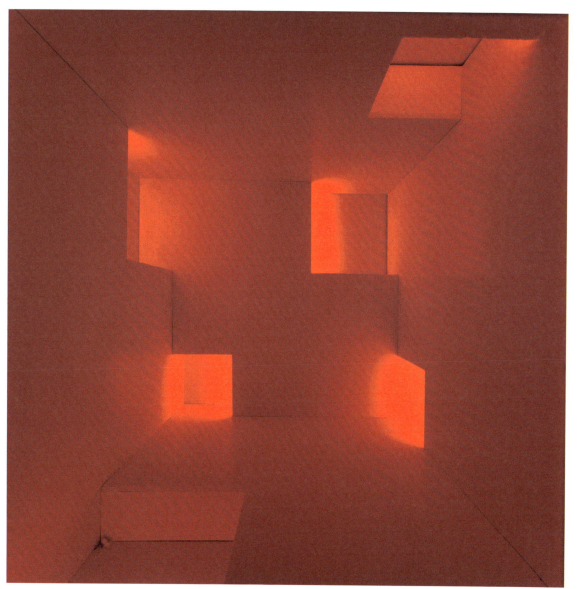

 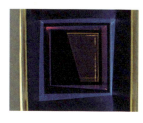 

Melek Dursun and Astrid Schmidt,
studies on colored light,
student assignments at h_da,
Darmstadt, 2014

Following pages:
Nicolas Dorval-Bory Architectes,
Apartment,
Levallois, France, 2013

COLORED LIGHT

Daylight is usually perceived as neutral, artifical light with a high color temperature seems cold, wheras a low color temperature seems warm. When daylight is mixed with cold artificial light, the difference in color temperature lets the daylight seem red.

In a Lisbon speech therapy clinic MMVarquitecto has used this phenomenon to create color zones that provide a structure to the available space, which can be flexibly divided with sliding elements. Here too the uniform white surfaces form the substrate for the play of the colored light. Due to the natural fluctuations in the daylight, the composition changes throughout the day.

Colored light and its reflections can immerse space in color, but beyond that it can also change the interpretation of the entire space. Students of h_da, Darmstadt, have restructured a long underground connecting passage between the Alice Hospital and the Darmstadt Children's Hospital using colored surfaces and colored light. Even though the different colored surfaces in plan have clearly different lengths, they appear to be of equal length when looked at from a perspective view due to the differences in their brilliance, which leads to a much shortened spatial effect. Ceilings coated with colored paint in combination with color-filtered light form spatial units that are varied with the asymmetrical arrangement of the lettering. The impression is that of walking through color portals, the flanks of which are completed solely through mirroring and reflection.

Julia Baumann, Nina Hofmann, and Natascha Roth,
students project at h_da,
new design for tunnel between the Alice Hospital
and the Children's Hospital,
Darmstadt, Germany, 2015

The space of the tunnel is segmented into color zones,
which are visually shortened colored light and
reflection.

MMVarquitecto,
Speech therapy clinic,
Lisbon, Portugal, 2010

Color space created by the interaction of blue-filtered
artificial light with daylight with a warm hue.

Tudor Vlasceanu,
Romanian Pavillon,
Biennale 2010, Venice, Italy

Homogeneous white, glossy surfaces combined with light
from above create an impression of dissolving corners.

The artist Carlos Cruz-Diez explores color as a completely autonomous medium, free from cultural conventions and established habits of seeing. He aims for a separation of pigment and object. In his color light spaces he refers to as *Chromosaturations*, color can be perceived directly by the visitors; the idea is that color unfolds as a situation that can be experienced physically. He created an environment that consisted of a sequence of three spatially limited zones that were defined by strong colored light. Visitors experienced intense monochrome shades of red, blue, and green. This monochrome coloring challenges our seeing habits because the brain usually expects different color stimuli to appear at the same time. At the open intersections, the colors react with each other in accordance with the laws of additive color mixing. The colors were deliberately chosen because the human cone cells responsible for color vision are sensible to the wavelenghts corresponding to these three colors. Due to density and intensity, the colored light became detached from the surface and seemed to float tangibly in space; it was perceived by observers as a physical sensation, like warmth or coldness. The artist achieved this light intensity by placing many neon tubes near one another, the light from which was colored through filter gels, dispersed, and projected onto white walls. Cubes placed at the border between two colored spaces act as multifaceted volumes, which render the different nuances of each color visible. The artist carefully calculates the effect of his environments beforehand.

"My work is about your seeing. There is a rich tradition in painting of work about light, but it is not light—it is the record of seeing. My material is light, and it is responsive to your seeing."[20] James Turrell

In his work, James Turrell relies on knowledge gained from his studies of psychology and mathematics, and refers to the findings of psychologists and perception researchers, in particular the work of Wolfgang Metzger in the 1930s, as well as the contemporary research at Pomona College in Claremont, USA, on the effect of homogeneous color fields. Turrell's works go one step further: he uses light and colored light as a space-forming and space-dissolving medium. His intention as an artist is to create situations that make it possible for visitors to direct their attention to the act of seeing; this is achieved by stimulating them to question their experience-based expectations and assumptions. Turrell uses physical and physiological effects of seeing, such as the reinforcement caused by complementary colors following each other. The minimum also plays an important role: the smallest possible perceivable color or light difference, or a space freed of all objects. In such carefully developed empty spaces, perception itself becomes the object through calculated visual irritation.[21]

Following pages:
Carlos Cruz-Diez, "Chromosaturation", 1965–2004,
exhibition "Carlos Cruz-Diez: Color in Space and Time",
2011, Museum of Fine Arts (MFAH), Houston/USA

20 Brown 1985, 42ff.
21 Böhme 1997, 28.

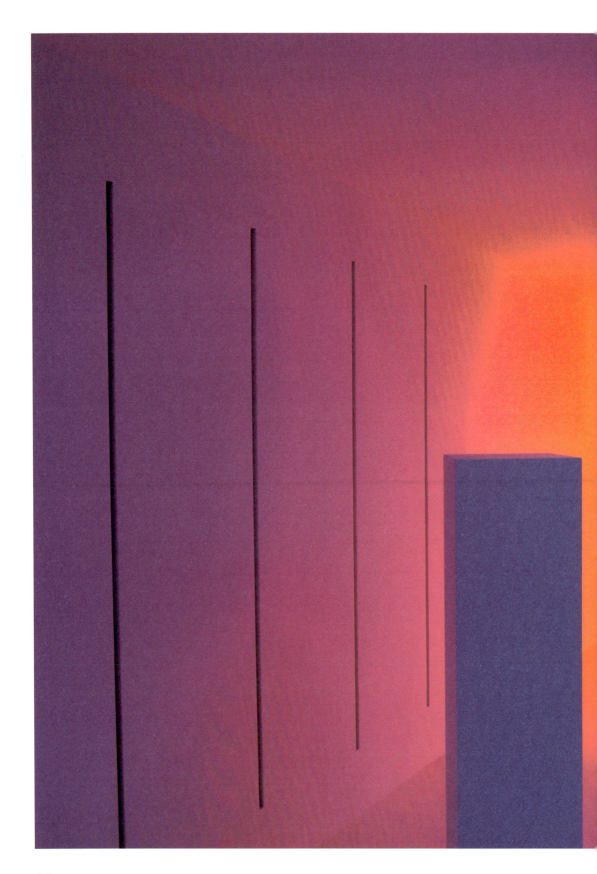

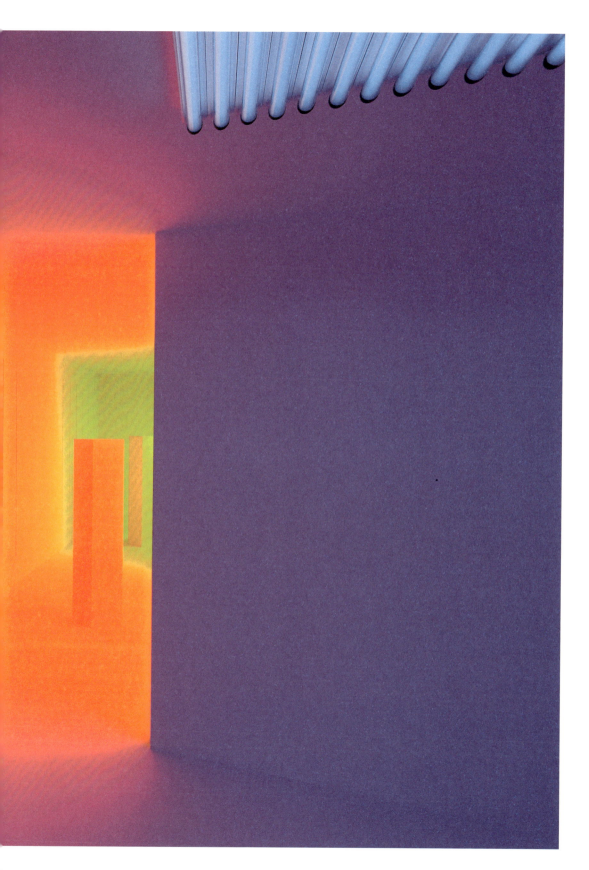

Turrell designs complex space sequences that are intended to promote impressive, concentrated experience. In a series of works called *Space Division Constructions*, he used colored light to generate an almost tangible material surface. The installation consisted of three rooms in sequence. A completely dark transition room served as preparation, as a zone in which to leave behind sense stimuli and to sharpen perception and concentration. When entering the next observation room, the visitor saw a rectangle with an even inherent luminance on the opposite head wall. The absence of any perspective effect and the experience of visiting exhibitions made visitors expect a two-dimensional "picture." This assumption remained in place even when they moved in the room. Only when they came quite close to the wall could visitors see the cutout in the wall that opened up to the light space lying behind the wall. The perceived surface of the light was not real.

This illusion was created by careful placement in space, by the optimal arrangement of the wall opening, and by room geometry, light intensity, color shade, and saturation. The walls of the observation room were lit in such a way that no light could reach the other parts of the room. The colored neon tubes in the light room were concealed and arranged around a cutout directed toward a pointed edge. The room's edges were rounded and the walls were painted in reflective white in order to enhance the detachment of the color from the surface. The space geometry and the size of the opening were designed such that, for visitors, the edges of the light room were concealed from almost all positions in the observation room. This created the illusion of a flat surface on the wall, like a seemingly "stacked atmosphere" of great brilliance. Visitors had to make an effort to interpret what could be seen, and had to continually question their interpretation as they moved through the room.[22]

In *Ganzfeld Pieces*, named after a phenomenon researched in parapsychology, the frame of the observation room was omitted. The visitor was immersed in a monochrome colored light field (also called *Ganzfeld*) that filled the entire range of vision and expanded seemingly into infinity, negating all laws of euclidean space. The colored mist took on an almost tangible intensity and materiality, the color floating like particles in space. The complete homogeneity in the *Ganzfeld* space challenges the system of seeing, which is based on changes in visual stimuli.[23] When one views it for longer periods, the ability to see is much reduced, to the point where only the noncolors black or gray can be distinguished; this is referred to as the blank-out effect. In addition, there is the visual irritation caused by the absence of a horizon and of the room edges as aids to orientation, which can lead to an impaired sense of balance and even to a feeling of dizziness.[24] This reduction of visual stimuli was made possible by concealed light sources, rounded room edges, and very homogeneous room surfaces.

22 Zschocke 2006, 144–54.
23 Ibid., 154–64.
24 Hoormann 2007, 112–34.
25 Böhme 1997, 26.

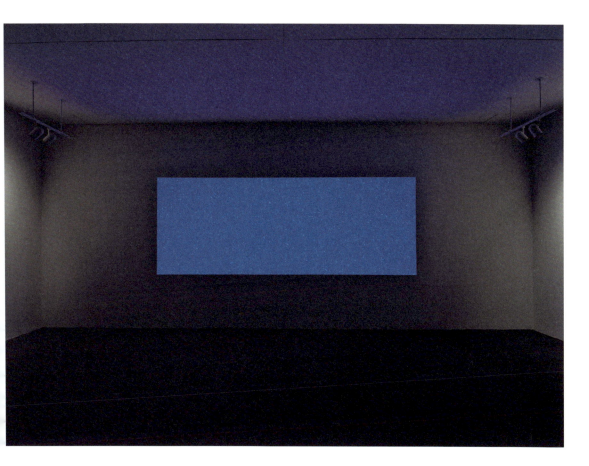

Even though the quality of the light substance cannot be touched, it can be physically felt.[25]
James Turrell

James Turrell,
"Two Blues", space-dividing construction,
space installation, 2008

Luminous color space creates the impression of a
flat area floating in front of a wall.

Dominique Coulon & associés,
Simone Veil School,
Colombes, France, 2015

Readability
and orientation

Information and interaction

People's orientation in space is primarily based on visual intuition. In this context, color is of crucial importance, because we receive the major part of all information via this sense medium. The perception of our environment with all its characteristics requires the interaction of several senses; however, space is primarily perceived and objects identified by visual characteristics such as size, form, and color.[1]

Organizing and guiding systems in buildings based on color can help to clarify the space situation. In this context, color is both a medium for transporting or supplementing new information that could not be understood from the existing room structure, and a means of reducing information within a complex structure of rooms and symbols and of developing clear points of reference. The role played by a hierarchical arrangement of the levels of interpretation and the importance of distinctively designed recognition elements becomes particularly evident when the legibility, and hence the orientation, is lost. Unfamiliar or labyrinthine spaces, like those we find in the typical settlements of an Arabic medina, prompt us to search for familiar organizing patterns and identification points. Unclear, incomprehensible, or unexpected space situations, such as those occurring in the dramaturgical/artistic arena, can trigger strong irritation and unease caused by provoked changes in perception. This occurs in particular when a clearly defined context is manipulated or a visual illusion is created.

In the architectural context, creating a visible order is an elementary requirement—depending on the functions to be managed. The means by which user orientation can be achieved are developed in the special discipline referred to as *signage*. Here, color is a key device used to help orientation and establish a system of order. Objective criteria, such as the routes and sequence of rooms determined in architecture, are supplemented by multilayered levels of perception. Orientation relies on both hard and soft factors. Likewise, higher-level aspects play a role, such as specific cultural influences or the importance of a place.

Color—as the inherent color of material or as color applied to a surface—can have many subtle effects as conveyor of space-related information and is capable of structuring the overall context. Back in 1977, with the Centre Pompidou in Paris, Renzo Piano and Richard Rogers created a building whose color scheme reveals otherwise hidden context. It is an example of genuine machine aesthetics, which governs all design decisions. All functions of the building are openly displayed and assigned via color, as on a diagram. In this building, color is used as a code; it marks both circulation routes and technical services installations. The colors form an abstract graphical line pattern, both at the facades and inside the building, where they become a decorative element in the otherwise plain space.

Every change in color coding also changes our perception. Depending on the chromaticity—either in the form of deliberate, clearly recognizable contrasts or as part of an agreed color scheme—different statements are generated by the color that are closely related to the compositional intent.

1   Buether 2014.

276

The arrangement of lines and two-dimensional components, structural and serial designs, or space-filling elements has a close relationship with the built structure.

Even just the accentuation or negation of room edges with color generates a new image of the space. Linear color routes in the form of horizontal or vertical stripes can help with the recognition and linking of series of rooms and can become part of an overarching space experience; staggered color spaces can counteract this recognition through strong contrasts. In this way, color emphasizes the change of functions in a more or less emphatic way. Special situations such as thresholds and transition spaces, voids, and access facilities need to be designed as such within the overall architecture. In the case of access and voids, this can be achieved using the vertical surfaces in order to identify the overall context between spaces.

Whereas pure, saturated color shades such as red hold our attention and are received directly, like a signal, desaturated colors that are used as a color wash in a balanced material or color scheme create atmospheric mood scenarios in space. However, the expression of the color design does not only depend on the selection of the color value; the involvement of the context and, above all, the presence or absence of light—daylight and artificial light—are essential for the desired effect. The recognizability of the intended information can be lost when it is exposed to unfavorable light conditions or is under the influence of light and shadow. Deficiencies in the design of spaces cannot be eliminated aesthetically through the use of color, but its competent application can support the architecture. Conversely, the application of color that leads to misinterpretation can have an adverse effect on the architectural logic.

Transition spaces

The term *transition space* comes from psychoanalysis and describes the space between the physical and psychological "interior and exterior worlds." In architecture too, threshold areas exist between public and private spaces. It is important to give this space the necessary attention and to express the shift between different uses and functions so that it is understood intuitively. As a purely functional interface, a transitional space can lead directly to the destination, but it can also trigger unexpected changes in direction as part of the intended layout. Special attention should be paid to transition spaces where different uses are to be accommodated, for example living and working.

In a house with an atelier, located in the Swabian Alb mountainous region and designed by kaestle&ocker Architects (previously C18 Architects) for an industrial designer, the functions of living and working are accommodated within a clear building volume. On the two sides, instead of two differentiated entrances, identical, symmetrical entrances lead to the atelier and the residence. Whereas one of the access doors leads directly to the atelier and the workshop, the other opens into a generous reception area that also connects the functions and levels via a void. The reception is located at street level, whereas the private living quarters unfold down the slope. The two levels are connected via a space-saving two-flight staircase. Within the white room-confining surfaces, the stairwell stands out almost like a canyon. With a magical attraction and spatial effectiveness symbolizing a gateway, the strong blue transition space marks the shift between the levels and between the public and private areas.

With its luminosity, a homogeneous mineral paint finish in deep blue, in the same shade as the high-gloss finish of the fitted furniture, leads visitors intuitively in the right direction. Depending on the daylight mood, this effect is enhanced by the light coming in through the roof light at the rear, which almost seems to dissolve the stairwell into something immaterial.

In 2013 Bernd Zimmermann Architects adopted a similar principle with the WZ residence in Ludwigsburg. This conversion of a 1950s residence illustrates, in a simple manner, how color—in this case, the noncolor black— can create an intuitive perception of zoning and thereby support clear orientation. The external shape of the house was retained, but the interior was largely stripped out, and with the help of voids and galleries, zones were created that link the different levels over split levels. The open living space is subdivided by two opposing access structures serving as a distribution spine. The focal point of the three-story void in the living area at garden level is a tree planted inside the house, above which a roof light ensures optimum lighting conditions. The color scheme is used to accentuate the space. Whereas the entire interior is finished in white, the transition space with its narrowing layout between stair sculpture and living space has been immersed in deep black on the floor, walls, and ceiling. The shift between the functions has been deliberately highlighted with a strong contrast.

kaestle & ocker Architects,
(formerly C18 Architects),
House with atelier in the Swabian Alb
mountainous region, Germany, 2008,
Color shade: blue, Keim Optil, color value 190 HBW 17

Following pages:
Bernd Zimmermann Architects,
WZ residence,
Ludwigsburg, Germany, 2013

TRANSITION SPACES

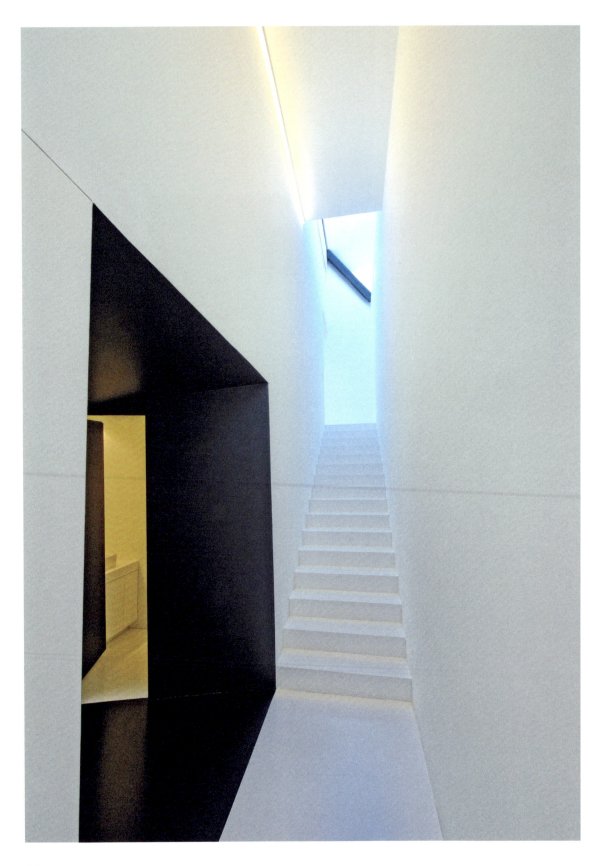

IDOM, architect Gonzalo Carro,
Archivo Histórico de Euskadi,
Bilbao, Spain, 2013

Precisely comosed spaces and calor create unique
experiendes of space and a continuous band for
orientation in the archive of the Basque country
in Bilbao.

By using space and color deliberately, the designers were able to open up quite distinct perception spaces and form a consistent orientation system in the new building of the history archive of the Basque country in Bilbao, Spain. With the archive, the architects of IDOM created a contemporary, open, and transparent structure. Of the total of eleven floors, seven are aboveground, accommodating the administration offices and reading and exhibition rooms. The comprehensive collection of historical documents has been housed underground and takes up the entire length and breadth of the site. The floors are connected via a central, high void beneath a roof light, which helps to direct daylight through to the corridors of the third underground floor. The lighting concept has been supplemented by wide light shafts located in the rear courtyard of the building. The juxtaposition of the protected underground archive with the bright, light-flooded building aboveground results in an exciting composition. The dominant color shade in the building is white. In addition, the application of selected color highlights and the selection of materials create a natural hierarchy in the order of space.

On the upper floors, the color of the internal corridor zones contrasts sharply with the work areas. Daylight can penetrate through glass partitions deep into the interior of the building, thus creating unreal, seemingly limitless zoning. This makes it possible to intuitively recognize the functions. The access to the archives is indicated by continuous stripes on floors, walls, and ceilings, the color of which varies from floor to floor. Within the archive rooms too, the color code points the way and, with its rhythmical application, breaks the monotony of the long corridors. The mobile archive shelves are also finished in the same strong color—a radiant yellow.

In the refurbishment of an indoor swimming pool in the Paris suburb of Bagneux by Dominique Coulon & associés in 2014, the color chosen ensured that the intuitive orientation complemented the architecture of the building. Prior to its refurbishment, the inconspicuous concrete building could hardly be distinguished from the surrounding housing estate. For cost reasons, the basic structure of the existing building was preserved and a new structure inserted that contains the additional functions. The large south-facing glass facade and the load-bearing structure of the slanting pillars were retained. Whereas originally the roof construction was visible, this has now been concealed by a homogeneous white ceiling. The new arrangement of the facility provides for a clear spatial separation of functions, not through separating walls, but through changes in the surface, color, and lighting scheme.

The color blue—a reference to the water—appears in many facets throughout the building. The entrance wall was given a bluish coating with tiny reflective glass beads. For the interior, a combination of different color shades was selected: black-blue for corridors and outside ceiling, gray-white for the walls of the pool area, and signal white. As contrast, the strong light-blue color completes the color palette. Solvent-free, microporous natural paint and concrete paint were used for coating the wall and ceiling surfaces.

Dominique Coulon & associés,
Indoor swimming pool, Bagneux, France, 2014

Color shade of corridors RAL 5004 black-blue,
color shades in pool area RAL 9002 gray-white and
RAL 9003 signal white, contrast RAL 5012
light-blue, solvent-free microporous natural paint
and concrete paint

The interplay of color and light is especially
impressive in the area of the grandstand,
which was constructed as a room within the pool space.

The effect of the interaction of color and light is particularly evident in the grandstands. The grandstand area was constructed as a room within the pool space. The strong, homogeneous blue coloring on floors, walls, ceilings, and seating areas creates a visually comprehensible transition space.

The extremely abrupt transition between the areas appears almost surreal. Depending on the incoming light and its intensity, the reflection of the color produces vivid blue shades on the ceiling that contrast with the otherwise colorless swimming area.

Orientation Systems

"All too often, 'orientation systems' are equated with 'signage' and are mostly not thought about until the main design tasks have already been completed." This is how the authors of the book *Signage: Spatial Orientation* describe the challenge of this still young discipline.[2] It is an undisputed fact that a good orientation system can not only provide information but also strengthen the space experience, and that this leads to greater identification with the building. Wayfinding is applied at different scales irrespective of whether its elements are added to the architecture or are developed as an interdisciplinary task in parallel with the hierarchy of information during the design process.

Taking school buildings as an example, it is obvious how important orientation in space is and that, at the same time, an atmosphere has to be created that promotes learning. Good orientation is the result of sight axes, relationships between rooms, and two- or three-dimensional space experience. Apart from aesthetic and psychological criteria, color is used as a device to enhance the users' comprehension of the surroundings. In order to guide the students, circulation areas, levels, and break areas can be differentiated with a color scheme. The spatial perception depends on the individual radius of movement and the user's own speed. The readability of the three-dimensional structure is related to the configuration and composition of building components, to the visual and haptic quality of materials and surfaces, as well as to the lighting.

The school in Schulzendorf, Germany, by zanderrotharchitekten is characterized by space-filling worlds of color. An existing school building from the 1960s in a growing community close to Berlin was refurbished and extended. Instead of building a new freestanding structure, and to comply with the new town planning order and the mandate for the preservation of open space, the existing building was supplemented by two horizontal building volumes, and the whole facility was unified by the application of a new homogeneous facade. The previously open courtyards were turned into internal, glazed atriums. The former external walls became internal facades along which the new circulation routes to the classrooms were created.

Cutouts on the ground floor interface the internal volume with the outside space and create a central atrium that can be used for school events. With wider areas and retreat spaces for the students, the circulation areas provide additional, special spaces for learning. A complex public color space runs through the building, with changing sequences across floors, walls, 2 Kling, Krüger 2013.

zanderrotharchitekten,
conversion and extension of the
Schulzendorf primary school,
Schulzendorf, Germany, 2007

Color shades green NCS S 1075-G-50Y,
orange NCS S 0580-Y-50R, yellow NCS S 0580-Y,
magenta NCS S 1070-R-20B, white

zanderrotharchitekten,
Conversion and extension of the
Schulzendorf primary school,
Schulzendorf, Germany, 2007

Diezinger & Kramer,
Color scheme Herbert Kopp,
Imma-Mack secondary school,
Eching, Germany, 2006

and ceilings. The colored surfaces provide a structure and emphasis to the room sequences, and identify individual rooms. The expression of the space is enhanced by the application of paint to the surfaces and, in combination with light, has an inviting and powerful effect. The scheme is designed less for its decorative effect than for guiding users intuitively.

The color concept is governed by a clear strategy: each floor level in each of the two atriums has its own color; however, this is assigned to individual building components. For example, the green of the ceiling in the floor level above is replicated on the floor and on the internal parapet, a scheme that is repeated on the next floor with the orange color. In contrast to the changing colors in the surrounding corridors, the verticality of the atriums is emphasized by the use of the strong colors yellow and magenta throughout the floor levels. The different colors in juxtaposition create intentional contrasts, which highlight the key elements of the architecture and, as in a sea of color, blur into one unit. The effect is accentuated by the roof lights above the atriums. The application of large colored areas provides a structure to the space and orientation in the otherwise monotonous configuration of the 1960s school.

Diezinger & Kramer too used color at the Imma-Mack secondary school in Eching, Germany, in order to provide structure to the corridors leading to the classrooms. In cooperation with the artist Herbert Kopp, they developed a color scheme for the definition of the "significant place" in an undistinguished location on the edge of Eching between a commercial estate and a new development. With their strong color, the external facades mark the building; a lilac color shade distinguishes the classrooms and a yellow-green the corridor zones. By contrast, in the interior the color was only continued on the floors, the palette being supplemented by a mustard yellow, spruce green, orange, light blue, and a rosé shade. In order to simplify the maintenance of the building and be able to carry out repair work more cheaply, all other areas were kept in white. However, depending on the daylight, these areas adopt a soft, changing color through reflection from the colored floors. The colors define zones in the corridors and, in the area of the central foyer, weave into an irregular chessboard pattern. The colors were chosen in accordance with the NCS system and were applied in a latex paint medium.[3]

The fact that orientation in buildings does not necessarily require the use of the entire color palette is illustrated by the Centre des métiers at the University for Applied Art and Technology, La Cité collégiale, in Orléans, Canada, by ACDF* ARCHITECTURE. The new research and training center for the building industry is located between the natural landscape of a river and a heavily trafficked highway. The architectural shape takes its cue from the topography and, with its flexible basic structure, is able to accommodate the building's various functions. Whereas the workshops face the road, the administration offices, the multipurpose room, and the classrooms are oriented toward the river landscape. The dividing line between the functions is clearly apparent in the selection of the colors black (workshops) and white (public areas). The yellow stairwell that stands out from the black block like a flow of lava creates a color highlight.

3   Paul 2007.

The conversion of the Toni Campus in Zurich, formerly Europe's largest milk processing operation, provided the opportunity to bring together the Zurich University of the Arts (ZHdK), which had previously been spread across dozens of sites, and two departments of the Zurich University of Applied Sciences (ZHAW) on a new university "super campus." The range of facilities was extended to include commercial spaces such as a cinema and a concert hall, a library, exhibition spaces, and gastronomic outlets, as well as one hundred apartments. In addition to integrating the many diverse functions, the architects faced the challenge of providing a meaningful structure to the development, which has a total of 1,400 rooms, without losing the industrial character of the place. Organized like a "city within a city," the existing ramp system is used as a vertical boulevard from which a series of halls, plazas, voids, and cascade-like stairwells lead off—all of which forms the internal space structure and allocates the functions. An orientation system using sculptural letters and numbers provides orientation within the main structure of the building.

Furthermore, internal corridors and staircases connect the rooms of the university, which have been arranged in functional groups. The character of the industrial ensemble has been retained through the unfinished concrete walls and floors. Depending on the adjacent functions and hence the materiality and light coming in, the gray of the concrete appears either warm or cold. Highlights were only accepted for certain exceptional functions, for example for the internal staircases, where the orientation system was supplemented with strong signal colors. Surfaces on the inside of the stairwells were painted a strong pink color shade: the steel structure and handrail of the spiral staircase, and both the gypsum board wall and in the adjoining space the leaf and frame of the door.

For the students' workplaces of the ZHAW, the architects chose another color shade. In the former drying tower, the students' workplaces are arranged on three levels. The spatial effect of the small cascade is reinforced by light color nuances. The warm green color of the workplace levels, staircases, and parapets changes in its three-dimensional effect from a dark color on the surface into a lighter color via the vertical stacking. Both foreground and background generate a vivid sculptural effect. The multilayered application of color gives this space a refreshing vivaciousness without detracting from its functional purpose.

A combination of a graphical guide system and color islands was used by iglesias-hamelin arquitectos in a bicycle station. Colored areas on the floor, walls, and ceiling are visible from far away and define the parking places for the bicycles; zebra crossings for pedestrians and the numbering of the places were left uncovered, thus showing the color shade of the in situ concrete substructure. This has allowed a clear organization of the space at reduced expense.

In the Wohnen mit scharf! project by Superblock in Vienna, the internal guide system was integrated at an early stage. The apartment block of fifty-one units was designed as an example of intercultural living for residents with different needs. The positioning of the building created a clear edge

ACDF* ARCHITECTURE,
Centre des métiers, La Cité collégiale,
Orléans, Canada, 2010

toward the road and made it possible to create a common outside space. This was achieved by raising the residential floors on pillars so that the first floor could be used for public functions. The conceptual design consists of a compact building structured by recesses and negative spaces. In contrast to the fair-faced concrete, the cantilevering balconies, and the concrete gray painting of the facade, the public circulation areas have been finished in a deliberately strong color—magenta. The vertical circulation space runs through the building like a gorge, providing horizontal and vertical orientation to the residents. The intense color with signal effect accompanies the residents from the outside to their private apartments and creates the block's recognition value, relating the inside to the outside. The deliberate contrast of the colors and volumes is supplemented by the pattern in the interior that has been applied by roller in the stairwell.

The multilayered application of color gives the space a refreshing vivaciousness without detracting from its functional purpose.

A

EM2N with Bivgrafik GmbH (signage),
Toni Campus,
Zurich, Switzerland, 2014

A   Small cascade, workplace:
    color shades wall and parapet green shades
    NCS S 1030-G30Y, NCS S 2030-G30Y, NCS S 3030-G30Y,
    staircases, parapet outside NCS S 1030-G30Y,
    NCS S 2020-G30Y, NCS S 2030-G30Y, NCS S 3030-G30
B   Staircase connection:
    color shades wall and doors NCS S 1060-R20B,
    staircase/steel structure pink NCS S 1060-R20B

B

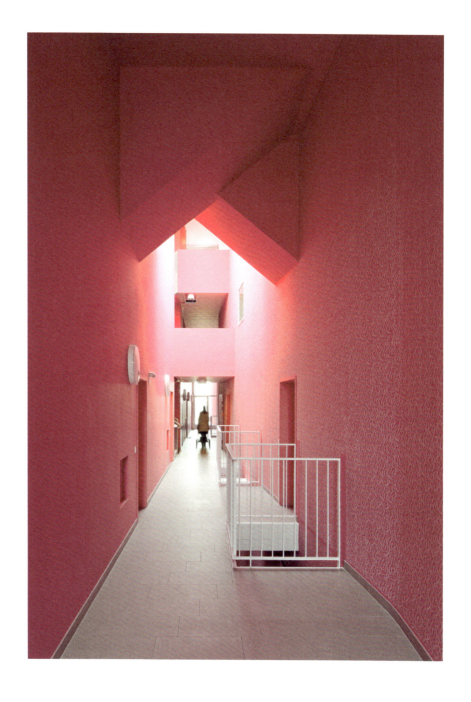

iglesias-hamelin arquitectos with
Verónica Gorri (graphic design),
bicycle parking station CTPM, Madrid, Spain, 2012,
Color shades: blue NCS S 1050-B20G,
gray NCS S 2010-B, black NCS S 9000-N

Superblock Architects,
Wohnen mit scharf! apartment block,
Vienna, Austria, 2014,
Color shade: magenta

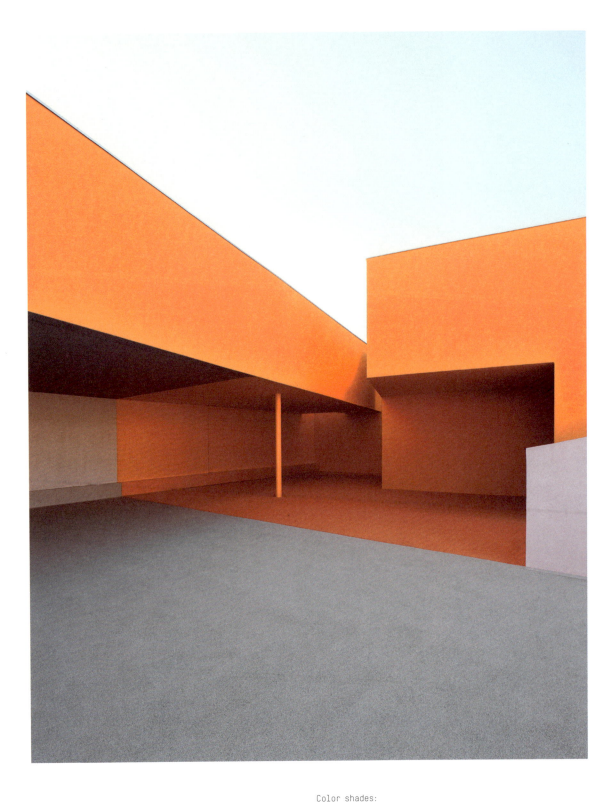

Dominique Coulon & associés,
Simone Veil School,
Colombes, France, 2015

Color shades:
orange Sikkens D6.58.58, corresponds to RGB value
240/118/44, gray Sikkens F2.05.55, corresponds
to RBG value 157/151/143, pink Sikkens Z8.18.63,
corresponds to RGB value 224/152/173

Color sequences and space sequences

As a design element, color can actively unfold its effect in different dimensions and complete the metamorphosis of a surface into space. The work of architect and painter Rupprecht Geiger (1908–2009) is strictly focused on reduction, clarity, and autonomy of color, detached from form. His interpretation of color harmonies is limited to two-dimensional basic forms, which, however, in their intensity and arrangement—as contrast or in a chromatic modulation merging into each other—result in an unexpected three-dimensional effect. The interaction of color and form challenges the viewer's perception and allows different interpretations of how this sense of space is created. The French architect Dominique Coulon also interprets color as an autonomous system, albeit as a "dynamic system of its own kind and in its own right." Color does not accompany architecture, but achieves the impression of space through a method of overlaying, of contradiction. Only when the geometric form and/or the existing room edges are negated is it possible to use color as an additional layer and to create a new three-dimensional relationship, and with that a changed perception. The exploration of the possibilities at the interface between surface and space leads to many diverse forms of expression, which support intuitive perception or deliberately confuse it. Both approaches are justified for the purpose of vitalizing the space.

The visual transformation of interiors by Dominique Coulon is a calculated act intended to deprive viewers of what they are used to. Like material and form, he looks upon color and color contrast as tools for the creation of certain atmospheres. Architecture influences its users—not only on a physical and behavioral level, but also in an expressive, emotional form. In school buildings in particular, Coulon's unconventional approach is particularly noticeable; precise geometry is applied in the interaction of light and strong colors. The new building for the Simone Veil school in Colombes, France, had to accommodate an extensive room schedule on a small site. The day nursery, primary school, gymnasium, canteen, and library are arranged vertically respecting their different need for privacy, common functions are more easily accessible on the lower floors and private functions located on the upper floors. The depth of the volume is structured by projections and recesses, a central void that provides views inside and out, and the choice of materials.

The functions are ordered in accordance with the age groups using the materials and color codes. Whereas the pure material color of wood and concrete is reserved for the primary school pupils, the children in the day nursery enjoy a colorful universe. Orange, magenta, and pink point the way—in the corridors, courtyards, and gymnasium. The crossover points vary deliberately in order to generate an additional quality of space.

Dominique Coulon & associés,
Simone Veil School,
Colombes, France, 2015

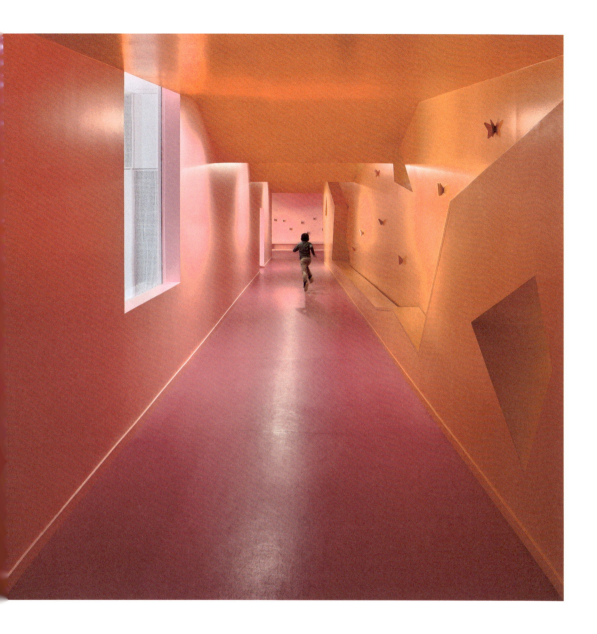

Because the site lies in an urban setting and does not benefit from inviting open space, the roof area was activated as a recreation area, playground, and school garden. The architects chose a deliberately autonomous, dynamic system of superimposition. Irrespective of the geometric form, the color space sequences are in deliberate contrast to the flow of spaces and do not unfold their effect unless they are lit. Geometry, colored form, and shadow result in a constantly changing play. Color becomes an element of experience. Whereas the surfaces of the recreation areas were finished with a sports flooring in colored EPDM granulate, the interior and exterior walls were finished with acrylic paint or colored plaster in the color shades orange, gray, and pink.

NIKKEN SEKKEI, Ryohin Keikaku, PARTY,
Terminal 3 at Narita International Airport,
Japan, 2015

An example of the two-dimensional effect of color sequences is the architectural orientation system of Terminal 3 at Narita International Airport, Japan. Tokyo's Narita airport was built in the 1970s as a relief airport for the capital's main airport, Haneda. As part of the last extension in 2015, Terminal 3 was built for economy airlines. In line with the use of the terminal by economy airlines, the budget was also reduced, which meant that a creative approach was needed with respect to readability and orientation. The architecture was reduced to the essentials; instead of homogeneous suspended ceilings and digital display boards, the architects opted for color and universally applicable symbols. Referencing the 2020 Summer Olympics in Tokyo, a guide system was chosen that consists of blue and red running tracks such as those featured in track and field sports. The tracks consist of polyurethane plastic finishes with EPDM granulates that are normally used in sports halls; in addition to helping with orientation, they are comfortable to walk on. All necessary information was applied with white paint directly to the tracks. Fair-faced concrete and light-gray walls make up the subdued background, without which the color coding—blue for the sky and hence departures, red for earth and hence arrivals—would not function.

How fine the line is between surface and space, and how a color code can become a space sequence, was illustrated in the *TDM5: Grafica italiana* exhibition project by Fabio Novembre in the Triennale Design Museum in Milan in 2012. The museum houses the most important collection of Italian design of the modern era and, in addition to the main exhibition, addresses a variety of themes in a changing exhibition cycle. With Fabio Novembre's exhibition design for *TDM5: Grafica italiana*, an extraordinary platform was provided to showcase the diversity of Italian graphic design. Seven two-meter-high walls project into the space like an open, empty notebook and ask visitors to move between the pages, both physically and intellectually. With the aid of a simple and succinct color coding system, the leap into the third dimension of the otherwise two-dimensional exhibits rearranges them in relation to each other and groups them into different subjects, from magazines to visual identities. For the color scheme, Novembre chose the colors of the rainbow, "Roy G. Biv"—red, orange, yellow, green, blue, indigo, and violet—in deference to the deity Iris from Greek mythology (Greek *iris* = rainbow; see Newton's color circle with seven colors, see p. 77–95).

Fabio Novembre,
TDM5: Grafica italiana,
exhibition design,
Triennale Design Museum,
Milan, Italy, 2012–13

In the interior of the offices of the PR agency Panama in Stuttgart, a conversion carried out by zipherspaceworks of an office building dating from the 1960s, intense color stripes are used as codes to guide visitors to functions and levels. The practice used an abstract, graphical stripe pattern with strong colors that follows the direction of movement and, in the entrance area, combines the ceiling, the back wall of the narrow space, and the counter into a unit that dominates the space. Colored spaces overlay the actual building structure and widen out or constrict depending on the information content. Arriving at the meeting spaces the interior is finished completely in white, in contrast to the orientation system. The room sequence follows the principle of gradation—from extremely colorful to completely achromatic—being based on a hierarchy of functions/sequence of spaces that can be intuitively experienced (see p. 174–219). This impression of space is further enhanced by a luminous wall surface and light bands that follow the dynamic. Contrasting tonal values cause the colors to seemingly project forward or recede into the background. On the narrow back wall, the stripes are seen as a built relief, which further reinforces their spatial effect with the help of concealed fitted light strips. The dynamic movement of a graphic flanked by a luminous wall surface directs visitors into the depth of the space and farther on, around the corner to the staircase to the second floor, in the anteroom of which the stripes widen out into areas only to disappear almost completely in the meeting rooms in favor of greater neutrality. Other elements, such as the staircase and parapet, recede due to their black paint finish and prevent the spread of the color in space through reflection. The colored stripes generate a directional dynamic in the space.

zipherspaceworks,
PR agency Panama,
Stuttgart, Germany, 2001

Hess/Talhof/Kusmierz,
Primary school am Arnulfpark,
Munich, Germany, 2012,
Floor finish: sports floor green

Peanutz Architects,
"Chorwurm", permanent exhibition
on the region's history of
choirs and singing at the district museum,
Finsterwalde, Germany, 2010

Space ribbons

A recognizable, seamlessly contiguous sequence of rooms of the same color can appear as a space ribbon. Space ribbons guide visitors through a building. If they are clearly visible, they support orientation even when the layout is very complex.

At the Munich primary school am Arnulfpark, the architects Hess/Talhof/Kusmierz use color as a linking element in the organizational concept of the four so-called learning houses. On the first floor, a green space ribbon that has been cut out of the building volume as a covered outside area links the external sports ground to the lowered sports hall. It is covered by a colored so-called Tartan floor finish, the color of which is repeated on the ceiling in the form of colored wood-wool boards; in addition to its linking function, the floor can be used as a running track or covered recreation area. In the multicultural center at Isbergues, France, Dominique Coulon used a yellow space ribbon, which he referred to as an "internal street," to link up all publicly accessible areas. As a central axis, it links the park with the city and opens the building toward both sides. All functions have been arranged along this space ribbon: on one side a theater, on the other a library. Their volumes intersect to create a varied intermediate space. The organizing yellow ribbon runs through this space, taking on various forms: a counter, a reading island, or the color surfaces along the circulation areas. The latter continue far into the building through their reflection and provide orientation with a signal effect.

In their design for the permanent *Chorwurm* exhibition, on the region's history of choirs and singing, in the district museum in Finsterwalde, Germany, Peanutz Architects filled a space ribbon with content. The ribbon is formed by a 75-centimeter-wide, 230-centimeter-high gray basic volume, which becomes a ribbon due to numerous cutouts and distortions. The ribbon runs centrally through the spaces of the district museum. The chronological storytelling structure of the exhibition is enhanced by color. Wherever there is a cut in the basic volume—at wall openings, display units, or seats—its "inner color" appears. Red is used in the exhibition area for the Middle Ages, green for the Reformation, blue for the Romantic period, brown for the Weimar Republic and Third Reich epoch, and yellow for the GDR period and the time since reunification. Owing to the emphasis on the areas of the ribbon that are part of the built fabric, the exhibition architecture does not have any front and rear sides. Numerous openings and cross-connections make it possible for visitors to move freely through the space without ever "losing the thread" owing to the ordering structure.

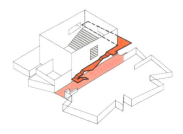

Dominique Coulon & associés,
Multicultural center,
Isbergues, France, 2013

The use of color for staging spatial events is based on a dialogue with plasticity and the elements of space.

SelgasCano Architects,
El Batel conference center,
Cartagena, Spain, 2011

Accentuation

Color is a means of expression with a strong, suggestive effect. The right measure of precision and the right choice of color influence this quality of spaces and can separate or negate functions and places within a larger whole. The idea of accentuation is to emphasize only the necessary elements in order to retain a calm overall impression in the space. For the zoning and orientation in the El Batel conference center in Cartagena, Spain, the architects of SelgasCano use only a few colors that draw their spectrums from nature and, in certain daylight moods, create a unit with the surroundings. The 200-meter-long conference center is located at the harbor in Cartagena. In a reference to the nearby container port, individual volumes of different heights and lengths can be seen above the facade ribbon in acrylic glass or polycarbonate, in alternating colors. In order to adapt to the height of the surrounding buildings, the auditoriums and event spaces were sunk into the ground. The different functions are strung along the length of the building like the pearls of a necklace. The walls widen out or close in on the circulation area, which is organized via two ramp systems.

Whereas the building has been kept in light colors such as white, light blue, and light gray, the recesses and the ETFE ceiling of the foyer are dominated by a strong orange shade. This spectrum of this color shade is derived from the particularly intense sunsets of this coastal region in the south of Spain. Necessary openings, such as entrances, as well as information panels and seating furniture, make a distinct break with the color of the building. In the event spaces, the orange color continues on the floor and ceiling in different materials. In combination with sunlight, the color chosen, similar to a sunset, creates a particularly inviting atmosphere that encourages visitors to pause. The large auditorium has been immersed in a contrasting blue, which makes reference to the room's position below sea level. In combination with daylight, the translucent materials polycarbonate and acrylic glass support the luminous effect of the multilayered surface.

The architects of MADE arhitekti pursued a different accentuation strategy when designing the Music and Art School in Saldus, Latvia. In order to benefit from space synergies, the rooms of the Music School and the Art School were intersected with each other in the new two-story building. In the center of the deep volume are the rehearsal rooms and libraries; at the edge are the classrooms. Light wells ensure that daylight reaches the shared public spaces. Concrete, wood, and glass are the materials used in the building; their natural color and texture are retained to exert their own effect. The symbolic separation, and thus orientation, is accomplished using internal colored surfaces. Staircases, walls, parapets, and doors are finished in light opaque colors that contrast with the fair-faced concrete surfaces of the floor and walls. The students of the music school orient themselves by the yellow-green colored surfaces, whereas the light-blue color is the orientation system for the art school students.

In a small space, such as the apartment at Elvaston Place in London designed by Michaelis Boyd, it is possible to use an individual element as a focal point by accentuating it. The newly inserted staircase in the entrance area connects the two levels of the apartment, which is mostly finished in neutral colors. Due to the interaction of color and form, the staircase appears like a sculpture in space. The structure, which seems translucent owing to the perforated metal sheeting, is highlighted by the strong red color; at the same time, its sophisticated construction is emphasized.

MADE arhitekti,
Saldus Music and Art School,
Saldus, Latvia, 2013,
Color shades blue NCS S0540 B30G,
gray NCS S0565 G50Y

Michaelis Boyd,
Staircase at Elvaston Place,
London, Great Britain, 2013,
Powder coating on steel,
color shade: red

Antonino Cardillo,
Event Space "Specus Corallii",
Trapani, Italy, 2016

Inherent color
and material color

Again and again there is the sensuality of the material—how it feels, what it looks like: does it look dull, does it shimmer or sparkle? Its smell. Is it hard or soft, flexible, cold or warm, smooth or rough? What colour is it and which structures does it reveal on its surface?[1]

Manfred Sack

Deubzer König + Rimmel Architects,
Interims-auditorium maximum,
Munich Technical University, Garching campus,
Munich, Germany, 2011

Shimmering, light, and elegant is how the auditorium presents itself with the wavy facade on the campus in Garching. The black stain finish on the rough-sawn spruce wood cladding and the sculptural detailing of the facade result in an appearance that is not homogeneously dark but offers a shimmering play of silvery shades of gray emulating the movement of waves. Depending on the viewing angle and position of the sun, the facade structure is more or less readable.

Material values

Materials have specific inherent colors. These colors characterize the respective material through the interaction of texture, structure, and light. A sense for the careful use of materials is considered essential for architecture and space quality. The architectural form and the use of materials are closely interrelated and must be viewed holistically. By selecting a material, a design attitude is formulated that is also articulated in the manner the material is worked or applied.

"Wood, metal, stone, and precious stone owe their particular beauty to the life shaped by working process, the traces of the tool, the various ways in which the inspired passion or sensibility of the artist who works with these tools expresses itself."[2] Henry van de Velde

Working appropriately with material requires knowledge of the interactions between the manufacturing process, the material, and the form. The surface treatment of a material in particular influences the readability of its substance and the characteristic of its inherent color or surface color. Depending on the properties of the material and how the surface is treated, the way the material appears changes as the color and incidence of the light changes

According to Gottfried Semper, the right choice of material is essential for architecture. Every building is to be constructed in a design that suits the material. He held that the properties of a product "are, so to speak, a natural, logically derived consequence of the raw material."[3]

The architectural debate on material and color and their appropriate use reached its climax with the arrival of the Arts and Crafts movement in the middle of the nineteenth century and with the Art Nouveau style. The value of materials and colors for the effect of space and architecture, and the relationship between art, crafts, and people, was considered important and was extensively discussed. The movement, in which the painter William Morris, amongst others, had considerable influence, understood itself as a countermovement to industrialization and was aimed at countering cheap mass production and at returning to the appreciation of the natural beauty of materials. This beauty was supposed to be achieved by returning to simplicity and to an appropriate use of materials, amongst other things.

"Now the subject of Material is clearly the foundation of architecture, and perhaps one would not go very far wrong if one defined architecture as the art of building suitably with suitable material."[4] William Morris

Another key figure of the movement, John Ruskin, vigorously promoted craft production, because he considered the quality of the work and the quality of the product to be inseparably interconnected. Following the arrival of mechanization in architecture and product design, controversial

1 Manfred Sack in
   Deplazes 2013, 19.
2 Van de Velde, 1902,
   in Rübel, 169–76.
3 Semper 1878, 90.
4 Morris, 1892,
   in Morris 2012, 403.

ideas regarding the handling of the material and the process of mechanization, similar to the polychromy dispute, were being discussed; an example
are the views of the Russian theorist Alexander Toporkov.

"The rebirth of crafts was the daydream of the new movement in the field
of artistic production that had been started by Ruskin and his followers. I
have already suggested that this ideal is retrospective. Ruskin's ideas are
from the Middle Ages."[5] Alexander Toporkov

Toporkov's approach was to understand material objectively, and in craft
production he saw too strong an individualization of the material. In his
view a new awareness was needed for industry and how it handled the
so-called objective manufacturing methods, which required a new understanding of technical form. There was consensus regarding quality and the
expression of artistic productions: the imitation of all historical styles and
craft products was wholly rejected.

"At this point, it is our task in the arts and crafts to follow up falsification
of material. Who would have ever dreamt that people would undertake
to seek to produce a surrogate for even such a cheap material as wood?"[6]
Heinrich Pudor

In his paper entitled "Lay sermons on arts and crafts," Henry van de Velde bemoaned the use of cheap materials for imitation: "As soon as a new
material is found or discovered today, you ask yourself immediately which
of the already existing materials could best imitate the new one—stucco,
cement, celluloid, and linoleum are to be considered."[7]
       In this debate, color became an essential subject since it was often
used to convey an illusion and to imitate the appearance of material such
as wood or marble. For example, with the use of the encaustic technique,
one of the earliest means of embellishing surfaces, natural stone and marble was imitated to make surfaces look surprisingly like the genuine material. The development of industrial paint production at the beginning of
the nineteenth century led to the invention of numerous new pigments.
Century-old stenciling techniques combined with the new color palette
were used to decorate and enhance rooms, creating colorful atmospheric
interiors.
       Newly developed building materials, such as concrete and steel, were
initially considered to be without character and, according to their critics,
required a form of refinement, for example with color. These critics feared
a tendency toward alienation and brutalization. However, the promoters
of these building materials saw modern society represented in them and
assigned them their own specific material aesthetic.
       Modern life had brought a real glut of materials to the market, and
cheap industrial products in the form of reproductions took the place of the
products of former craft enterprises. This development in materials supply
prompted the architect and chairman of the Werkbund, Hans Schwippert,

to draw this conclusion in his lecture in the context of the 1952 Darmstädter Gespräche on the subject "Man and Technology": "The world of materials has been infinitely expanded" and "What we love in the finished work, that is, to see a trace of the work, is no longer there."[8]

In view of these statements, Toporkov's distinction between the technical material, which is characterized by neutral properties such as fractures or cracking behavior, and the crafted material, which is to be allocated to sentient, perceiving individuals, is interesting. This confirms that the visual impression of material and color is more than a purely atmospheric phenomenon, because the entire perception of space, color, and materials is defined by the presence of the material in interaction with a viewer.[9]

Raw material and processing

When dealing with the pure material in particular, the different qualities in processing reveal the true value of the raw material. Whereas master decorator Hugo Hillig figuratively refers to the "iron ligaments" of reinforced concrete,[10] Le Corbusier spoke strongly in favor of the unfalsified appearance of concrete: "On the raw concrete you see the smallest random patterns of the shuttering: the joints of the boards, the wood fibers, the knots, etc. [...] Well, these things are wonderful to behold. They are interesting to observe and enrich those who have a little imagination."[11]

However, even though Le Corbusier praised the tactile characteristics and the surface texture of concrete resulting from the shuttering process, it was the color of the material that led to controversial discussions. "Formerly, people were of the opinion that cement comes across as sad because it has a sad color. This opinion is just as wrong as the claim that a color is inherently sad. A color obtains its value only through its surroundings."[12]

Meanwhile, the journalist Erich Lüth pleaded with town planners and architects: "Do not create dark gray concrete deserts. Rescue the amenity value of our architecture by using color in any way you see fit: by using colored material and structure, also in the fight against sterilizing prefabrication of building components."[13] By contrast, wood is said to have a warm and cozy character that is partly due to the color of the material and partly due to the material's naturalness and "authenticity." Wood, which formerly was considered a common, simple, and almost poor building material, and at best was used for stables, is used in many contemporary buildings, taking into account the current interest in natural materials, and in order to create a certain expression and atmosphere in a building.

The French sociologist and theorist Jean Baudrillard sees the reason for this in the fact that "it takes its substance from the earth, because it lives, breathes, and 'works.' It possesses a hidden warmth, it does not just shine like glass, but it burns from within. In its fibers it has captured time; it is therefore an ideal vessel and, at the same time, a content that you want to extract from the grip of time. Wood has a unique smell and even its own parasites. In short, this material is a living thing."[14]

5   Toporkov in Rübel 2005, 294.
6   Pudor 1910, 26.
7   Van de Velde 1902, 165.
8   Schwippert, 1952, in Rübel 2005, 86.
9   Torpokov, 1928, in Rübel 2005, 290–94.
10 Hillig 1914, 66.
11 Boesinger 1966, 192.
12 Ibid.
13 Lüth 1972, 70–71.
14 Baudrillard, 1968, in Baudrillard, 1991, 50–51.

The architects Andreas Fuhrimann and Gabrielle Hächler combined the properties of wood and concrete in terms of both atmosphere and construction in the new building of a family residence in Engelberg, Switzerland. The formation and the effect of the space is the result of separating the structural, load-bearing material concrete from its enveloping wood cladding. While the load-bearing structure has been formed from raw, untreated fair-faced concrete in reference to the rough appearance of the surrounding rock formations, a contrast is created by the cladding of the fixtures with large, industrially produced plywood panels in light silver fir. The precision of the joinery demonstrates a great craftsman's understanding of the materials and their effect on the space. The light coming in from the ceiling gives the room an almost surreal sculptural effect.

For the Haus am Moor in Krumbach, Austria, the wood was selected by the architect Bernardo Bader from the private woodland in Schwarzenberg, where it was felled, sawn, and worked during the right moon phase. A total of sixty fir, spruce, and elm trees were used for the construction, the wall surfaces, doors, floor joists, and floorboards. The natural material was deliberately used without cutting out knots and blemishes in order to preserve and keep visible the natural vibrancy of the wood. Untreated silver fir is used to line the living areas, which creates a sensual space impression due to the modesty and unadorned nature of the wood. The individual boards were carefully put together taking into account their grain.

Untreated wood naturally displays much variation depending on the type of tree and how it is worked and fitted. The effect of the weather and the intensity of solar irradiation change the color of the natural material and influence the aging processes. The centuries-old farmhouses in Vorarlberg, Austria, with their characteristic small shingles can be found next to modern buildings with the same materials and, by virtue of the wood as a natural building material, form a certain consistency. Wood seems to become gray in a matter-of-fact way, and results in a rich play of color.

Depending on the region, the color of materials such as stone or wood can vary in accordance with local sources, whereas the color of artificially produced materials such as concrete, plaster, or glass can be predefined. Even so, these colors look different depending on the context. The characteristic appearance of natural stone is governed by the area the material comes from and by the geological process. Working processes include dressing, bush-hammering, charring, and polishing.

Metals obtain their natural color through the composition of the base materials and alloying. Metallic surfaces reflect and distribute light, whereas cementitious surfaces can produce density and dullness. Surfaces or facade skins can appear nebulous or monumental, irritating or pleasing. Depending on the solar irradiation and the viewing angle, the material changes its appearance according to the relief structure, perforations, and surface coatings.

bernardo bader architekten,
Haus am Moor,
Krumbach, Austria, 2013

The appearance of the untreated and sanded fir
wood in the interiors creates a high-quality
and calm atmosphere owing to the careful detailing.

Andreas Fuhrimann, Gabrielle Hächler,
Family residence,
Engelberg, Switzerland, 2009

The lounge in parts extends over two stories and forms
the center of the house. The varying spatial effects
are further enriched by the multifaceted appearance of
the rough-sawn wood and sharp-edged concrete.

For the architects of the Pitagoras Group, who produced a design for a new cultural center as a platform for art and creativity on the former marketplace of Guimarães, Portugal, the challenge was to find a material that would link the existing buildings of the old city with the new development and, at the same time, dematerialize the large volume. The architects succeeded in finding a contemporary material for a calm facade consisting of metallic, shimmering brass bars, which also resonates with the surrounding buildings in terms of scale and proportion. The abstract design of the buildings and the cube-like impression is reinforced by the use of the monochrome material with its distinctive color. The metal surfaces appear light and elegant. They shimmer in various color nuances. Depending on the time of day and year, the projections and recesses of the building create a subtle play of light in combination with the dark base areas.

The untreated steel sculptures by the American sculptor Richard Serra appear raw and monumental. The symbiosis of form and material of the larger-than-life volumes determines the space surrounding them. Richard Serra says: "for me, space is material"[15]; he lets viewers walk amongst the steel walls and physically experience the space sequences formed by the steel. Owing to the changing effects of the light coming in, in combination with the space composition and the material structure, the color of the objects is subject to subtle changes. This results in very fine color nuances and constant new color impressions, which are difficult to determine with color charts. Overall, the brownish-red color has a full and dense presence.

In architecture, materiality is normally associated with texture in the form of elements, joints, or joint patterns. In Serra's sculptures, it is impressive that these elements feature very few seams, thereby indicating the enormous size of the curved steel plates.

Whereas architecture involving elements or brickwork lets us understand the construction process, Serra's sculptures appear like three-dimensional monuments in spite of the plate material, while the brick facade of the architect Alvar Aalto's summerhouse looks more like a fabric. The summerhouse was used by the Finnish architect as an experimental project. The facade has a material-like feel due to the different nuances of red and various brick formats, combined with an array of laying patterns. The color of the bricks links the building with the forecourt.

15 Serra in Freund 2007.

Pitagoras Group,
cultural center,
Guimarães, Portugal, 2012

The surface with its golden sheen changes throughout the day and creates contrasting, even dematerialized facade impressions.

Alvar Aalto,
Summerhouse,
Muuratsalo, Finland, 1953

Brick wall panels with different bonds and different brick colors provide a kind of test field in the ensemble, which, with its main house, guest wing, and some sheds and stores, surrounds an inner courtyard. Aalto ordered some of the bricks to be specially produced and fired for this house.

Richard Serra,
Torqued Ellipses, 1996–98, sculpture, steel

The large, raw, and rusty steel sculptures develop a wide spectrum of brown and red shades with many facets.

RAW MATERIAL AND PROCESSING

The architect Heinrich Seipp was fascinated by the color mood projected by brickwork: "Everybody knows about the great variety of moods projected by brickwork walls depending on the color resulting from the firing, ranging from a full, warming red-brown that can already be seen on the outside of the house and spreads a certain sense of well-being, through to a certain sober and frosty pale yellow; also familiar is the extraordinarily enlivening and lifting effect of glazed bricks, which is based on their usually more vivid color, their reflective gloss, and the contrasting effect with the other materials."[16] In buildings that are just rendered, which Seipp referred to as "desolate and bleak," he considered it necessary to apply color or ornamentation.

For Franz Geiger, rendered buildings "had nothing to do with a genuine essence of Modernism, because the render conceals the construction and often amounts to an architectural lie; the render also conceals the inherent color of the natural material and, in order to achieve this, resorts to artificial means [...]. Appropriateness of the material is one of the foremost requirements of the true art of building, and this is missing in rendered buildings. [...] Rendering a wall is a surrogate for building with proper masonry units."[17]

Material versus color

The pavilion designed by Mies van der Rohe for the International Exposition in Barcelona in 1929 (rebuilt true to the original in 1983–1986) is probably the best-known example of material chromaticity in the history of architecture. What was new was not the use of material with its inherent color but the clear, rigorous composition, the precision of the jointing, and the use of marble in the form of room-high patterned panels. The ordering wall planes consisting of different types of marble allow a free plan layout in which the interior and exterior merge. Through reflections on the external water surface and the highly polished material, the interior appears as if expanded into infinity, following the idea of the open flow of space. For the plinth and the floor, a light Roman travertine was used, which, when exposed to sunlight, almost seems to dissolve into immateriality. The principle of the freestanding space-forming walls was combined with the idea of displaying the textile-like yellow-red onyx marble (serpentinite). Used over large areas and in prominent positions, the valuable material provides a counterpoise to the architectural aesthetic defined by the use of steel and glass. Similarly, the green marble walls confining the rooms (vert antique and Tinos marble) have been arranged in an almost sculptural way (see p. 37–76).

16 Seipp 1902, 372ff.
17 Geiger 1902, 370.

Materials should be the only colors in architecture.[18]
John Ruskin

Carlo Scarpa,
Fondazione Querini Stampalia,
Venice, Italy, 1963

Using metal, stone, and ceramic elements of various sizes,
Scarpa produces a collage-type space composition
in which different material colors and degrees of reflectiveness interweave with the existing building fabric.

The architect Carlo Scarpa also used the inherent color of material in a complete way in his compositions. In addition to the theme of arranging spaces in the form of layered collages, which keeps recurring in his work, his architecture is characterized by an understanding of material and precise detailing. He used architectural components in the way of a collage, which allowed him to place new elements in combination with existing building fabric.

In the library of the Fondazione Querini Stampalia in Venice, his specific way of handling light, material, color, and water is clearly discernible. The interior is characterized by an arrangement of steps and staircases, as well as a floor mosaic that consists of square, seemingly randomly arranged marble tesserae. The dynamic surface is bordered by stone upstands, which means that any water coming into the building during floods is included in the design. With his choice of material for the flooring, Scarpa separated different functional zones, which are not necessarily identical to the spatial arrangement. Colored wall and ceiling panels and the contrast between reflective and matt surfaces, strong chromaticity and muted materials, give the areas their specific atmosphere, creating a collage of spaces rich in detail.

Tool marks, signs of aging, and the traces of wear or damage are woven into the scheme and become the motif of the project. They provide important information on the materials used and their structure. The resulting atmosphere places the architecture into a larger sense context and allows a wide range of associations. The materials become living substances, which represent a kind of inherent life owing to the changeability granted them.

Scarpa deliberately places intersecting two-dimensional elements of different sizes in relation to one another. He often uses tesserae of different colors, small square blocks of stone or ceramic, laid on floors as part of mosaic designs.

18 Ruskin in Meerwein
    2007, 50.

De architectengroep and SeArch,
Dutch embassy in Addis Ababa, Ethiopia, 2005

The dyed deep-red concrete makes reference to the red
rock formations found in the north of Ethiopia.

Colored material

By dyeing or coating a material it is possible to create material alienation, because the coloring is perceived as an application, something that covers the original material. When material is treated with pigment throughout, its properties such as absorbency or inhomogeneity are not negated but appear more prominent, which leads to a perceived vibrancy; the character of the material is retained. This process lends itself particularly to concrete, the mixture of which ordinarily already consists of 80 percent aggregate and additives. Besides the raw materials, the intensity of the coloring also depends on the production process.

Inspired by the red rock formations in the north of Ethiopia, the architects De architectengroep and SeArch used a red pigment for coloring the in situ concrete for the Dutch embassy in Addis Ababa in 1998–2005. The incoming light causes the dyed material to glow intensely or to significantly change its color hues. The concrete was shuttered and poured on-site. The texturing of the facades coincides with the position of the shuttering boards. In this way, the building makes reference to its surroundings rather than appearing like a foreign body.

Whereas prior to the industrial revolution only a limited color palette was available for building production, which frequently resulted from the inherent color of the material—fired brick/clinker, sandstone, tiles, or colored cement—or from technical constraints such as the need for durable binding agents, new possibilities opened up with the artificial production of pigments and colorants. This also changed the way color was used. The best-known example of this is the technical administration building of Hoechst AG, a factory founded in 1863 for the production of synthetic colorants, which was built by architect Peter Behrens between 1920 and 1924.

The Expressionistic building, which is now listed as a historic monument, symbolizes the idea of an industrial culture in which room sequences, light, and color come together in a comprehensive work of art. The most conspicuous part of the building is the central five-story cupola hall, which is lit via three crystalline glass domes. Owing to the scarcity of material resources, the originally planned extensive use of sandstone was abandoned in favor of regionally available bricks. The load-bearing pillars look like stalactites, which increase in mass and number of bricks toward the top and reinforce the flowing space impression of the building. The gaze is directed upward and the perceived image seems to vibrate due to the light coming in from the top. The pillars have been coated with a thin color wash in the spectral colors.

From the green on the lower ground floor, which is still faintly detectable, the colors build up on the stepped pillars, from blue and red through to a light yellow beneath the domes. Through the increasing brightness in the upper floors, the colors counteract the heavy appearance of the pillars that close in on the space as they become thicker near the top. Floor mosaics made of bricks with different glazes and laid in complex bonding

The materiality of the substrate shines through "so that the painting combines like a transcendent heavenly sphere with the earthly architectural shell to make a sacral statement."[19]

patterns are found on the first floor and on the galleries and support the sacral atmosphere. Behrens cleverly interlaced the aesthetic appearance with the architectural manifestation of the business fields of the original client. The color scheme was not only used for identifying window frames, doors, and walls or functional content, but was also used in three-dimensional space. Through the manner in which the color shades are arranged spatially and systematically, the abstract and the transcendent are combined, as are two essential basic approaches to the application of color.

The monochrome blue color wash in the prayer room of the Dominikuszentrum in Munich, a spiritual center with social facilities built by Meck Architects in 2003–8, develops a symbolic power. The building, which is accessed via a deliberately low entrance with bronze-clad revolving doors, surprises visitors with an unexpected, intense space experience. The color blue forms the inner architectural envelope of the prayer room and gives the room a spiritual atmosphere in addition to the special color mood of the light. Blue is the symbol of the heavenly, the divine, and is the color of Mary. The monochrome wall picture *Raumikone 2* by the artist Anna Leonie continues the concept of the blue room in a multifaceted way. Twenty-seven pigmented color washes were manually applied to the peat-fired bricks, which makes the color blue appear in different degrees of luminosity. The materiality of the substrate shines through "so that the painting combines like a transcendent heavenly sphere with the earthly architectural shell to make a sacral statement."[19]

19 Leonie 2008.

Peter Behrens,
Administration building of Hoechst AG,
Höchst, Germany, 1924

In this interior by Peter Behrens, color, form, and light
develop an intense interplay and a sacral atmosphere.
The color scheme causes the verticality of the pillars
to be structured and interwoven at the same time.

eck Architects and Anna Leonie (wall picture),
rayer room, Dominikuszentrum,
unich, Germany, 2008

Group of architects Saad El Kabbaj, Driss Kettani,
and Mohamed Amine Siana,
Laayoune Technology School,
Ajun, Morocco, 2014

The complex intersections of color and form, and the
different possibilities for interpreting the two-
dimensional areas and three-dimensional bodies, interact
with the changing play of light and shadow, and repeatedly enter into new combinations.

Material, color, and appearance

In his writings on polychromy, the architect and journalist Arthur Rüegg distinguishes between material color—components such as stone, wood, and concrete, and surface finishes such as plaster, stucco, glass, and metal that are left in the honest, intrinsic color of the material—and paint color that is applied to surfaces. Within this distinction, a number of different appearance phenomena can be observed. Depending on the specific type of material, with textured or grained material in particular, the effect is determined by the light's depth of penetration and the type of reflection. Within the texture, the shadow creates a different color, and this "shadow color" creates a differentiated and lively color impression for the viewer. The use of jointing or shuttering material can create a particular sense impression, also from materials that at first sight appear quite nondescript. Polishing material or applying a clear lacquer can accentuate inherent structures and turn dull material into an ornamental embellishment. On the other hand, color has an inherent potential to alienate material or bring out its texture. The way color is received and therefore the color effect depends directly on the properties of the carrier surface. When applied to different substrates, the same color will have a different appearance in each case.

The systematic use of color can indicate religious or cultural habits used to encode spaces, to indicate the content and purpose of functions, and thereby—beyond the aesthetic component—to convey messages, make distinctions, and provide orientation signals. It is also possible, however, to modify traditional patterns by relatively simple means. Perception is relative and depends on the respective surroundings. A color family can have a linking effect, can strengthen or differentiate and alienate an ensemble.

The selection of materials and colors is not only based on considerations relating to the construction or the use of regional resources, but is frequently closely related to the regional context, the identity and culture of the region, and the traditions and crafts dominating in that region. Local colors and building materials specific to certain regions have developed over a long period of time. The intensity and luminosity of the colors of North Africa have been exciting people for centuries. Cobalt blue, which is also called Majorelle blue after its inventor Jacques Majorelle, and lemon yellow are just two color shades that dominate the famous Jardin Majorelle garden in Marrakesh, Morocco. Special plastering techniques such as *tadelakt*, in which lime is applied as a plaster, reinforced with stones, and then polished, blur the boundaries between material color and paint color. The fourteen buildings of the new university campus of Laayoune Technology School, which were built in 2014 by the group of architects Saad El Kabbaj, Driss Kettani, and Mohamed Amine Siana, are distributed away from the city center of Ajun, Morocco. The reinforced concrete structure, which was covered with a rough coat of render and in turn painted with an ochre-colored vinyl paint, reinterprets the old Moroccan clay buildings

Ricardo Bofill,
La Muralla Roja apartment building,
Calp, Spain, 1973

With the help of the color, the building volumes become modulated sculptures that develop their own identity within the color units of sky blue, indigo, and violet assigned to the circulation spaces.

MATERIAL, COLOR, AND APPEARANC

and the colors of the Sahara. Even though the architectural repertoire is reduced and remains strictly geometrical, the play of intersections and recesses results in a kind of visual transposition of the forms. Light and shadow generate complex graphical shapes in the form of a temporary color canon.

The radiance of the La Muralla Roja apartment building by architect Ricardo Bofill in Calp, Spain, is no less intense. Designed like a fortress, the complex has been built on the rocky cliffs of the Spanish coast and the design follows the Constructivist principle of putting together individual modules. The external facades appear in different shades of red in order to highlight the contrast with the surrounding landscape. Although inspired by the Arabic buildings in the Mediterranean area, the traditional casbahs and citadels have been reinterpreted with towers, pinnacles, and battlements. What at first sight appears confusing proves to be a precise geometric plan layout. This has created an ensemble of internal courtyards, staircases, wall openings, and cantilevers that are linked with each other, providing a surprise around every corner and intended to encourage a new communication. The application of a spectrum of different color worlds is intended to identify the different architectural elements in accordance with their structural functions.

Staircases and circulation areas were rendered in different shades of blue, such as sky blue, indigo, and violet. Depending on the time of year and the position of the sun, this creates a strong contrast with the sky or else blends with the color of the firmament. The intensity of the colors is influenced by the light and the depth, which, while maintaining the same color, change the illusion of space. The strong colors separate the areas from each other but do not emphasize the two-dimensionality of various parts of the building. Quite the opposite: by continuing the color scheme across the building volumes, the architect has, in combination with the varying effects of the light, created sculptural space volumes.

Fronleichnam Church in Aachen, Germany, which was built in 1930 to plans by Rudolf Schwarz, deftly deviates from the conventions of New Gothic church designs that were dominant until then. Schwarz himself referred to it as uncompromising for its time. The elongated, angular space has been completely reduced to the noncolors black and white. The white-plastered, unembellished side walls and the white altar wall contrast with the black of the natural stone. The dark-blue Belgian stone seamlessly continues from the floor via the altar steps to the altar area. The black-stained wood pews match the inherent color of the floor material so that both are perceived as a unit.

The unconventional use of traditional materials and building forms affects and irritates the habitual way of seeing. For the change of use of a former slaughterhouse into a professional cookery school, the architects of Sol89 have taken and rearranged the typical building shapes and colors of the surroundings. As a result of the all-embracing use of color and material, the new roof landscape appears abstract and homogeneous. Its different elements are visually connected and given a new identity. Instead of the traditional rounded, earth-colored clay tiles, the architects used flat ceramic units with a strong red color for the new sloping roof. This contemporary intervention links the ensemble to form a plausible unit, but nevertheless preserves the tradition of the surroundings.

Sol89,
Change of use of a former slaughterhouse
into a cookery school, Medina, Spain, 2011

The topographic effect of the roof landscape is generated
with the application of the red color and the precise,
sharp-edged transition between wall and roof surface.

Rudolf Schwarz,
Fronleichnam Church,
Aachen, Germany, 1930

A high, light-flooded white room forms a strong contrast
with the black color of the floor, which, in combination
with the pews, appears like a relief.

The alienation of the material

Untreated, natural, and pure material stands in opposition to material that has been deliberately alienated, for example by the application of color. Smooth or rough, shiny or matt, dense or porous, shimmering or plain, surfaces can be manipulated in such a way that their overall appearance is exclusively defined by color. It is mainly a question of strategy as to where color is to be applied, what color carrier is selected, and in what form and for what function it is to be used. Unlike at the time of the modernist movement, today no color theory exists that can claim to be generally applicable. Color can function as material, and material can be part of a color scheme. If color is deliberately used in a new color and material context, it can have unexpected new effects.

A project that questions architectural and aesthetic conventions is the Dirty House in London by David Adjaye. Designed deliberately to counter the "mainstream architecture of the 2000s," the black building with deeply recessed window openings and a floating, white, flat roof throws up many questions. The simple fire protection coating, which covers streetlamps and electricity boxes all over the city, enhances the undesigned and, highlights the antiarchitecture.

The Dutch architectural practice MVRDV has taken an even more extreme approach with its Didden Village in Rotterdam. Built on the roof of a former clothes factory, the project is not only a provocative gesture aimed at the establishment, but also a prototype for increasing the density in old, existing urban quarters on the tops of hitherto unused roofs. Instead of an outsized volume, the architects created a differentiated living space, a city in miniature. The entire construction was sealed with a polyurea spray coat and then colored with an additional top coat in light-blue polyurethane. The coating layer has seamlessly sealed the terrace, roof, and facades of the structures on the roof, thus creating a tough waterproof membrane around the prefabricated timber frame walls. The color shade NCS 1560-R90B was chosen to replicate the color of the sky. In bright sunshine, the artificial character of the luminous roof structures is particularly apparent.

Shortly beforehand, the artist Florentijn Hofman used a similar concept to draw attention to a row of houses in Rotterdam that was threatened with demolition. He covered the entire facade, including all windows and openings, with blue latex dispersion paint.

Florentijn Hofman,
"Beukelsblauw",
Rotterdam, The Netherlands, 2004–6,
15 m × 15 m,
Latex dispersion on buildings

With blue paint used as a means of alienation,
the modest, dilapidated row of houses became
a focus of attention. This did not, however, prevent
them from being demolished.

Following pages:
MVRDV, Didden Village,
Rotterdam, The Netherlands, 2006

The homogeneous color coating links the individual
building components to create one large, almost
surreal whole, to which the details are subordinated.

THE ALIENATION OF THE MATERIAL

In the House of Dust project in Rome, Antonino Cardillo works with few but effective material interventions at the border between reality and fiction. In an apartment dating from the 1960s, identical color shades are interpreted in completely different ways using colored surface textures of various roughness, which are placed in strong contrast to each other. In parts this has created strong color worlds that, under the effect of light and shadow, generate an array of atmospheres. The application of rough earth-colored plaster—the so-called dust layer—up to the level of an artificial horizon, which also connects with all windows and openings, generates a cave-like feeling. The rough plaster, which has been manually applied with a trowel and colored subsequently, and the polished cement plaster determine the interior of the main room. A change in color—from gray-brown to a shade of pink—separates the public and private areas of the apartment. The alienation of the material using the devices of color and texture surprises and, at the same time, generates a feeling of security. The mood in the rooms changes depending on the light situation. This demonstrates clearly how relative our perception of color is.

An example of the use of new production methods that make possible a particular design expression is the extension of the Museum of Fine Arts in Chur, Switzerland, which was built by the architects Barozzi Veiga in 2012–2017. The towerlike circulation building features an envelope of a light, nearly translucent relief that replicates the ornamentation of the existing building. This does not consist of individual three-dimensional elements but of prefabricated light-gray concrete elements, the surfaces of which were modified using textured templates. The ornaments measuring 50 by 50 centimeters were joined together to form prefabricated panels measuring 4 by 4 meters, which were fitted to the shell building on-site. The cassettes for the openings were built in several sections as grid-like components in fair-faced concrete quality. The ornamental principle is continued on the metal door to the delivery area. However, the door's ornamental three-dimensionality can only be detected on closer inspection. The light color of the facade was produced with a special concrete mixture consisting of white cement and Jura limestone.

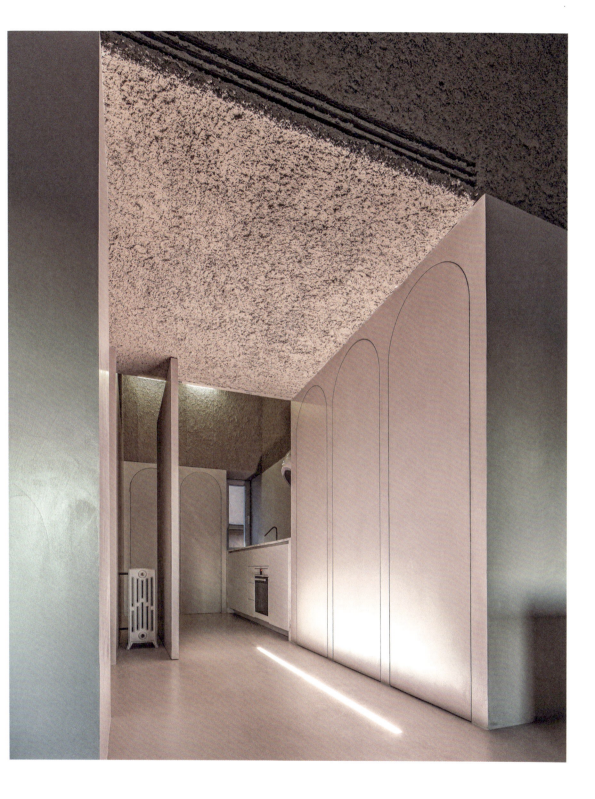

Antonino Cardillo,
House of Dust, residence,
Rome, Italy, 2013

Rough plaster contrasts with smooth surfaces and,
through the shared color, generates a cohesive perception
of the space in spite of different surface textures.

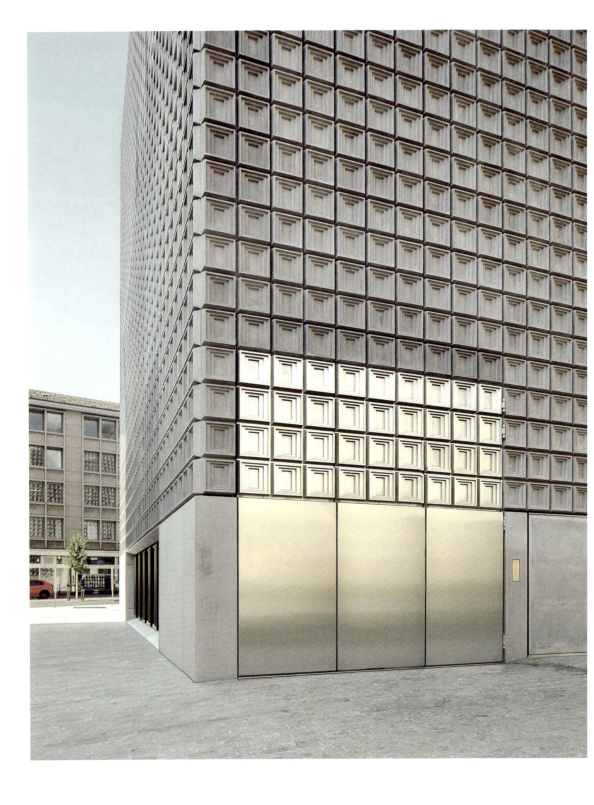

Barozzi Veiga,
Extension to the Museum of Fine Arts,
Chur, Switzerland, 2016

The highly precise finish of the horizontally and
vertically applied facade pattern could only be achieved
using prefabricated elements.

Part 3

Appendix

Glossary

Absorption
Absorption of light is a physical process whereby light transfers its energy to matter. A fully absorbent surface appears black. The opposite of absorption is reflection. The chromatic effect of surfaces is the result of certain wavelengths' being absorbed and others reflected.

Abstraction
Abstraction is a mental process focused on reduction to what is essential and on omitting details to achieve complete simplification. In a color context abstraction is achieved, when color overlays a room so that its details and edges visually merge into the background until spatial depth is completely dissolved.

Achromatic colors
The colors black and white, as well as the gradations between them in the form of gray shades, are referred to as achromatic colors.

Adaption
Adaption refers to the ability of the eye to adapt to different light conditions.

Afterimage
An afterimage of the eye refers to a phantom image that is still perceived when the original light stimulus has subsided. There are two types of afterimages. A positive afterimage is created through a very short and intense exposure of the retina; the colors correspond to the light stimulus. When different images alternate very quickly, genuine images and afterimages merge into a new image. This effect generates the impression of moving pictures in a film projection that consists of a fast series of individual pictures. When a colored surface is looked at for a longer period of time, a negative afterimage may be created because the stimulated receptors are slowly desensitized. If subsequently one looks at a neutral surface, the nondesensitized receptors react more strongly, creating an afterimage in which the values for lightness and color are reversed.

Application of a color scheme
Color is used to modify the appearance of rooms and substrates in order to create more or less emphasis.

Autonomy
The color is used as a medium independent of the carrier (for example, the picture surface, room surface).

Coating
Coating is a general term covering all paint finishes, lacquers, and also protective systems and skim coats in construction. In DIN EN ISO 4618 Coating materials–Terms, the designation is defined in accordance with the following criteria:

Binders or resin
Water-soluble (e.g. acrylate dispersion, epoxy resin dispersion, electro-deposition, polyurethane dispersion, silicate paint, and others); containing solvent (alkyd resin coating, epoxy resin coating, polyurethane coating, polyester coating, and others)

Application
Powder lacquer, powder coating, stove enamel, cathodic dip-coating, coil coating material, and others

Position in the coating system
Priming material, undercoating material, top-coat material or gloss.

The German standard DIN 55945 Coating materials and coatings–Additional terms to DIN EN ISO 4618 adds further definitions to this standard to include designations for individual coating materials. With reference to the building physics characteristics of coating materials, DIN EN 1062-1 Paints and varnishes–Coating materials and coating systems for exterior masonry and concrete, Part 1: Classification defines key variables such as water vapor diffusion resistance, water permeability, carbon dioxide permeability, degree of gloss, layer thicknesses, grain size, and others.

Color
The German term for color (Farbe) is also used to refer to the material used for coatings.

Definition in accordance with DIN 5033
Color is the visual sensation associated with a part of the field of vision that appears to the eye to be without structure, which is the only way that this part, viewed with one unmoving eye, can be distinguished from another area that is also without structure and seen at the same time.

Nonluminous color
Color reflected from surfaces is referred to as nonluminous color. When neutral light that is perceived as being colorless falls on a colored surface, certain spectral components are withdrawn from the light through absorption. The remaining reflected radiation arriving at the eye triggers the sensation of color; this means that the color of the surface results from the nonabsorbed components of the color spectrum of the light. The surfaces of solid materials have a continuous reflectivity or absorption spectrum; this means that they reflect and absorb light energy of any wavelength. The proportion of absorbed and reflected energy components can be different in different parts of the spectrum, thus creating a different color impression as light conditions change.

Luminous color
Color generated by colored sources of light or filtered light is referred to as luminous color. Short-wave light creates the blue spectrum, mediumwave light the green spectrum, and long-wave light the red spectrum.

Pigment
Pigments are the basic ingredients of paints used by artists and in architecture. They come in the form of powder consisting of microscopically small particles of a solid material, and are not soluble in liquid. When they are used to coat a surface, they are mixed with binders, fillers, and solvents. Minerals occurring in nature, so-called earth pigments, have been used for the production of pigments since time immemorial. Since the eighteenth century, chemical processes have been used to produce synthetic pigments.

Color mixing

Subtractive color mixing
The mixing of nonluminous colors is referred to as subtractive color mixing because, in this process, light is "subtracted," that is to say, it is absorbed. The base colors of subtractive color mixing are magenta, cyan blue, and yellow. These base colors can be used to create all other colors. When all colors are mixed together in subtractive color mixing, the result is black; when a surface appears black, it absorbs the radiation of all wavelengths.

Additive color mixing
In additive color mixing, the different wavelengths of light combine to form a new luminous color. The base colors of additive color mixing become visible when daylight is refracted into its color components via a prism: red, green, and violet-blue. When these are added back together, they become white light.

Color rendering
The relationship between luminous and nonluminous color leads to a dependency between the color we see and light; this needs to be taken into account particularly in the design of artificial light. DIN 6169, Color rendering; general terms, defines color rendering as the relationship between the original color of an object and its rendered color. The rendered color index describes the quality of the color rendering of light sources. The index covers a range from 1 to 100, with all grades above 80 considered good color rendering.

Color shade
The three characteristics color shade, lightness, and color saturation describe a color. The color shade defines the fundamental distinction between one color and another, for example red, yellow, and green. The lightness and color saturation describe variations of the color shade.

Color wash
A color wash is a pigmented translucent coating. In painting it is used because of its transparent properties; in architecture it is mostly used to protect building components. The characteristic properties of the material remain visible.

Contrast
Colors are never isolated; they react to their surroundings. In his 1961 color theory, Johannes Itten defined seven color contrasts:

Color per se contrast
Arises between at least two colors in pure, unbroken form.
Light/dark contrast
Arises due to the different color lightness of two colors.
Cold/warm contrast
The effect is based on the subjective perception that colors appear warm or cold.
Complementary contrast
Arises between two complementary colors.
Quality contrast
Arises from differences in the color quality, that is, between saturated, luminous colors and muted, matt, dull colors.
Quantity contrast
Arises from the juxtaposition of colored areas of different sizes.

Simultaneous contrast
Describes the interaction of adjacent color fields that have a mutual effect on each other; this means that the neural processes in the brain create so-called induced colors, which in reality are not there.

Degree of gloss
DIN EN 1062-1 distinguishes between G1 high gloss, G2 medium gloss, and G3 matt. The relationship between a beam of light falling on a surface and the light reflected from the surface at a certain defined angle of measurement is measured with a device called a glossmeter. The unit of measure is GU (gloss unit); values range from 100 GU to the minimum value of 0 GU for an absolutely matt surface.

Dematerialization
Color contributes to the seeming dissolution of the substrate or the room geometry.

Diffusion
Scattering of light and colored light from a rough surface in many directions due to reflection from small surfaces. Diffuse light is nondirectional and hardly casts any shadow. The colors of the sky that change throughout the day are the result of the scattering of the different components of sunlight when it hits the gas molecules of the earth's atmosphere.

Diffusivity
Diffusivity refers to a diffuse, that is, unclear, unordered, contourless, or fuzzy, characteristic of an object or sense impression.

Dissonance
Intentional breaking of the laws of the theory of harmony results in dissonance.

Illusion
An illusion is a deception of the senses in the form of a false interpretation of sense perceptions, such as visual stimuli.

Interference
Interference refers to a change in the amplitude of two or more light waves due to addition when superpositioning. When light is reflected from thin, transparent layers within a material, it is possible for color phenomena to be created that are eferred to as "interference colors."

Kinetics / kinetic effect
Kinetics is a branch of physics that deals with the relationships between forces and the resulting movements of a solid. When an object seems to change as a result of the movement of the viewer, one refers to this as a kinetic effect.

Light
Electromagnetic radiation that is visible to the human eye is referred to as light. The wavelengths are between 380 and 760 nanometers. Radiation in the adjacent areas is no longer visible and is referred to as ultraviolet and infrared "light" respectively.

Glossary

Light spectrum / spectral colors
Each source of light—sunlight and artificial light—has its own characteristic spectral composition. For example, when light is refracted through a prism, the individual colors of the different wavelengths become visible. When refracted, neutral light is seen in the colors of a rainbow, with the spectral colors violet, blue, green, yellow-green, yellow, orange, and red merging into each other without distinct steps.

Mirroring
In mirroring, nearly all the light falling on an object is reflected. A clearly recognizable mirror image is created.

Monochromy
Monochromy refers to the use of a single color.

Physiology
Physiology is the study of normal physical and biochemical processes in cells, tissues, and organs of all living beings, taking into account all life processes in the entire organism.

Polychromy
The art of painting in several colors.

Primary color / base color
Primary colors are any of a group of colors from which all other colors can be obtained by mixing. In subtractive color mixing, which is used in painting and printing, these colors are cyan, magenta, and yellow, also referred to as base colors; in additive color mixing, these colors are the three luminous colors red, yellow, and blue.

Reflection
Depending on the material, color, and surface, objects impermeable to light reflect part of the light that falls on them. Light areas reflect much light, whereas dark areas absorb a large proportion of the energy of the light falling on them. Light rays are reflected at the same angle at which they fall on the surface. If the surface is uneven, this angle will vary in accordance with the grain, and the light rays are reflected in many different directions. This is referred to as diffusion or scatter, and can be used deliberately to distribute light or luminous color in space.

Seeing
The retina reacts to even very small light stimuli and can distinguish between fine nuances of lightness and color. The processing of light stimuli involves a number of different mechanisms. For the distinction between light and dark, the retina has so-called rods. They register different intensities of light and thus degrees of lightness. Colors are distinguished with the help of cones, which react to the different spectral composition of the light. The cones are less sensitive than the rods. Whereas the rods react to even very small quantities of light, significantly more light is required to activate the cones. In broad daylight, both rods and cones are active. As darkness increases, it becomes more and more difficult to detect colors. In a dark environment or at night, only the rods are active; seeing is restricted to the distinction between light and dark. The retina is a highly sensitive organ, but very small particle shapes and rapidly changing light stimuli cannot be perceived separately by the retina. Stimuli that are too close together or that follow each other too rapidly are not perceived as separate by the eye.

Structure
The relationship of elements to each other and their composition; the set of rules used to organize the composition of a picture, the decoration of a surface, a relief, or a room.

Synesthesia
Synesthesia is the ability to make a connection between physically separate areas of perception; only some people have this ability. For example, certain musical tones are perceived as very specific colors.

Texture
The term is derived from the Latin word *textura* (fabric) and refers to the feel, appearance, or consistency of surfaces. The texture of a surface determines its visual and aesthetic appearance, as well as its haptic qualities. It is independent of color.

Three-dimensionality
Three-dimensionality refers to the spatial characteristics of an object. Color and light can enhance or reduce the three-dimensional effect of a surface or a room/space.

Tonal value
Tonal value refers to different degrees of lightness of a color shade, between light (in color systems, usually a high proportion of white) and dark (in color systems, usually a high proportion of black).

Index of names

Index of names

Index of subjects

H

hard-edge painting – 26, 128
harmony – 89, 92
hierarchy – 101, 284, 288, 305
homogeneous – 31, 141, 171, 269, 288

I

identity – 39, 41, 60, 138, 158, 219, 333
illusion – 107, 113, 209, 241, 272
illusionism – 26
immaterial – 69, 119, 171, 278
Impressionism – 11, 16
improvisation – 24
individualization – 62, 318
inherent color – 38, 69, 276, 317, 325, 329
inside space – 121
instability – 33, 81, 111
intensity – 100, 238, 269, 272
interaction – 21, 23, **50 ff.**, 90, 117, 135, 204, **238 ff.**, 276
interference – 50, 126, **229**
interlacing – 99, 154
intermediate shades – 90
intermediate tones – 125
intersection – 113, 195, 223
inversion – 99

J

joint – 81, 168, 323

K

kinetics/kinetic effect – 113

L

lacquer – 30, 117, 230, 333
layer – 185, 195, 204, 229, 233, 299, 338, 342
layering – 15, 111, 152, **228 ff.**
light – 10 ff., 59 ff., 80 ff., 111 ff., 222, 238 ff.
light spectrum – 80, 89, 262
lightness – 80 ff., 90 ff., 119
line – 9, 21, 303
luminosity – 10, 26, 278, 330, 333
luminous color – 80, 262

M

marble – 42, 186, 318, 325, 327
mass – 48, 67, 101, 164, 317, 329
mass production – 44, 82, 317
material – **30 ff.**, 117, 177, **317 ff.**
material color – 59, 240, 299, 327, **333**
materiality – 56, 119, 222, 256, 323, 330
materialization – 262
metal – 30 ff., 230 ff.
microstructure – 222, 233
minimal art – 26, 128
mirroring – 238 ff.
mist – 256, 262, 272
mixing – **79 ff.**, 90 ff., 230, 240
modeling – 15, 16, 20
modulation – 299
monochromatic space – 149
monochromy – 30
Munsell color system – 91
mural – 17
music – 10, 94, 103, 312

N

NCS system – 82, 291
neoplasticism – 21, 101
niche – 65, **152 ff.**, 189
nonluminous color – 119
nuance – 9, 81, 204

O

object – 16, 80, 113, 183, 189, 269
op art – 203
orientation – 51, 186, **276**, **278**, **288 ff.**
orientation system – **288**, **292**, 303 ff., 312
ornament – 40
overlaying – 59, 117, 126, 141, 230, 299

P

paint – 42, **229**, **230**, 284, 291, 333
Pantone system – 94
pattern – 126, 195, 203
perception of color – 9, 38, 204, 342
perspective – 12, 113, 126, 135
photography – 67, 81, 209, 240, 256
physiology – 204
pictorial arrangement – 107
pigment – 51, 65, 72, 171, 229, 329
pixel – 15, 222
plan layout – 56, 136, 213, 325, 335
Pointillism – 15, 16, 41
polychromy – **39**, **40**, 45, 52, 72, 222, 318, 333
Pop Art – 67, 94
postmodernism – 67
primary color – 84
prism – 84, 89
projection – 17, 164, **255**
proportion – 15, 20, 82, 90, 240
public space – 149, 219, 312
Purkinje effect – 240

Index of subjects

Literature

The autonomy of color

Albers, Josef.
Interaction of Color.
New Haven: Yale University Press, 2006.

Albrecht, Hans J., and Robert Delaunay.
Farbe als Sprache:
Robert Delaunay, Josef Albers, Richard Paul Lohse, 3rd ed.
Cologne: DuMont, 1979.

Baumann, Felix, et al.
Cézanne: Vollendet Unvollendet.
Exh. cat. Kunstforum Wien; Kunsthaus Zürich.
Ostfildern: Hatje Cantz, 2000.

Bauermeister, Christiane, and Nele Hertling.
Sieg über die Sonne:
Aspekte russischer Kunst zu Beginn des 20. Jahrhunderts.
Exh. cat. Akademie der Künste, Berlin, and the
Berliner Festwochen. Berlin: Frölich & Kaufmann, 1983.

Beyme, Klaus.
Das Zeitalter der Avantgarden:
Kunst und Gesellschaft 1905–1955. Munich: Beck, 2005.

Bocola, Sandro.
Die Kunst der Moderne: Zur Struktur und
Dynamik ihrer Entwicklung. Von Goya bis Beuys.
Gießen: Psychosozial-Verlag, 2013.

Bronner, Susanne, and Renate Wiehager.
Minimalism and After: Traditions and Tendencies
of Minimalism from 1950 up to the Present.
Ostfildern: Hatje Cantz, 2007.

Brunner, Michael, and Andrea C. Theil.
Venezianische Malerei von 1500 bis 1800: Kontur oder Kolorit?
Ein Wettstreit schreibt Geschichte. Exh. cat. Städtisches
Museum Engen + Galerie. Engen: Städtisches Museum Engen
+ Galerie, 2003.

Buchloh, Benjamin H. D.
"The Primary Colors for the Second Time:
A Paradigm Repetition of the Neo-Avant-Garde,"
October 37 (1986): 41–52.

Cézanne, Paul.
Über die Kunst: Gespräche mit Gasquet: Briefe.
Munich: Mäander, 1980.

Chilova, Alla.
Rodtschenko: Eine Neue Zeit. Munich: Hirmer, 2013.

Danzker, Jo-Anne Birnie, ed.
Theo van Doesburg: Maler-Architekt. Munich: Prestel: 2000.

Delaunay, Robert, and Pierre Francastel.
Du cubisme à l'art abstrait: Documents inédits publiés
par Pierre Francastel et suivis d'un catalogue de l'oeuvre de R.
Delaunay par Guy Habasque.
Paris: S.E.V.P.E.N. 1957.

Doesburg, Theo van.
"Die Grundlage der konkreten Malerei."
In *Konkrete Kunst: Manifeste und Künstlertexte,*
edited by Margit Weinberg Staber. Zurich: Stiftung für
konstruktive und konkrete Kunst Zürich, 2001.

Du, no. 872, *"Konstruktive Kunst"* (December 2016).

Ecker, Berthold, and Wolfgang Hilger.
Vom Selbstzweck der Farbe: Monochromie als Prinzip.
Vienna: VBK, 2001.

Elger, Dietmar, ed.
Donald Judd: Farbe. Ostfildern: Hatje Cantz, 1999.

Essers, Volkmar.
Henri Matisse: 1869–1945: Meister Der Farbe.
Cologne: Taschen, 2016.

Frank, Herbert.
Vincent von Gogh: Briefe an seinen Bruder Theo.
Leipzig: E. A. Seemann, 1997.

Friedel, Helmut, ed.
Wassily Kandinsky: Gesammelte Schriften 1889–1916.
Munich: Prestel, 2007.

Gage, John.
Color and Culture:
Practice and Meaning from Antiquity to Abstraction.
Berkeley: University of California Press, 1993.

Gassen, Richard W.
Die Neue Wirklichkeit: Abstraktion als Weltentwurf.
Exh. cat. Wilhelm-Hack-Museum Ludwigshafen am Rhein.
Ludwigshafen am Rhein: Wilhelm-Hack-Museum, 1994.

Grynsztejn, Madeleine, and Julian Myers.
Ellsworth Kelly in San Francisco.
Berkeley: University of California Press. 2002.

Haftmann, Werner.
Malerei im 20. Jahrhundert. Munich: Prestel, 1965.

Hager, Frithjof, ed.
Geschichte denken: Ein Notizbuch für Leo Löwenthal.
Leipzig: Reclam, 1992.

Hauser, Arnold.
Sozialgeschichte der Kunst und Literatur.
Munich: Beck, 1991.

Helfenstein, Heinrich, and Jean Pfaff.
Farben sind wie der Wind:
Jean Pfaffs Architektonische Farbinterventionen.
Basel: Birkhäuser, 2001.

Hilova, Alla, Ortrud Westheider, and Hubertus Gassner.
Rodtschenko: Eine neue Zeit.
Exh. cat. Bucerius Kunst Forum, Hamburg.
Munich: Hirmer, 2013.

Literature

Hofmann, Werner.
Die Moderne im Rückspiegel:
Hauptwege der Kunstgeschichte.
Munich: Beck, 1998.

Hofstätter, Hans. H.
Gustave Moreau: Leben und Werk.
Cologne: DuMont, 1978.

Holm, Michael Juul, ed.
Color in Art.
Cologne: DuMont, 2010.

Irwin, David.
Winckelmann: Writings on Art.
London: Phaidon, 1972.

Janssen, Hans.
Piet Mondrian: Die Linie.
Ex cat. Martin-Gropius-Bau, Berlin.
Berlin: Martin-Gropius-Bau, 2015.

Liesbrock, Heinz, and Gotthard Graubner.
Gotthard Graubner: Gespräch mit Josef Albers.
Exh. cat. Josef Albers Museum, Bottrop.
Düsseldorf: Richter, 2012.

Liesbrock, Heinz, and Michael Semff, eds.
Malerei auf Papier Josef Albers in Amerika.
Ostfildern: Hatje Cantz, 2010.

Matisse, Henry, Jack D. Flam.
Matisse on Art.
Berkeley: University of California Press, 1995.

Nitschke, August.
Jahrhundertwende:
Der Aufbruch in die Moderne, 1880–1930, 2 vols.
Reinbek: Rowohlt, 1990.

Neubert, Jens, ed.
Expressiv Konkret/Expressively Concrete:
Jean Baier (1932–1999).
Ostfildern: Hatje Cantz, 2014.

Newman, Barnett, John Philip O'Neill, John Philip,
and Mollie McNickle.
Barnett Newman: Selected Writings and Interviews.
Berkeley: University of California Press, 1992.

N.N.
Hommage à Claude Monet.
Exh. Cat. Grand Palais, Paris. Paris, 1880.

Richter, Horst.
Malerei der sechziger Jahre.
Cologne: DuMont, 1990.

Rowell, Margit, and Ad Reinhardt.
Ad Reinhardt and Color.
New York: Guggenheim Museum, 1980.

Schröder, Klaus Albrecht, and Heinz Widauer, eds.
Matisse und die Fauves.
Cologne: Wienand, 2013.

Signac, Paul.
Von Eugene Delacroix zum Neo-Impressionismus.
Berlin: Schnabel, 1908.

Staber, Margit.
Konkrete Kunst: 50 Jahre Entwicklung
Exh. cat. Helmhaus Zürich.
Zurich: Zürcher Kunstgesellschaft, 1960.

Stadt Bottrop, ed.
5 × 5: Quadrat Bottrop. Zeitlauf 1976–2001:
Rückschau und Ausblick.
Schwelm: Meinersdruck, 2001.

Wallner, Julia.
Farbe Raum Farbe.
Berlin: Georg Kolbe Museum, 2013.

Walter, Bettina-Martine, and Bernhart Schwenk, eds.
Die Große Utopie: Die Russische Avantgarde 1915–1932.
Exh. cat. Schirn-Kunsthalle, Frankfurt.
Frankfurt am Main: Schirn-Kunsthalle, 1992.

Weimann, Robert, Hans. U. Gumbrecht, and Benno Wagner.
Postmoderne Globale Differenz.
Frankfurt am Main: Suhrkamp, 1991.

Welschedel, Wilhelm, ed.
Immanuel Kant: Kritik der Urteilskraft.
Berlin: Suhrkamp, 1996.

Widauer, Heinz, Klaus Albrecht Schröder,
and Michael Baumgartner.
Wege des Pointillismus: Seurat, Signac, Van Gogh.
Munich: Hirmer Verlag, 2016.

www.fondation-monet.com, accessed on July 18, 2018.

Positions on color in architecture

Apollinaire, Guillaume.
"*Die Maler des Kubismus:*
Ästhetische Betrachtungen, Paris 1913."
In Kunsttheorie im 20. Jahrhundert,
edited by Charles Harrison and Paul Wood.
Ostfildern: Hatje Cantz, 1998.

Archithese, no. 6,
"*Farbige Räume – espaces en couleur*" (June 1994).

Arch+, no. 48.
"*Julius Posener: Vorlesungen zur Geschichte der*
Neuen Architektur" (December 1979).

Arch+, no. 53.
*"Julius Posener: Vorlesungen zur Geschichte der
Neuen Architektur II: Die Architektur der Reform (1900–1924)"*
(September 1980).

Arch+, no. 194.
"Bruno Taut: Architekturlehre" (October 2009).

Barthel, Albrecht.
Wenzel Hablik, Farbräume der Moderne.
Heide: Landesamt für Denkmalpflege
Schleswig-Holstein, 2007.

Batchelor, David.
The Luminous and the Grey.
London: Reaktion Books, 2014.

Blotkamp, Carel, et al., eds.
Theo van Doesburg, Maler-Architekt.
Munich: Prestel, 2000.

Boesiger, Willy, ed.
Le Corbusier et Pierre Jeanneret: Oeuvre complete, 8 vols.
Paris: Les Editions d'Architecture, 1967.

Brenne, Winfried, and Bruno Taut.
Meister des farbigen Bauens in Berlin.
Berlin: Braun, 2005.

Buether, Axel.
Colour: Design fundamentals.
Munich: Institut f. intern. Architektur-Dok, 2013.

Carranza, Luis E., Fernando L. Lara, and Jorge F. Liernur.
*Modern Architecture in Latin America:
Art, Technology, and Utopia.*
Austin: University of Texas Press, 2014.

Choisy, Auguste.
L'art de bâtir chez les Romains.
Paris: Ducher, 1873.

Conrads, Ulrich.
Programs and Manifestoes on 20th-century Architecture.
Cambridge, MA: MIT Press, 1975.

Daidalos, no. 51,
"In Farbe/In Colour" (March 1994).

Doesburg, Theo van.
*Über europäische Architektur:
Gesammelte Aufsätze aus Het Bouwbedrijf 1924–1931.*
Basel: Birkhäuser, 1990.

Doesburg, Theo van.
Grundbegriffe der neuen gestaltenden Kunst, 2nd ed.
Mainz: Kupferberg, 1981.

Dörries, Cornelia.
Wer hat Angst vor Farbe, dabonline.de, March 1, 2006.

Droste, Magdalena, and Peter Gössel.
Bauhaus.
Cologne: Taschen, 2015.

Fontana, Lucio.
Manifesto blanco, 1946.
Milan: Galleria Apollinaire, 1966.

Frampton, Kenneth.
Modern Architecture: A Critical History.
London: Thames & Hudson, 2014.

Ghirardo, Diane Yvonne.
Architecture after Modernism.
London: Thames and Hudson, 1996.

Giedion, Sigfried.
Space, Time and Architecture: The Growth of a New Tradition.
Harvard: Harvard University Press, 2008.

Gigon, Annette, and Mike Guyer.
Gigon Guyer Architekten: Arbeiten 2001–2011.
Baden: Lars Müller Publishers, 2012.

Gropius, Walter.
Architektur: Wege zu einer optischen Kultur.
Frankfurt am Main: Fischer Bücherei, 1956.

Heer, Jan.
*The architectonic colour:
Polychromy in the purist: Architecture of Le Corbusier.*
Rotterdam: 010 Publishers, 2009.

Holm, Michael Juul, ed.
Color in Art. Cologne: DuMont, 2010.

Itten, Johannes.
*Kunst der Farbe: subjektives Erleben und
objektives Erkennen als Wege zur Kunst.*
Freiburg: Christophorus, 1961.

Jones, Owen.
The Grammar of Ornament. London: Day and Son, 1865.

Judd, Donald.
*Some Aspects of Color in General and Red
and Black in Particular.*
Sassenheim: Sikkens Foundation, 1993.

Kandinsky, Wassily.
Über das Geistige in der Kunst: Insbesondere in der Malerei.
Munich: Piper, 1911.

Klinkhammer, Barbara.
*"After Purism: Le Corbusier and Colour",
Preservation Education & Research 4* (2011): 19–38.

Klinkhammer, Barbara.
*"Ineffable Space: Le Corbusier's Colour Schemes for the
Monastery Sainte Marie de La Tourette," WIT Transactions on
The Built Environment* 118 (December 2011): 115–28.

Literature

Krischanitz, Adolf.
Architektur ist der Unterschied zwischen Architektur.
Ostfildern: Hatje Cantz, 2010.

Krischanitz, Adolf.
"Farbtopoi in der Architektur:
Meine Zusammenarbeit mit Oskar Putz."
In *Veröffentlichte Kunst, Kunst im öffentlichen Raum.*
Berlin: Springer, 1991.

Krischanitz, Adolf, and Helmut Federle.
Neue-Welt-Schule. Ostfildern: Hatje Cantz, 1994.

Le Camus de Mézières, Nicolas.
Le génie de l'architecture, ou l'analogie
de cet art avec nos sensations.
Paris: Benoit, 1780.

Le Corbusier.
"L'espace indicible," l'Architecture d'Aujourd'hui (1946).

Le Corbusier.
"Pessac," L'Architecture Vivante (Fall/Winter, 1927).

Léger, Fernand.
Mensch Maschine Malerei: Aufsätze und Schriften zur Kunst.
Bern: Benteli, 1971.

Loos, Adolf.
Spoken into the Void: Collected Essays, 1897–1900.
Cambridge, MA: MIT Press, 1987.

Mack, Gerhard, ed.
Colours: Rem Koolhaas/OMA, Norman Foster,
Alessandro Mendini.
Basel: Birkhäuser, 2001.

Malevich, Kazimir.
The Non-Objective World by Kazimir Malevich,
translated by Howard Dearstyne.
Chicago: Paul Theobald and Company, 1959.

McLachlan, Fiona.
Architectural Colour in the Professional Palette.
London: Taylor & Francis, 2012.

Michels, Norbert.
Architektur Und Kunst:
Das Meisterhaus Kandinsky-Klee in Dessau.
Leipzig: Seemann, 2000.

Moravánszky, Ákos.
"Askese und Opulenz," werk, bauen + wohnen 6 (2016).

Moravánszky, Ákos, ed.
Architekturtheorie im 20. Jahrhundert:
eine kritische Anthologie. Vienna: Springer, 2003.

Nierendorf, Karl, and Hans Maria Wingler.
Staatliches Bauhaus Weimar 1919–1923.
Munich: Kraus Reprint, 1980.

N.N.
"Die neuen Wohnviertel Frugès in Pessac (Bordeaux):
Architekten Le Corbuiser und Pierre Jeanneret,"
Das Werk: Architektur und Kunst 2 (1927).

Pastoureau, Michel.
Blau: Die Geschichte einer Farbe.
Berlin: Klaus Wagenbach, 2013.

Pauly, Danièle.
Barragán: Space and Shadow, Walls and Colour.
Basel: Birkhäuser, 2008.

Pauly, Danièle.
Le Corbusier: Die Kapelle von Ronchamp.
Basel: Birkhäuser, 1997.

Putz, Oskar.
"Über das Verhältnis von Farbe und Architektur am
Beispiel Bruno Taut," UmBau, no. 8 (1984).

Roth, Alfred.
"Von der Wandmalerei zur Raummalerei, Farbe als
architektonisches Gestaltungselement,"
Das Werk: Architektur und Kunst 2 (1949).

Rübel, Dietmar, Monika Wagner, and Vera Wolff.
Materialästhetik:
Quellentexte zu Kunst, Design und Architektur.
Berlin: Reimer, 2005.

Sartoris, Alberto.
Colour in Interior Architecture in Circle:
International Survey of Constructive Art.
London: Faber and Faber, 1937.

Sauerbruch, Matthias, and Louisa Hutton.
Sauerbruch Hutton Archive.
Baden: Lars Müller Publishers, 2006.

Schiess, Adrian, Max Wechsler, and Heinz Wirz.
Adrian Schiess. Farbräume Zusammenarbeit mit den
Architekten Herzog & de Meuron und Gigon/Guyer 1993–200
Luzern: Quart, 2004.

Schumacher, Fritz.
Streifzüge eines Architekten. Nendeln: Kraus Reprint, 1976.

Semper, Gottfried.
The Four Elements of Architecture and Other Writings.
Cambridge: Cambridge University Press, 1989.

Semper, Gottfried.
Style in the Technical and Tectonic Arts, Or, Practical Aesthetics,
translated by Harry F. Mallgrave.
Los Angeles: Getty Research Institute, 2004.

Steiner, Dietmar.
Siedlung Pilotengasse Wien:
Herzog & de Meuron, Steidle + Partner, Adolf Krischanitz.
Zurich: Artemis, 1992.

Svestka, Jiri, ed. Andor Weininger:
Vom Bauhaus zur konzeptuellen Kunst.
Düsseldorf: Kunstverein f. d. Rheinlande u. Westfalen,
Kestner-Gesellschaft, 1990.

Taut, Bruno.
Frühlicht 1920–1922:
Eine Folge für die Verwirklichung des neuen Baugedankens.
Basel: Birkhäuser, 2014.

Temkin, Ann.
Color Chart: Reinventing Color 1950–Today.
New York: Museum of Modern Art, 2008.

Trautwein, Katrin.
"Rekonstruktion der Polychromie der Villa La Roche I:
Farbe als Material, Architektur als Skulptur,"
Coviss (March 2012).

Trautwein, Katrin.
"Rekonstruktion der Polychromie der Villa La Roche II:
Le Corbusiers Prinzipien der Farbgestaltung,"
Coviss (April 2012).

Ursprung, Philip ed.
Herzog & de Meuron: Natural History.
Exh. cat. Canadian Centre for Architecture, Montreal.
Baden: Lars Müller Publishers, 2005.

Valdensová, Lucia.
"Familien-Affären:
Adolf Loos als Designstar des Pilsener Bürgertums,"
Bauwelt 32–33 (2015): 20–25.

Van der Laan, Hans.
Architectonic Space:
Fifteen Lessons on the Disposition of the Human Habitat.
Leiden: Brill, 1983.

von Moos, Stanislaus.
"Der Purismus und die Malerei Le Corbusier,"
Das Werk: Architektur und Kunst 53 (1996).

von Vegesack, Alexander, ed.
Verner Panton, das Gesamtwerk.
Weil am Rhein: Vitra-Design-Museum, 2000.

Venturi, Robert, Denise Scott Brown, and Steven Izenour.
Learning from Las Vegas.
Cambridge, MA: MIT Press, 1972.

Welsch, Wolfgang, ed.
Wege aus der Moderne:
Schlüsseltexte der Postmoderne-Diskussion.
Weinheim: VCH Verlagsgesellschaft, 1988.

Wick, Rainer.
"Bauhausarchitektur und Farbe,"
Wissenschaftliche Zeitschrift der Hochschule für
Architektur und Bauwesen Weimar 5/6 (1983).

Winckelmann, Johann Joachim.
The History of ancient Art, vol. 2, edited by J. R. Osgood,
translated by Giles Henri Lodges.
Boston: James Munroe and Company, 1849.

Seeing and categorizing color

Albers, Josef.
Interaction of Color.
Yale: Yale University Press, 2006.

Bachmann, Ulrich.
Colour and Light/Farbe und Licht.
Sulgen: Niggli, 2011.

Bollnow, Otto Friedrich.
Mensch und Raum.
Stuttgart: Kohlhammer, 1976.

Elíasson, Ólafur, and Jonathan Crary.
Ólafur Elíasson: Minding the World.
Ostfildern: Hatje Cantz, 2005.

Gage, John.
Color and Culture:
Practice and Meaning from Antiquity to Abstraction.
Berkeley: University of California Press, 1993.

Glasner, Barbara, and Petra Schmidt, eds.
Chroma: Chroma: Design, Architecture and Art in Color.
Basel: Birkhäuser, 2009.

Holm, Michael Juul, ed.
Color in Art.
Cologne: DuMont, 2010.

Klassik Stiftung Weimar, ed.
Goethes Farbenlehre.
Weimar: 2011. Source: www.klassik-stiftung.de.

Meerwein, Gerhard, Frank H. Mahnke, and Bettina Rodeck.
Color: Communication in Architectural Space.
Basel: Birkhäuser, 2007.

Oswald, Martin.
"Farbenblinde sehen besser," lecture given at the Akademie
der Bildenden Künste München, July 10, 2002,
www.kunstpaedagogik.userweb.mwn.de/VortragOswald.pdf.

Richter, Gerhard.
Text: Writings, Interviews and Letters 1961–2007.
London: Thames & Hudson, 2009.

Schmalenbach, Werner.
Paul Klee: Die Kunst-Reihe in Farben.
Berlin: Deutsche Buch-Gemeinschaft, 1959.

Spillmann, Werner, and Verena M. Schindler.
Farb-Systeme 1611–2007:
Farb-Dokumente in der Sammlung Werner Spillmann.
Basel: Schwabe, 2010.

Literature

St. Clair, Kassia.
The Secret Lives of Colour.
London: John Murray, 2016.

Stromer, Klaus, ed.
Farbsysteme in Kunst und Wissenschaft.
Cologne: DuMont, 2005.

Temkin, Ann.
Color Chart: Reinventing Color 1950 to Today.
New York: Museum of Modern Art, 2008.

Welsch, Norbert, and Claus Christian Liebmann.
Farben: Natur, Technik, Kunst.
Heidelberg: Spektrum, 2012.

Wittgenstein, Ludwig.
Remarks on Colour, edited by G. E. M. Anscombe,
translated by Linda L. McAlister and Margarete Schattle.
Berkeley: University of California Press, 2007.

Zwimpfer, Moritz.
Licht und Farbe: Physik, Erscheinung, Wahrnehmung.
Sulgen: Niggli, 2012.

Color as two-dimensional, structural and spatial element

Aargauer Kunsthaus, ed.
Bridget Riley: Bilder und Zeichnungen 1959–2005.
Aarau: Aargauer Kunsthaus, 2005.

Albrecht, Hans J., and Robert Delaunay.
Farbe als Sprache:
Robert Delaunay, Josef Albers, Richard Paul Lohse, 1st ed.
Cologne: DuMont, 1974.

Bendin, Eckhard.
Zur Farbenlehre: Studien.
Dresden: Die Verlagsgesellschaft, 2011.

Bielefelder Kunstverein.
Neuer Konstruktivismus.
Bielefeld: Kerber, 2007.

Breuer, Leo, Richard W. Gassen, and Andreas Pohlmann.
Leo Breuer: 1893–1975: Retrospektive.
Heidelberg: Ed. Braus, 1992.

Camille Graeser Stiftung Zürich, Kunstmuseum Stuttgart,
Aargauer Kunsthaus, eds.
Camille Graeser und die Musik.
Cologne: Wienand, 2015.

Du, no. 872, *"Konstruktive Kunst"* (December 2016)

Fleck, Robert.
Mack: Reliefs.
Munich: Hirmer, 2015.

Gage, John.
Color and Culture:
Practice and Meaning from Antiquity to Abstraction.
Berkeley: University of California Press, 1993.

Galerie Denise René, ed.
Cruz-Diez. Exh. cat.
Paris: Galerie Denise René, 1973.

Gassen, Richard W, and Vera Hausdorff.
Camille Graeser: Vom Entwurf zum Bild:
Ideenskizzen und Entwurfszeichnungen 1938 bis 1978,
edited by the Camille Graeser-Stiftung.
Cologne: Wienand, 2009.

Güse, Ernst-Gerhard, and Martina Plümacher.
Reflexionen no. 4.1. Bild – Handeln.
Luxemburg: Éditions MediArt, 2017.

Haupenthal, Uwe, and Gudrun Piper.
Konstruktiv–Konkret: Malerei, Plastik, Grafik. Exh. cat.
Richard-Haizmann-Museum Niebüll; Museum für
Konkrete Kunst Ingolstadt. Husum: Verl. der Kunst, 2008.

Holeczek, Bernhard.
Richard Paul Lohse, 1902–1988. Exh. cat.
Wilhelm-Hack-Museum, Ludwigshafen am Rein.
Heidelberg: Ed. Braus, 1992.

Jaffé, Hans L. C.
Mondrian und De Stijl.
Cologne: DuMont, 1967.

Kepes, György.
Modul, Proportion, Symmetrie, Rhythmus.
Brussels: La Connaissance, 1969.

Liesbrock, Heinz, ed.
Anni und Josef Albers: Begegnungen mit Lateinamerika.
Ostfildern: Hatje Cantz, 2007.

Liesbrock, Heinz, and Gotthard Graubner.
Gotthard Graubner: Gespräch mit Josef Albers. Exh. cat.
Josef Albers Museum, Bottrop. Düsseldorf: Richter, 2012.

Liesbrock, Heinz, and Michael Semff, eds.
Malerei auf Papier Josef Albers in Amerika.
Ostfildern: Hatje Cantz, 2010.

Lorenz, Kuno.
Reflexionen no. 5: Können in den Künsten und Wissen
in den Wissenschaften: Trennendes und Verbindendes.
Luxembourg: Éditions MediArt, 2017.

Muthofer, Ben.
Geometrie Farbe Licht. Exh. cat. Kunstforum Ostdeutsche
Galerie Regensburg. Regensburg:
Kunstforum Ostdeutsche Galerie Regensburg, 2012.

Neubert, Jens, ed.
Expressiv Konkret/Expressively Concrete:
Jean Baier (1932–1999).
Ostfildern: Hatje Cantz, 2014.

Riley, Bridget, and Robert Kudielka.
Malen um zu Sehen:
Bridget Riley: Gesammelte Schriften, 1965–2009.
Munich: Hirmer, 2012.

Rompza, Sigurd.
Reflexionen no. 1: Als Künstler über Kunst schreiben.
Luxembourg: Éditions MediArt, 2015.

Rompza, Sigurd.
Reflexionen no. 2: Arbeitsnotizen 2010–2015.
Luxembourg: Éditions MediArt, 2015.

Rompza, Sigurd.
Reflexionen no. 3: Thesen zu meiner künstlerischen Arbeit.
Luxembourg: Éditions MediArt, 2016.

Rompza, Sigurd.
"*Reflexionen no. 4: Zu den Farb-Licht-Modulierungen der*
Jahre 2002–2004 künstlertheoretische." In *Relief:*
Konkret in Deutschland Heute, edited by Jo Enzweiler.
Saarbrücken: Galerie St. Johann, 1981.

Rompza, Sigurd, and Monika Bugs.
Sigurd Rompza im Gespräch mit Monika Bugs.
Saarbrücken: Verl. St. Johann, 2000.

Rotzler, Willi.
Konstruktive Konzepte. Zurich: ABC, 1977.

Stocker, Esther, and Günter Oberhollenzer, eds.
Esther Stocker: Verrückte Geometrie.
Bielefeld: Kerber, 2015.

Svestka, Jiri, ed.
Andor Weininger: vom Bauhaus zur konzeptuellen Kunst.
Düsseldorf: Kunstverein f. d. Rheinlande u. Westfalen,
Kestner-Gesellschaft, 1990.

Uelsberg, Gabriele.
H. H. Zimmermann:
Das konkrete Konzept: Acrylmalerei, Zeichnungen,
Collagen, Druckgraphik, edited by Jürgen Becks.
Exh. cat. Städtisches Museum Wesel, Galerie im Centrum.
Wesel: Stadt Wesel, 2006.

Wiehager, Renate, ed.
Jan van der Ploeg: Selected Works, 2009–2016.
Exh. cat. Kunsthaus Baselland, Muttenz.
Cologne: Snoeck, 2016.

Zimmermann, H. H.
Notizen aus dem Atelier-Arbeitsbuch 1982–2012,
edited by Jörg Loskill. Essen: Klartext, 2012.

Areas of color and room surfaces

Adam, Hubertus.
"*Patrick Gmür/Peter Roesch: Schulhaus Scherr Zürich,*"
Archithese (May 2003).

Albrecht, Hans J., and Robert Delaunay.
Farbe als Sprache:
Robert Delaunay, Josef Albers, Richard Paul Lohse, 1st ed.
Cologne: DuMont, 1974.

Bachmann, Wolfgang.
"*Voller Farbe: Primarschule Hinter Gärten in Basel-Riehen,*"
Baumeister (April 2007).

Barragán, Luis, and Fernández A. Toca.
Barragán: Das Gesamtwerk.
Basel: Birkhäuser, 1996.

Elíasson, Ólafur, and Jonathan Crary.
Ólafur Elíasson: Minding the World.
Ostfildern: Hatje Cantz, 2005.

Elser, Oliver.
"*Wohnhaus Schwarzer Laubfrosch,*" Bauwelt, no. 35 (2004).

Esch, Phillip.
"*Farbe vollfett: Erweiterung des Schulhauses Scherr, Zürich,*
von Patrick Gmür Architekten," Werk, Bauen + Wohnen
(November 2003).

Gage, John.
"*Rothko: Color as Subject.*" In *Mark Rothko,* edited by
Jeffrey Weiss. Exh. cat. National Gallery of Art, Washington,
DC. New Haven: Yale University Press, 1998.

Krischanitz, Adolf.
Architektur ist der Unterschied zwischen Architektur.
Ostfildern: Hatje Cantz, 2010.

Lorenzini, Karl.
"*Nicht jeder Mensch braucht die selben Farben,*"
Modulor Magazin (January 2015).

Marchal, Katharina.
"*Das Leben mit Farben: Über die Arbeit des Farbkünstlers*
Jörg Niederberger," Modulor Magazin (January 2015).

Meerwein, Gerhard, Frank H. Mahnke, and Bettina Rodeck.
Color: Communication in Architectural Space.
Basel: Birkhäuser, 2007.

Stadler, Hilar.
"*All Over: Hilar Stadler im Gespräch mit Peter Roesch.*"
In *Prix Meret Oppenheim 2007.*
Bern: Bundesamt für Kultur, 2008.

Van der Laan, Hans.
Der architektonische Raum: Fünfzehn Lektionen über die
Disposition der menschlichen Behausung.
Leiden: E. J. Brill, 1992.

Literature

von Drathen, Doris.
"Anish Kapoor, die Unendlichkeit der Mathematik,"
Kunstforum, no. 169 (2004).

Zschocke, Nina.
Der irritierte Blick: Kunstrezeption. Paderborn: Fink, 2004.

Autonomous color strategies

Dekel, Gil.
"I Am a Painter: Perspective-localized painter,
Felice Varini, interviewed by Gil Dekel, May 26, 2008."
Last updated October 2, 2014,
www.poeticmind.co.uk/interviews-1/i-am-a-painter.

De Koning, Krijn.
Krijn de Koning. binnen buiten.
Rotterdam: NAI Publ., 2002.

Magrou, Rafael.
"Man with a Plan: Dominique Coulon Is a Blueprint Believer,"
Mark, no. 62 (2016).

Putz Oskar.
"Bindung und Autonomie der Farbe am Bau:
Thesen zur Polychromie," Archithese (June 1994).

Putz, Oskar, and Irene Nierhaus.
Korrespondenzen: Zu Arbeiten von Oskar Putz.
Exh. cat. Wiener Secession.
Vienna: Galerie Wiener Secession, 1992.

Rousse, Georges.
Georges Rousse, Architectures.
Paris: Bernard Chauveau Édition, 2010.

Sauerbruch, Matthias, and Louisa Hutton.
Sauerbruch Hutton Archive 2.
Zurich: Lars Müller Publishers, 2016.

Tebbe, Friederike, and Christiane Fath.
Farbräume = Color Spaces. Berlin: Jovis, 2009.

Wilson, Rob.
"From A to B and Back Again:
The Work of Ola Kolehmainen with Sauerburch Hutton,"
www.uncubemagazine.com/blog/12652765.

Diffusivity, color reflection, and colored light

L'Architecture d'aujourd'hui.
Carlos Cruz-Diez: Construire l'art avec l'espace.
Paris: Archipress & Associés, 2016.

Architectural Record, no. 10, *"Projects – Steven Holl"* (2010).

"AVA Talks to staat Creative Agency, May 1, 2012."
Accessed April 26, 2017, blog.bloomsburyvisualarts.com.

Bachmann, Ulrich.
Colour and Light/Farbe und Licht. Sulgen: Niggli, 2011.

Baunetzwissen. Dichroitisches Glas. Accessed April 26, 2017,
www.baunetzwissen.de/glossar/d/dichroitisches-glas-51651.

Blum, Elisabeth.
Atmosphäre:
Hypothesen zum Prozess der räumlichen Wahrnehmung.
Baden: Lars Müller Publishers, 2010.

Böhme, Hartmut.
"Das Licht als Medium der Kunst: Über Erfahrungsarmut
und ästhetisches Gegenlicht in der technischen Zivilisation."
In Licht, Farbe, Raum: Künstlerisch-wissenschaftliches
Symposium, Braunschweig, edited by Michael Schwarz.
Krefeld: Leporello, 1997.

Brown, Julia, ed.
Occluded Front: James Turrell.
Los Angeles: Fellows of Contemporary Art, 1985.

Crary, Jonathan.
"Your Colour Memory: Illuminationen des Ungesehenen."
In *Nachbilder: Das Gedächtnis des Auges in Kunst*
und Wissenschaft, edited by Werner Busch and Carolin Meister.
Zurich: Diaphanes, 2011.

Elíasson, Ólafur, and Jonathan Crary.
Ólafur Elíasson: Minding the World.
Ostfildern: Hatje Cantz, 2005.

Gage, John.
Colour in Turner: Poetry and Truth.
London: Studio Vista, 1969.

Gage, John.
Color and Culture:
Practice and Meaning from Antiquity to Abstraction.
Berkeley: University of California Press, 1993.

Hagendorf, Herbert, Joseph Krummenacher, Hermann-Josef
Müller, and Torsten Schubert.
Wahrnehmung und Aufmerksamkeit.
Allgemeine Psychologie für Bachelor.
Berlin: Springer, 2011.

Hoormann, Anne, Dieter Burdorf, Dieter, Mechthild Fend,
and Bettina Uppenkamp.
Medium und Material:
Zur Kunst der Moderne und der Gegenwart.
Munich: Wilhelm Fink, 2007.

Hotze, Benedikt.
"Museum Brandhorst," Baunetzwoche 125, May 15, 2009.

ICA News Release.
Holiday Home, Ben van Berkel and Caroline Bos.
Philadelphia: ICA, 2006.

Kuhnert, Nikolaus.
"Matthias Sauerbruch und Lousia Hutton im Gespräch mit
Nikolaus Kuhnert und Anh-Linh Ngo," Arch+, no. 194,
"Lernen von Bruno Taut" (October 2009).

Meerwein, Gerhard; Frank H. Mahnke, and Bettina Rodeck.
Color: Communication in Architectural Space.
Basel: Birkhäuser, 2007.

Parker, Dorothea.
"Museum Brandhorst: Kopfbau für das Kunstareal,"
Bauwelt (July 2009).

Kraft, Benedikt.
"Zum Reinbeißen schön:
Die Fassade des Museums Brandhorst in München,"
DBZ, (September 2009).

Noever, Peter.
James Turrell: The Other Horizon.
Ostfildern: Hatje Cantz, 1999.

Sauerbruch, Matthias, and Louisa Hutton.
Sauerbruch Hutton Archive.
Baden: Lars Müller Publishers, 2006.

Sauerbruch, Matthias, and Louisa Hutton.
Sauerbruch Hutton Archive 2.
Zurich: Lars Müller Publishers, 2016.

Schick, Ulrike, ed.
Peter Zimmermann: Pool.
Vienna: Verlag für Moderne Kunst, 2017.

Schlereth, Thomas.
"Mit den Farben auf dem Weg," laudatory speech on the
occasion of the award of the Reinhold-Schneider-Stipendium
to Andreas von Ow, Freiburg im Breisgau, April 7, 2016.

Schlereth, Thomas.
Zwischenraum_01. Berlin: Hackesche Höfe:
Malerei von Andreas von Ow.
Berlin: Zwischenraum, 2012/2013.

Schmal, Peter Cachola.
Der Pavillon. Lust und Polemik in der Architektur.
Ostfildern: Hatje Cantz, 2009.

Schumacher, Ulrich.
Carlos Cruz-Diez. Exh. cat. Quadrat Bottrop,
Josef Albers Museum.
Bottrop: Stadt Bottrop, 1988.

Suárez, Osbel.
Carlos Cruz-Diez: Color Happens.
Madrid: Fundación Juan March, 2009.

Tietz, Jürgen, Nicolette Baumeister, et al.
Baukulturführer 107. Immanuelkirche Köln.
Architekten. Sauerbruch Hutton.
Berlin: Koch, Schmidt u. Wilhelm, 2016.

Welsch, Norbert, and Claus Liebmann.
Farben. Natur, Technik, Kunst.
Heidelberg: Spektrum, 2012.

Winterhager, Uta.
"Immanuelkirche Köln," Bauwelt (September 2014).

Zschocke, Nina.
Der irritierte Blick: Kunstrezeption und Aufmerksamkeit.
Paderborn: Fink, 2004.

Zwimpfer, Moritz.
Licht und Farbe: Physik, Erscheinung, Wahrnehmung.
Sulgen: Niggli, 2012.

Readability and orientation

Binder, Ulrich.
"Farbraum Stadt." In Farbraum Stadt. Box ZRH.
Zurich: Kontrast, 2010.

Bruns, Margarete.
Das Rätsel Farbe: Materie und Mythos.
Stuttgart: Reclam, 2012.

Buether, Axel.
Colour: Design Fundamentals.
Munich: Institut f. intern. Architektur-Dok, 2013.

Glasner, Barbara, and Petra Schmidt, eds.
Chroma: Chroma: Design, Architecture and Art in Color.
Basel: Birkhäuser, 2009.

Heller, Eva.
Wie Farben wirken.
Hamburg: Rowohlt, 1989.

Kling, Beate, and Torsten Krüger.
Signaletik: Orientierung im Raum.
Munich: Detail, 2013.

Meerwein, Gerhard, Frank H. Mahnke, and Bettina Rodeck.
Color: Communication in Architectural Space.
Basel: Birkhäuser, 2007.

Paul, Jochen.
"Staatliche Realschule in Eching," Bauwelt (April 2007).

Reichel, Alexander, and Kerstin Schultz, eds.
Einrichten und Zonieren:
Raumkonzepte, Materialität, Ausbau.
Basel: Birkhäuser, 2014.

Schittich, Christian, ed.
Erschließungsräume.
Munich: Detail, 2013.

www.farbaks.de

Literature

Inherent color and material color

Archithese, no. 5, *"Farbe/La couleur"* (May 2003).

Archithese, no. 6, *"Farbige Räume – espaces en couleur"* (June 1994).

Detail, no. 12, *"Architektur und Farbe"* (December 2016).

Baudrillard, Jean.
"Stimmungswert Material. Naturholz und Kulturholz (1968)."
In idem., *Das System der Dinge:*
Über unser Verhältnis zu den alltäglichen Gegenständen.
Frankfurt am Main: Campus, 1991.

Blaser, Werner, and Johannes Malms.
West Meets East: Mies van der Rohe.
Basel: Birkhäuser, 2001.

Boesiger, Willy, ed.
Le Corbusier et Pierre Jeanneret: Oeuvre complete, 8 vols.
Paris: Les Editions d'Architecture, 1967.

Deplazes, Andrea.
Constructing Architecture:
Materials, Processes, Structures: A Handbook.
Basel: Birkhäuser, 2013.

Freund, Michael.
"Der Raum ist das Material: Richard Serra,"
Der Standard, July 13, 2007.

Geiger, Franz.
"Putzbau," Deutsche Bauhütte, no. 49 (December 1902).

Giedion, Sigfried.
Space, Time and Architecture: The Growth of a New Tradition.
Cambridge, MA: Harvard University Press, 2008.

Hegger, Manfred, Hans Drexler, and Martin Zeumer.
Basics Materials.
Basel: Birkhäuser, 2014.

Hillig, Hugo.
"Der Betonbau und die Dekorationsmalerei,"
Kunstgewerbeblatt 25, no. 4 (January 1914).

Huber, Hans Dieter.
"Oberfläche, Materialität und Medium der Farbe."
In *Who is afraid of: Zum Stand der Farbforschung*
edited by Karl Schawelka and Annette Hoormann.
Weimar: Universitätsverlag, 1998.

Leonie, Anna.
Dominikuszentrum München, www.meck-architekten.de.

Lüth, Erich.
"Ich finde Beton zum Kotzen," Berichte:
Jahrbuch der freien Akademie der Künste in Hamburg
(1971/1972).

Meerwein, Gerhard, Frank H. Mahnke, and Bettina Rodeck.
Color: Communication in Architectural Space.
Basel: Birkhäuser, 2007.

Olgiati, Valerio.
Valerio Olgiati: Lecture.
Basel: Birkhäuser, 2011.

Pudor, Heinrich.
Deutsche Qualitätsarbeit.
Gautzsch b. Leipzig: Dietrich, 1910.

Rübel, Dietmar, Monika Wagner, and Vera Wolff.
Materialästhetik:
Quellentexte zu Kunst, Design und Architektur.
Berlin: Reimer, 2005.

Seipp, Heinrich.
"Materialstil und Materialstimmung in der Baukunst,"
Deutsche Bauhütte, no. 6 (1902).

Semper, Gottfried.
Style in the Technical and Tectonic Arts, Or, Practical Aesthetics,
translated by Harry F. Mallgrave.
Los Angeles: Getty Research Institute, 2004.

Spiro, Annette, Hartmut Göhler, and Pinar Gönül.
Über Putz: Oberflächen Entwickeln und Realisieren.
Zurich: gta Verlag, 2015.

van de Velde, Henry.
"Die Belebung des Stoffes als Prinzip der Schönheit (1910)."
In idem., *Zum neuen Stil.*
Munich: Piper, 1955.

van de Velde, Henry.
Kunstgewerbliche Laienpredigten.
Leipzig: Seemann, 1902.

Image Credits

P. 5: Philadelphia Museum of Art. Purchased with funds contributed by C. K. Williams II (by exchange) © Ellsworth Kelly Foundation – P. 8: Isabella Stewart Gardner Museum, Boston, MA, USA / Bridgeman Images – P. 13: (t.) © Kunsthall Bremen / Lars Lohrisch / Artothek (image); (b. l.) Los Angeles, The J. Paul Getty Museum / bpk / adoc-photos; (b. M.) Paris, Musée d'Orsay / bpk / RMN - Grand Palais / Patrice Schmidt (image); (b. r.) Moskau, Staatliches Puschkin-Museum der Bildenden Künste / bpk / Alinari Archives / Alinari – P. 14: Kunsthaus, Zürich, Switzerland / Bridgeman Images; (b.) Paris, Musée d'Orsay / bpk / RMN - Grand Palais / Patrice Schmidt (image) – P. 18: (t.) © Fine Art Images – Artothek © Succession H. Matisse / VG Bild-Kunst, Bonn 2018; (b.) © Museum Folkwang Essen - Artothek – P. 27: (t.) © Camille Graeser-Stiftung / VG Bild-Kunst, Bonn 2018 (b.) © Kate Rothko-Pritzel & Christopher Rothko / VG Bildkunst, Bonn 2018. – P. 28: (t.) Collection Stedelijk Museum Amsterdam / Barnett Newman Foundation / VG Bild-Kunst Bonn 2018; (M.) The Solomon R. Guggenheim Museum, New York. Gift of the artist (by ex-change), 1972 © Ellsworth Kelly Foundation; (b.) © Whitney Musem (digital image) © Judd Foundation / VG Bild-Kunst, Bonn, 2018 – P. 29: (t.) bpk / Kunstsammlung Nordrhein-Westfalen, Düsseldorf / Achim Kukulies (image) © VG Bild-Kunst, Bonn 2018; (M.) Sammlung Schauwerk Sindelfingen, Germany / Ulrich Ghezzi (image) / Courtesy Galerie Thaddaeus Ropac; (b.) © Städel Museum – Artothek © VG Bild-Kunst, Bonn 2018 – P. 32: Syquali Crossmedia AG (Reto Rodolfo Pedrini) – P. 35: ©Tate, London 2018 / VG Bild-Kunst, Bonn 2018 – P. 37: Petr Jehlik – P. 41: © Victoria and Albert Museum, London – P. 43: Petr Jehlik P. 44: © Pepo Segura - Fundacio Mies van der Rohe / VG Bild-Kunst, Bonn 2018 – P. 46: © Sönke Wurr – P. 49: (t. l.) Collection Het Nieuwe Instituut/ collection Van Eesteren-Fluck & Van Lohuizen Foundation, Amsterdam or Het Nieuwe Instituut /on loan from collection EFL Foundation, Amsterdam archive (code): EEST inv.nr.: 3.181; (t. r.) Collection Centraal Museum, Utrecht / Kim Zwarts 2005 / Pictoright / VG Bild-Kunst, Bonn 2018; (b. l.) Collection Het Nieuwe Instituut, donation Van Moorsel, archive (code): DOES, inv.nr.: AB5209; (b. r.) Diane Lahumière / Galerie Lahumi-ère – P. 54: Jeroen Kolkman (image) © F.L.C. / VG Bild-Kunst, Bonn 2018 – P. 57: (t.) © F.L.C. / VG Bild-Kunst, Bonn 2018; (b.) Paul Kozlowski (Image) © F.L.C. / VG Bild-Kunst, Bonn 2018 – P. 58: (t.) P. De Prins (Image) © VIOE / F.L.C. / VG Bild-Kunst, Bonn 2018; (b.) Olivier Martin-Gambier (image) © F.L.C. / VG Bild-Kunst, Bonn 2018 – P. 61: www.tautes-heim.de / Ben Buschfeld (image) – P. 64: M. Gabriela Bermeo Castrejón (image) © Barragan Foundation / VG Bild-Kunst, Bonn 2018 – P. 66: Agostonio Osio (image) Courtesy Pirelli HangarBicocca, Milan © Fondazione Lucio Fontana / VG Bild-Kunst, Bonn 2018 – P. 68: Gregor Julien Straube – P. 70: (t.) Architekturzentrum Wien, Austria, collection / Margherita Spiluttini (image) © VG Bild-Kunst, Bonn 2018; (M.) SIK-ISEA, Zürich © VG Bild-Kunst, Bonn 2018; (b.) Architekturzentrum Wien, Austria, collection / Margherita Spiluttini (image) – P. 73: © Heinrich Helfenstein (image) / VG Bild-Kunst, Bonn 2018 – P. 75: © Gigon/ Guyer, Christian Brunner (Image) / VG Bild-Kunst, Bonn 2018; (b.) © Heinrich Helfenstein (Image) / VG Bild-Kunst, Bonn 2018 – P. 77: © Gerhard Richter 2018 (0166) – P. 78: (l. + r.) courtesy of the artist; Niels Borch Jensen Galerie und Verlag, Berlin; neugerriemschneider, Berin; Tanya Bonakdar Gallry, New York © Olafur Eliasson – P. 85–88: Color Systems own drawings acc. Stromer 2005 – P, 97: ©Tate, London 2018 / Bridget Riley 2018. All rights reserved – P. 98 © Camille Graeser-Stiftung / VG Bild-Kunst, Bonn 2018 – P. 100: Peter Cox, Eindhoven, The Netherlands (image) / Collection Van Abbemuseum, Eindhoven, The Netherlands – P. 102: (t.) Collection of the Gemeentemuseum Den Haag ©2018 Mondrian/Holtzman Trust; (b. l.) Harvard Art Museums / Busch-Reisinger Museum, Gift of Eva Weininger, 1996.315 Art / Imaging Department © President and Fellows of Harvard College (Image) © Estate of Andor Weininger / Licensed by VAGA, New York, NY / VG Bild-Kunst, Bonn 2018; (b. r.) Ketterer Kunst © VG Bild-Kunst, Bonn 2018 – P. 104: Horst Bartnig – P. 105: Museum für Konkrete Kunst, Ingolstadt, Germany © Richard Paul Lohse-Stiftung, Zürich / VG Bild-Kunst, Bonn 2018 – P. 106: © Camille Graeser-Stiftung / VG Bild-Kunst, Bonn 2018 – P. 108 + P. 109: © 2018 The Josef and Anni Albers Foundation / Artists Rights Society (ARS), New York / VG Bild-Kunst, Bonn 2018 – P. 110: (t.) © VG Bild-Kunst, Bonn 2018; (b.) © 2018 The Josef and Anni Albers Foundation / Artists Rights Society (ARS), New York / VG Bild-Kunst, Bonn 2018 – P. 112: Jacques Breuer (image) © VG Bild-Kunst, Bonn 2018 – P. 114: (t. + b.) Edgar Diehl – P. 115: Kunstforum Ostdeutsche Galerie, Regensburg, Germany © VG Bild-Kunst, Bonn 2018 – P. 116: (t.) Dirk Rausch (image) © VG Bild-Kunst, Bonn 2018; (b.) © VG Bild-Kunst, Bonn 2018 – P. 118: © Collection Museum Ritter, Waldenbuch, Germany / VG Bild-Kunst, Bonn 2018 – P. 120: (t. + b.) © VG Bild-Kunst, Bonn 2018 – P. 121: Jean-Louis Losi © VG Bild-Kunst, Bonn 2018 – P. 122: Tanja Locke – P. 123 - 125: (all) Kristof Lemp – P. 127: (t.) © Oliver Ottenschläger (image); (b. l.) Hilti Art Foundation © VG Bild-Kunst, Bonn 2018; (b. r.) Architekturmuseum der TU München, Germany / © VG Bild-Kunst, Bonn 2018 – P. 129: (all) Jan van der Ploeg Studio – P. 131: courtesy of Ricardo Bofill – P. 132: © Eugeni Pons – P. 137: (l.) Ilya Ivanov; (r.) Vito Stallone – P. 139: (t.) Stephen Silverman (Image) © Barragan Foundation / VG Bild-Kunst, Bonn 2018; (b.) Armando Salas Portugal (image) © Barragan Founda-tion / VG Bild-Kunst, Bonn 2018 – P. 140: (all) Menga von Sprecher – P. 142: Lucas Bols – P. 143: Andreas von Einsiedel – P. 145 - 147: Heinz Unger, Zürich (image) / Daniele Marques, Marques Architekten AG, Luzern / © VG Bild-Kunst, Bonn 2018 – P. 148: (t.) Luc Boegly; (b.) Sergio Grazia – P. 150: João Morgado – P. 151: ©Iwan Baan – P. 153: (t. l.) Bigoni Mortemard Architectes; (t. r.) © Ossip van Duivenbode; (b.) Arkitema Architects / Kontraframe – P. 155: (all) © Paul Ott – P. 156: (all) Filip Dujardin; P. 157: (t.) John Golling; (b.) Serge Technau – P. 159: (all) i29 interior architects – P. 160: Arkitema Architects / Kontraframe – P. 161: (t.) Beppe Giardino; (b.) © David Romero-Uzeda – P. 162: Duzan Doepel, Eline Strijkers with Stefan Meyer – P. 165: (t.) Thomas Ott; (b.) Kraenk Visuell – P. 166 + 167: © Fernando Guerra (image) / spacerworkers – P. 169: (t.) José Hevia; (b. l. + b. r.) Lyndon Douglas – P. 170: © VG Bild-Kunst, Bonn 2018 – P. 172: Hugo Santos Silva – P. 173: (t. + b.) Han Kyung Woo – P. 174: Pasquale Formisano – P. 176: Stefan Müller © VG Bild-Kunst, Bonn 2018 – P. 178: Friederike Tebbe © VG Bild-Kunst, Bonn 2018 – P. 179: (all) Kristof Lemp – P. 180 + 181: (t.) Djan Chu; (b.) Alan Chu – P. 182: © Eugeni Pons – P. 184: © Iwan Baan – P. 187: (t. l. + t. r.) Hans Jürgen Landes; (b.) Lukas Roth – P. 188: Architekturzentrum Wien, Austria, collection / Margherita Spiluttini – P. 190: Jan Bitter – P.191: Collection Centraal Museum, Utrecht (image & copyright) – P. 192: (t.) B.P. Navy Photo Courtesy of Naval History and Heritage Command; (b.) Matthew Cianfrani – P. 194: (all) own image – P. 196 + 197: Laurent Clément Photographe – P. 198 + 199: Fingerle&Woeste – P. 200: Katherine Lu – P. 202: Kazuyasu Kochi – P. 205: (t.) Iwan Baan; (b.) Jens Markus Lindhe – P. 206: (t.) Jan Bitter; (b.) Rolando de la Fuente (image), Adagp, Paris 2018 © VG Bild-Kunst, Bonn 2018 – P. 207: Courtesy of the Philadelphia Museum of Art © VG Bild-Kunst, Bonn 2018 – P. 208: (all) Kristof Lemp – P. 210 + 211: Georges Rousse © VG Bild-Kunst, Bonn 2018 – P. 212 + 213: Malka Architecture – P. 214 + 215: © Eugeni Pons – P. 216: (t. + b.) VOX Architects – P. 217: (t. + b.) Jan Bitter – P. 218 + 219: Boa Mistura – P. 220: Studio Olafur Eliasson, Courtesy of ARoS Aarhus Kunstmuseum, Denmark, © Olafur Eliasson – P. 223: Daisuke Shima – P. 224: (t. + b.) Annette Kisling – P. 225: Werner Huthmacher, Berlin – P. 226: Tham & Videgard Arkitekter – P. 227: Åke E:son Lindman – P. 228: (t.) Andreas von Ow, (b.) Christian Richters – P. 231: Bas Princen – P. 232: (l. + r.) © Andreas Lechtape – P. 234 + 235: Bernhard Straub (image) © VG Bild-Kunst, Bonn 2018 – P. 236 + 237: People's Architecture Office – P. 239: Erin O'Keefe – P. 242: Daniel Buren / © DB-ADAGP Paris / © VG Bild-Kunst, Bonn 2018 – P. 243–245: (all) Dennis Brandsma & Ewout Huibers – P. 246 + 247: own image – P. 248 + 249: UNStudio © Michael Moran – P. 250: Guillaume Wittmann (Dominique Coulon et associés) – P. 252 + 253: (all) Kristof Lemp – P. 254: Erin O'Keefe – P. 255: Michael Latz (Image) © Universität Konstanz – P. 257: COORDINATION ASIA – P. 258 + 259: (all) Fernando Alda – P. 260: (t. + b. r.) Thilo Frank / Studio Olafur Eliasson; (b. l.) Ole Hein Pedersen (all) Courtesy of ARoS Aarhus Kunstmuseum, Denmark, © Olafur Eliasson – P. 263: (all) Kristof Lemp – P. 264: Nicolas Dorval-Bory Architectes – P. 266: Kristof Lemp – P. 267: © Fernando Guerra, FG+SG – P. 268: Unulaunu – P. 271: Atelier Cruz-Diez Paris (image) © Carlos Cruz-Diez / ADAGP Paris / VG Bild-Kunst, Bonn 2018 – P. 273: James Lattanzio (image) – P. 274: ©Eugeni Pons – P. 279: kaestle&ocker / Brigida González (image) – P. 280 + 281: Valentin Wormbs – P. 282 + 283: (all) Aitor Ortiz, IDOM – P. 285–287: Clement Guillaume Photographe – P. 289: Andrea Kroth – P. 290: (t. l. + r.) Andrea Kroth; (b.) Stefan Müller-Naumann – P. 293: Marc Cramer – P. 295: (t. l.) Roger Frei; (t. r.) Niklaus Spoerri; (b.) Filip Dujardin – P. 296: Salva López – P. 297: Hertha Hurnaus – P. 298: ©Guillaume Wittmann – P. 300 + 301: ©Eugeni Pons – P. 302: Kenta Hasegawa (OFP) – P. 304: Pasquale Formisano – P. 305: Zooey Braun – P. 306: (t.) Philipp Lohöfener; (M.) Florian Holzherr; (b.) Stefan Meyer – P. 308: David Romero-Uzeda (Dominique Coulon et associés) – P. 309: Guillaume Wittmann (Dominique Coulon et associés) – P. 310: © Iwan Baan – P. 312: Ansis Starks – P. 313: © Agnese Sanvito – P. 314: Antonino Cardillo – P. 316: Henning Koepke – P. 321: (t.) Adolf Bereuter (image) / bernardo bader architekten; (b.)Andreas Fuhrimann, Gabrielle Hächler – P. 322: João Morgado – P. 324: (t.) Moritz Bernoully; (b.) own image / Richard Serra © VG-Bildkunst, Bonn 2018 – P. 326: Christiano Corte – P. 328: Christian Richters – P. 331: (t.) Michael Heinrich (image) © VG Bild-Kunst, Bonn 2018; (b.) Nikolaus Heiss – P. 332: doublespace photography – P. 344–335: (all) courtesy of Ricardo Bofill – P. 336: Fernando Alda – P. 337: Florian Monheim / Bildarchiv Monheim GmbH – P. 339: Rick Messemaker – P. 340: courtesy of MVRDV © Rob 't Hart (image) – P. 342 + 343: Antonino Cardillo – P. 344 + 345: (all) © Simon Menges

Abbreviations:
t. = top, b. = bottom, l. = left, r. = right, m. = middle

Imprint

Concept
Kerstin Schultz,
Hedwig Wiedemann-Tokarz,
Eva Maria Herrmann

Collaboration
Marina Baumgärtner,
Anna Bingenheimer,
Alina Maria Fernández Rädecke,
Annika Griewisch,
Tobias Klodt,
Jule Bierlein

Special thanks to
Caparol Farben Lacke Bautenschutz GmbH
and Knauf Gips KG.

Translation German into English
Hartwin Busch
Copyediting
John Sweet
Project management
Alexander Felix, Katharina Kulke
Production
Heike Strempel
Book design
Peter Dieter, Dorothea Talhof
www.formalin.de

Paper
Munken Kristall Rough, 120 g/m²
Printing
Kösel GmbH & Co. KG, Altusried-Krugzell

Library of Congress Control Number
2018955063

ISBN
978-3-0356-1596-8
e-ISBN (PDF)
978-3-0356-1840-2
German Print-ISBN
978-3-0356-1595-1

© 2019 Birkhäuser Verlag GmbH, Basel
P.O. Box 44, 4009 Basel, Switzerland
Part of Walter de Gruyter GmbH, Berlin/Boston

9 8 7 6 5 4 3 2 1
www.birkhauser.com

**Bibliographic information published by the
German National Library**
The German National Library lists this publication in
the Deutsche Nationalbibliografie; detailed
bibliographic data are available on the Internet at
http://dnb.dnb.de